Collins Gem

MODERN HISTORY

BASIC FACTS

HarperCollins*Publishers*

HarperCollins*Publishers*
Westerhill Road, Bishopbriggs, Glasgow G64 2QT

First published 1985
Second edition 1993
Third edition 2002

Reprint 10 9 8 7 6 5 4 3 2
© HarperCollins*Publishers* 1985, 1993, 2002

ISBN 0 00 712180 6

Designed and typeset by Book Creation Services Limited

Printed in Italy by Amadeus S.p.A.

Introduction

Collins Gem Modern History is one of a series of
illustrated dictionaries of the key terms and concepts
used in the most important school subjects. With its
alphabetical arrangement, the book is designed for
quick reference to explain the meaning of words used in
the subject and so provides a companion both to course
work and during revision.

Bold words in an entry identify key terms which are
explained in greater detail in entries of their own;
important terms that do not have separate entries are
shown in *italic* and are explained in the entry in which
they occur.

Other titles in the *Basic Facts* series include:
Gem *Biology*
Gem *Chemistry*
Gem *Computers*
Gem *Business Studies*
Gem *Mathematics*
Gem *Geography*
Gem *Physics*
Gem *Science*
Gem *Technology*

A

Abdication Crisis (1936) A constitutional crisis that arose when Edward VIII wished to marry Wallis Simpson, a divorced American woman, and chose to renounce the throne (abdicate) in favour of his brother, George VI. The British and Dominion governments considered that his intention of marrying a divorcée conflicted with his position as monarch and head of the Church of England.

Abyssinia see Ethiopia.

Accession, Treaty of A treaty signed in Brussels in 1972 by the six members of the EC, plus Denmark, the Republic of Ireland, Norway and the UK. The treaty concerned the admission of these four new members to the EC and the **European Atomic Energy Community (Euratom)**. The countries were required to hold referendums, as a result of which Norway refused to join.

Acheson, Dean (1893–1971) The US Secretary of State from 1949 to 1953. A keen supporter of the Western Alliance, he assisted in the setting up of UNRRA (1945), the **Truman Doctrine** (1947), and the **Marshall Plan** (1948). He also gained the agreement of the USA to join the North Atlantic Treaty (1949) and the commitment of US troops to NATO (1951).

Act of Parliament A law which has completed all the required discussion procedures in the lawmaking body, Parliament. In the UK, an Act of Parliament results when a Bill (a proposed piece of legislation) has been approved in all stages by both Houses of Parliament.

> **First Reading** (*Title*)
> **Second Reading** (*Details*)
> **Committee Stage** (*Details considered by a Committee of the House*)
> **Third Reading** (*The House takes a final decision on the Bill*)
> All these stages take place in both Houses, usually the Commons first, then the Lords.

Act of Parliament *The stages a Bill must pass through.*

When it receives the royal assent the Act becomes a Statute, but in practice the terms *Act* and *Statute* have become interchangeable.

Aden The capital of the People's Democratic Republic of Yemen. It was a British possession from 1839 to 1967, but with a decline in importance after WWII became part of the South Arabian Federation of Arab Emirates in 1963. It was overrun by the National Liberation Front (NLF) in 1967. The NLF was the victor in a civil war with the Front for the Liberation of South Yemen (FLOSY), and took over the country when the British left Aden.

Adenauer, Konrad (1876–1967) A German politician, first chancellor of the Federal German Republic (1949–63), Foreign Minister (1951–55), and founder and leader of the CDU party (*see* **Christian Democrats**) in 1945. He dominated West German politics and was responsible for his country joining the Atlantic and European alliances, as a partner and not a former enemy. He also worked for reconciliation with France, and accepted German responsibility for Nazi crimes against the Jews.

Afghanistan A republic of SC Asia. Area: 636,000 sq km. Pop: 22,600,000. Languages: Pushtu, Persian. Religion: Islam. Cap: Kabul.

The country has long been a victim of foreign interference because of its geo-strategic importance – it is situated between Russia and the Indian sub-continent. Its history in the 20th century has been turbulent, with the tribes violently resisting centralised government.

The monarchy was overthrown in 1973, and since then government has been unstable. Fighting developed between the Muslim fundamentalist tribal groups and the pro-Soviet regime, and in 1979 the USSR sent troops into Afghanistan to support the left-wing government. The Russian action provoked anger in the West and helped to bring about the breakdown of **détente**. It involved the Russians in a fierce struggle against well-organized rebels who saw them as foreign invaders. Despite superior equipment and control of the air, the Russians could not prevail, and withdrew in 1987–9. The left-wing regime fell in 1992, but conflict continued between the victorious rebel groups. Islamic extreme fundamentalist **Taliban** forces had gained control of most of the country by the late 1990s. The Northern Alliance gained control in 2002.

African National Congress (ANC) A movement founded in South Africa in 1912 to unite African opinion and to draw white attention to the problems of blacks by demonstrations, deputations and overseas delegations. The leaders were mainly Christian, middle-

class and Western-educated, and believed constitutional
progress could be made by argument and passive
resistance rather than violence. It formally renounced
non-violence after the Sharpeville massacre in 1960, at
which point it was also banned. Guerrilla activity
associated with the movement became widespread in
South Africa. The release from prison of its leader
Nelson **Mandela** in 1990 and the ending of the ban on
the ANC led to hopes of reconciliation between blacks
and whites. In 1991 the **apartheid** laws were abolished.
Following a referendum a multiracial constitution was
agreed, and Mandela became president of South Africa
when the ANC won the 1994 election. Mandela was
succeeded as president in 1999 by Thabo M'Beki, who
had become leader of the ANC in 1997.

African Nationalism A major force in the political
awakening of Africa, and in the rebellion of its peoples
against colonial rule. An important element was the
development among the native populations of a sense of
identity as black Africans rather than as subjects of
colonial powers, and this was combined with a
determination to achieve independence.

As Africans came into contact with Europeans they
realized that a gap existed between colonial policies and
Western political ideas such as democracy and freedom.
The European policy of racial discrimination and
separation, as shown in reserving the best land for
whites, and in politics and education, naturally angered
native Africans. Conditions of life did not necessarily
improve for the native peoples and in some cases
became worse as a result of European colonialism.

Isolated rebellions took place against European colonization and rule. Despite their political differences, the African nations saw themselves as united in the struggle against 'white colonialism' and sought a distinctive third alternative, influenced by socialism, between East and West.

Forty nations in Africa became independent between 1956 and 1975. However, changing preindustrial living conditions to meet the needs of the modern world was a huge task; difficulties included tribal factions, political instability and grave socio-economic problems, which led to demands for development aid.

Agadir A port in SW Morocco which in 1911 became the centre of an international crisis with the arrival of the German gunboat *Panther*. The Germans claimed that the *Panther* was in Morocco to protect German nationals and commercial interests, but in fact it was intended to counteract what Germany thought was French expansionist policy in Morocco. In the end Germany recognized French rights in Morocco in exchange for territory in the Congo.

Alamein *see* **North African Campaigns**.

Albania A republic of SE Europe. Area: 28,748 sq km. Pop: 3,422,000. Language: Albanian. Religions: Islam, Christianity (Eastern Orthodox) before 1967, now atheist. Cap: Tirana.

Albania became an Islamic independent principality in 1912 after more than four centuries of Turkish rule. A republic was established in 1925 and Ahmed Bey Zogu became President and later king with the title of King Zog I. The country was economically dependent on

Italy, which occupied it in 1939, deposing Zog.

After Italy's defeat in WWII a communist republican government was established (1946). Albania was a member of the **Council for Mutual Economic Assistance** and the **Warsaw Pact** but was expelled from the former (1961) because it sided with China in the **Sino-Soviet Split** and for what the USSR considered to be its deviationist policies (*see* **deviationism**). Albania withdrew from the Warsaw Pact in 1968 because it disapproved of the invasion of **Czechoslovakia**. It was economically and ideologically linked with China from 1968 to 1978, when the association was ended by China. Albania was the last Eastern European country to abandon Communism during the upheavals of 1991–2, but remained impoverished and politically unstable until the end of the century; economic hardship caused serious unrest in 1997.

Al Fatah The Palestine National Liberation Movement. Fatah (*Arabic* conquest) was the first Palestinian guerrilla organisation set up to liberate Palestine from Israeli occupation. Syria has provided arms, money and training facilities. Its leader is Yasser **Arafat**. *See also* **Palestine Liberation Organisation**.

Algeciras, Conference of (1906) An international meeting called to discuss the internal government of Morocco. In the resulting Algeciras Act, France and Spain had to respect Morocco's independence, but it permitted both nations jointly to police the country under a Swiss inspector-general. The **Entente Cordiale** (1904) was strengthened by British support of the settlement, which Germany opposed.

Algeria A republic of NW Africa. Area: 2,381,745 sq

km. Pop: 30,480,793. Language: Arabic. Religion: Islam. Cap: Algiers.

The country was colonised by the French during the 19th century. While settlers enjoyed most of the privileges of citizens of France, the native population had practically none, and it was only after WWII that promises were made of political and social equality. Because these were slow to materialize, the rise of **nationalism** among the native population led to a revolution (1954–62) which was waged by the National Liberation Front (NLF) in the form of guerrilla warfare. The independence struggle ultimately led to the destruction of the Fourth Republic in France (1958). French military officers fighting in Algeria suspected that the French government would negotiate a settlement with the FLN, and by their insistence on keeping Algeria French they and the settlers brought down the government. They tried to do the same with the Fifth Republic when the Secret Army Organisation (OAS) under General Salan (1899–1984) on several occasions attempted to assassinate **de Gaulle**. The OAS ceased to function when its leaders either dispersed or were captured. Eventually independence was achieved in 1962. The first president was **Ben Bella** who was deposed in 1965 by Colonel Houari Boumédienne (1925–78), a left-wing socialist whose repressive regime and hostility towards Algeria's neighbours only ceased with his death. His successor, Bendjedid Chadli, restored relations with neighbouring states and France.

Following widespread protests against Chadli's rule in

1988, constitutional changes introduced limited political pluralism. The fundamentalist Islamic Salvation Front (FIS) won preliminary elections in 1991, but a military coup in 1992 prevented the formation of an FIS government. The FIS then commenced a bloody terrorist campaign against the military government.

Allende, Salvador (1908–73) A Chilean politician. He was a co-founder of the Chilean Socialist Party, and in 1970 became the world's first democratically elected Marxist head of state. Allende tried to establish a socialist society while maintaining parliamentary government, but was increasingly opposed by business interests supported by the CIA (*see* **Central Intelligence Agency**). Industrial unrest, followed by strike action and violence (1972–73), brought about a right-wing military coup, during which he was killed.

Alliance, the *see* **Social Democratic Party**, **Liberal Party**.

Alsace-Lorraine A region of NE France. Area:14,522 sq km. Ceded to Germany by the Treaty of Frankfurt (1871) after the French defeat in the Franco-Prussian War (1870–71), it was restored to France after WWI by the Treaty of **Versailles** (1919). From 1871 to 1914 it was the major cause of bitterness between France and Germany, each of which sought control of its prosperous steel industry. During WWII it was under German occupation (1940–5).

Amin, Idi (1926–) A Ugandan political leader. In 1971 he led a military coup while President Milton Obote was abroad, proclaimed himself head of state, and dissolved parliament. His tyrannical regime caused the deaths of numerous opponents. Most Asians and many British were expelled in 1972 and their business interests confiscated. He was chairman of the OAU (1975–76). In 1979 Obote regained power in a coup supported by Tanzanian forces, and Amin went into exile.

Amritsar A city of NW Punjab, India, centre of the **Sikh** religion. In 1919, 379 people were killed and over 1,200 wounded when British troops opened fire on unarmed supporters of Indian self-government. The Indian nationalist movement was strengthened by the widespread anger at this appalling loss of life. In 1984, Sikh separatist extremists took refuge in the Sikh Golden Temple in Amritsar and were defeated after heavy fighting with government troops. Shortly afterwards, Indira **Gandhi** was assassinated by two of her Sikh bodyguards.

Anarchism A political doctrine which states that all forms of authority interfere with individual freedom and that government and the state should be replaced by communities in voluntary cooperation with one another. Modern anarchist theories developed in the 19th century. Anarchists have proposed various strategies for achieving their ends, ranging from violent direct action to passive resistance or civil disobedience. Whereas communists, such as Lenin, believed the state must ultimately wither away, leaving a voluntary regime without class or government, anarchists have generally opposed all state systems, whether capitalist or communist. Anarchist movements were politically important in the Ukraine, France, Italy and Spain at various times in the late 19th and early 20th centuries, and were particularly prominent on the Republican side in the **Spanish Civil War**. Anarchist ideas were revived by student activists in the 1960s, but have failed to gain widespread support.

ANC *see* **African National Congress**.

Andropov, Yuri Vladimirovich (1914–84) A Soviet politician. He was head of the KGB (1967–82), then General Secretary of the Communist Party (1982–4) and President of the USSR (1983–4).

Anglo-French Entente *see* **Entente Cordiale**.

Anglo-German Naval Agreement (1935) An arrangement which permitted Germany to construct a fleet to 35 per cent of the Commonwealth's strength, except for submarines, which could be up to equal tonnage but should not exceed 45 per cent of the Commonwealth total without prior notice to the UK. The agreement effectively encouraged Germany to break the Treaty of **Versailles**.

Anglo-Irish Agreement (1985) An agreement that provides for consultation between the British and Irish governments over Northern Ireland. It has been bitterly opposed by parts of the **Ulster Loyalist** community.

Anglo-Russian Entente (1907) An agreement designed to check German influence in the Middle East and to end Anglo-Russian mistrust. It also provided for the division of Persia (Iran) into spheres of influence; for the maintenance of Tibet as a buffer state under a degree of Chinese control; for the recognition in Afghanistan of special British interest; and for Russian control of the Bosporus and the Dardanelles subject to other powers' agreement. *See also* **Triple Entente**.

Angola A republic of SW Africa, formerly the colony

of Portuguese West Africa. Area: 1,247,000 sq km. Pop: 9,767,000. Cap: Luanda. The country has rich mineral resources.

Civil uprisings in the 1960s were repressed, but the country achieved independence in 1975 following the change of government in Portugal. Civil war followed between the various liberation movements, principally the Marxist-Leninist MPLA and the South African backed UNITA. With Soviet aid and the assistance of Cuban troops the MPLA achieved victory in 1976, though guerrilla warfare continued until 1992 when a precarious peace was agreed, and the MPLA won a large majority in free elections. A national unity government was formed in 1997 after renewed civil war, but fighting resumed between government and UNITA forces from 1998.

Anschluss The political union of Austria and Germany (1938–45). Hitler's plans for union had been checked in 1934 when Mussolini sent troops to the Brenner Pass to safeguard Austria's independence. By 1937 Mussolini was in the **Axis** camp and Hitler was able to put pressure on Chancellor **Schuschnigg** to legalize the Austrian Nazi Party. The Party stirred up unrest and in 1938 Hitler demanded that Schuschnigg postpone a planned plebiscite to determine Austria's future. Schuschnigg resigned and the Nazi **Seyss-Inquart** became chancellor. He invited the Germans to occupy the country and restore order. After the occupation Hitler held a plebiscite in which nearly all Austrians approved Austria's inclusion in 'Greater Germany'.

Anti-Comintern Pact An agreement between

Germany and Japan in 1936 in which both countries declared their hostility to international Communism. Italy joined in 1937; Hungary and Spain in 1939.

Anti-Semitism The persecution of or discrimination against Jews. In Europe, insistence on religious conformity often concealed envy of Jewish commercial success. Racist prejudice was evident especially in France, Germany and Tsarist Russia.

From the 1920s the Nazis used the Jews as a scapegoat for every German misfortune. A theory of an 'Aryan master race' was developed, though without any scientific basis. Under the Nuremberg Laws (1935). Jews were forbidden to marry 'Aryan' Germans and were denied German citizenship. Between 1939 and 1945 the Nazis killed more than one third of the total Jewish population of the world: over 6 million Jews died in **concentration camps** (*see* **Holocaust**).

Since 1945, hostility towards the state of **Israel** and **Zionism**, especially in the USSR, has been seen as disguised anti-Semitism.

Antonescu, Ion (1882–1946) A Romanian general and dictator, closely associated with the Iron Guard Fascist movement (*see* **Fascism**). In 1940 he became leader of a right-wing government and proclaimed himself 'Conductor', allying his country with the Axis powers in WWII. Heavy Romanian losses in battles in the USSR undermined his position and he was executed in 1946.

ANZUS Pact (1951) A security treaty between Australia, New Zealand and the USA. It provided mutual defence should any of the countries be a victim of an armed attack in the Pacific area. For Australia and

New Zealand the Pact meant a lessening of their dependence upon the UK and a closer collaboration with the USA. However, with New Zealand's adoption of a non-nuclear defence strategy in 1984–96, the USA refused to cooperate with New Zealand on defence matters, though the treaty remained technically in force.

Apartheid The official South African government policy of racial segregation and 'separate development' from 1948 until 1991. *See diagram p. 14.*

In 1960 the introduction of identity cards for non-whites and the suspension of their parliamentary representation was followed by widespread demonstrations, often violently suppressed – as at **Sharpeville**. Among the policies which aroused hostility around the world and at the UN were segregated education, a prohibition of mixed marriages, and the deportation of blacks from specified districts.

The policy of 'separate development' led to the Bantu Self-Government Act. which provided for the establishment of seven native African areas with non-white chief ministers, e.g. the Transkei in 1963; these self-governing territories later became independent, though they were not widely recognized as such internationally. South Africa left the Commonwealth in 1961 rather than modify its apartheid policies, but in 1985 it began to do so, and in 1991 the apartheid laws were abolished, paving the way for multiracial government. *See* **South Africa**.

Appeasement A form of foreign policy that seeks to avoid war by making concessions to a potential enemy. Such a policy was unsuccessfully followed by British and

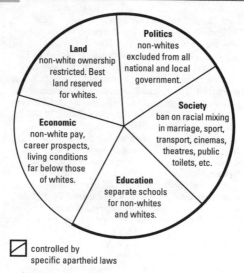

Land
non-white ownership restricted. Best land reserved for whites.

Politics
non-whites excluded from all national and local government.

Society
ban on racial mixing in marriage, sport, transport, cinemas, theatres, public toilets, etc.

Economic
non-white pay, career prospects, living conditions far below those of whites.

Education
separate schools for non-whites and whites.

controlled by specific apartheid laws

Apartheid

French governments towards Germany between 1936 and 1939. *See also* **Rhineland**, **Munich Agreement**.
Arab-Israeli Wars A series of conflicts, culminating four times (1948, 1956, 1967, 1973) in outright war between Israel and Arab countries over the existence in Palestine of the independent Jewish state of Israel.
The 1948 War The creation of the state of Israel

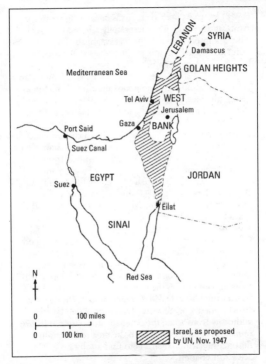

Arab-Israeli Wars

(1948) led to its immediate invasion by neighbouring Arab states, which was successfully resisted by Israel. The UN intervened and in 1949 established an armistice: Jerusalem was partitioned, the **West Bank** became Jordanian, and the **Gaza Strip** Egyptian.

The 1956 War As a result of **Nasser**'s anti-Israeli Pan-Arab policy and Egyptian nationalisation of the Suez Canal, the Israelis invaded Egypt in 1956, supported by British and French military action, and occupied the Gaza Strip and most of Sinai. The invasion was condemned by the UN, which secured a ceasefire and the withdrawal of the occupying forces. *See also* **Suez Crisis**.

The 1967 War The 'Six Day War' resulted from border incidents, increased action by Palestinian guerrillas, and the Egyptian blockade of the Gulf of Aqaba to Israeli shipping. Israel secured a rapid victory over Egypt, Syria and Jordan, and occupied Sinai, the Gaza Strip, the West Bank of the Jordan, and the Golan Heights.

The 1973 War The 'Yom Kippur War' was launched by Egypt, but after early Arab victories, Israeli forces crossed the Suez Canal. In 1974, after Arab states imposed a ban on oil exports to the West, Egypt and Syria agreed to stop the fighting.

After the **Camp David Agreement** in 1979, Egypt and Israel signed a peace treaty, following which Israel withdrew from Sinai; the other territories seized in 1967 remain occupied. Tensions in the area remained high despite international efforts to find a solution. *See also* **Lebanon**.

Arab League An organisation to promote inter-Arab

cultural, technical and economic links and to prevent conflict between Arab states. A pact was signed in 1945 by eight states. A council was established in Cairo, but the League remained an essentially loose grouping of states and never acquired a strong central authority. Until 1967 the League was concerned with organizing opposition to Israel, but after the PLO's increase in strength, the League became a mouthpiece of moderate Arab opinion and a body favouring economic unity. It now has 19 member states.

Arab Nationalism A sense of shared cultural background and common political interests expressed by members of Arab states in the face of outside influences and pressures.

The Pan-Arab movement was led by **Nasser** from 1954 to 1970. Plans for unification of the various Arab states could not conceal rivalries among the leadership nor tensions between various factions. Pan-Arab policy only tended to retain its appeal as long as it was directed against Israel (*see* **Arab-Israeli Wars**). Attempts at unification by Egypt and Syria as a United Arab Republic 1958–61 were not very effective. The main concerns of Arab nationalists continue to be the existence of the Jewish state of Israel and the rights of the Palestinian Arabs in the self-governing territories Israel has permitted in the West Bank and Gaza.

Arafat, Yasser (1929–) Palestinian nationalist, co-founder of **Al Fatah** and, since 1969, President of the **Palestine Liberation Organisation**. In 1993 he played a key role in the Middle East settlement and became leader of the resulting Palestinian-controlled areas, on the West Bank and in Gaza.

Ardennes Offensive (1944) The last major German offensive of WWII intended to split the Allied armies and capture Antwerp and Liège. After initial successes, the German forces were driven back and the last German reserves were exhausted.

Argentina A republic of South America. Area: 2,776,000 sq km. Pop:39,995,000. Language: Spanish. Religion: Christianity RC. Cap: Buenos Aires.

The country achieved independence from Spain in 1816. In the 20th century, elected presidents have been overthrown by military coups on numerous occasions.

In 1946 Juan Perón was elected President. He offered policies combining nationalism and state socialism, known as Perónism. However his power was largely dependent on the popularity of his wife Eva (known as Evita). She died in 1952 and he was overthrown in 1955, returning from exile 18 years later to become President again, with his second wife, Maria Estella, as vice-president. He died 9 months later and was succeeded by his wife, but economic crises and urban guerrilla activities led to her downfall in 1976.

The subsequent military regime carried out a 'dirty war' against its opponents, during which thousands of people 'disappeared'. In 1982 the regime invaded the **Falkland Islands**. Following the Argentinian defeat, the regime fell and was replaced by a democratically elected government. In December 2001 an economic crisis culminated with the resignation of President La Rua. Adolfo Rodriguez was appointed, but also resigned after a few days. On 1 January 2002 Eduardo Duhalde became president. At that time the country's debt was reported at $141bn.

Armistice An agreement between opposing armies to stop fighting in order to discuss peace terms.

The most important armistice negotiations at the end of WWI were between Germany on the one side and Britain, France and the USA on the other. In WWII, an armistice was concluded between Italy and the Allies in 1943, and the USSR signed with Romania, Finland and Hungary in 1944–5. No formal armistice was concluded with Germany or Japan in 1945: individual fighting fronts simply surrendered.

The Korean War was ended by the Panmunjom Armistice in 1953.

Arnhem, Battle of (1944) An Allied military disaster which resulted from the 1st Airborne Division's attempt to secure the bridge over the Rhine at Arnhem in Holland. The attempt failed owing to the slowness of the advance from the dropping zones, as well as stiff German resistance and well-organized countermeasures.

ASEAN *see* **Association of Southeast Asian Nations**

Asquith, Herbert Henry, Earl of Oxford and Asquith (1852-1928) A British Liberal politician, PM from 1908 to 1916. He was Chancellor of the Exchequer (1905–08), and as PM his administrations were notable for the maintenance of free trade, the 'People's Budget' of 1909 (which led to the **Parliament Act** of 1911), the establishment of old age pensions and national insurance schemes, the introduction of the payment of MPs and the disestablishment of the Church of Wales

During Asquith's administrations there occurred pressure for Irish Home Rule, agitation for **women's suffrage**, the **Easter Rising** and the first half of WWI.

Association of Southeast Asian Nations (ASEAN) An association established in 1967 in Bangkok by Indonesia, Malaysia, the Philippines, Singapore and Thailand to work for economic progress and to increase stability in SE Asia. Brunei joined in 1984, Vietnam in 1995, and Laos and Burma in 1997.

Atatürk (Mustafa Kemal) (1880–1938) The founder of modern Turkey, and president from 1923 to 1938. Kemal took part in the Young Turks revolt (1908), and won fame as the defender of Gallipoli (1915). In the 1920s he led Turkish resistance to Allied plans for the division of Turkey, and successfully drove out the Greek invading armies (1919–22).

After the Treaty of **Lausanne** (1923) with the Allies, Kemal assumed the name Atatürk ('father of the Turks') and ruled as a dictator. He introduced radical, generally Westernising reforms: the separation of state and religion, the introduction of Western law in place of Islamic, the abolition of the caliphate, the emancipation of women, and the abandonment of the Arabic for the Latin alphabet.

Atlantic, Battle of the The struggle for control of the sea routes around the UK during WWII. It lasted for the whole period of the war but was particularly severe between 1940 and 1943 when Allied convoys were attacked by **U-Boats** (frequently operating in packs), armed surface raiders, and long-range aircraft. Allied countermeasures included the escorting of convoys by warships, and the use of special escort aircraft carriers, armed merchant cruisers, submarines, land-based air cover, radar, and the underwater detection device Asdic. After severe losses in 1940 and early 1941, the Allies slowly gained the upper hand, not least because of the mobilisation of the USA's huge shipbuilding capability.

Atlantic Charter A declaration of common objectives signed by Roosevelt and Churchill in 1941. It contained plans for the postwar world: the right of all peoples to choose their own governments and to live free from fear and want; no territorial changes to be made without the consent of the peoples involved; the disarmament of aggressive nations; a wider and permanent system of international security; and access to essential raw materials through trade between all nations combined with freedom of the seas

Atomic Bomb *see* **nuclear warfare**.

Attlee, Clement (1883–1967) A British politician, PM from 1945 to 1951. Attlee became leader of the Labour Party in 1935. He entered the wartime coalition with Churchill, and was deputy PM (1942–5). As PM in the postwar Labour government, he was responsible for the creation of the **Welfare State**. He ended his career as Leader of the Opposition 1951–55, receiving an earldom in 1955.

Auschwitz The most notorious of the Nazi **concentration camps** in which mass extermination was carried out, mainly of Jews. The camp was built in 1940 near Cracow in Poland, and the organized killings on a massive scale began there in 1941. *See* **Holocaust**.

Australia The world's largest island and smallest

continent, situated in the Southern Hemisphere between the Indian and Pacific Oceans. Area: 7,687,000 sq km. Pop: 18,235,600. Language: English. Religion: Christianity (Protestant, RC). Cap: Canberra.

In 1900 the Australian Commonwealth Act united six former British colonies (now the six states) into an independent Commonwealth Dominion with a federal government, which came into being in 1901. The Labor Party was the dominant political grouping in the new country, but was not strong enough to gain clear electoral victory until 1914. During WWI about 20 per cent of the 300,000 Australian volunteers were killed in Europe and the Middle East fighting for the Allies.

Between the Wars there was inter-state and federal disagreement over taxation in relation to defence expenditure, which nearly led to the break-up of the federation. This was prevented by increased prosperity as wool prices rose, and by a growing awareness of Japan's aggressive intentions in the Far East and Pacific.

Australia entered WWII in 1939, its forces being active principally in North Africa and the Far East. As a result of WWII, defence links were formed with New Zealand and the USA (the **ANZUS Pact**), as a result of which troops were sent to serve in Vietnam in 1965.

Industrial growth followed the Second World War. The huge Snowy River hydroelectric scheme in New South Wales contributed to this growth. Trade has developed with Japan and the USA but declined with Britain especially after the latter joined the Common Market in 1973. The Liberal Party (more or less equivalent to the British Conservative Party) has been

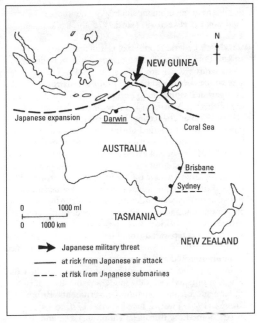

Australia *The country in danger, 1942.*

dominant in government since WWII, although Labor held power between 1972 and 1975 and again from 1983 to 1996.

Austria A Federal republic of C Europe. Area: 84,000 sq km. Pop: 8,054,000. Language: German. Religion: Christianity (RC). Cap: Vienna.

With the defeat and break-up of the **Austro-Hungarian Empire** at the end of WWI, a republic was established in Austria in 1918, with Karl Renner (1870–1951) as chancellor. The 1920s were marked by much social and political unrest, with frequent clashes between Fascist and socialist supporters. These led to serious riots in Vienna in 1927. **Dollfuss** became chancellor in 1932 but his home and foreign policies pleased neither left nor right and he was assassinated by a group of Nazis. He was succeeded by **Schuschnigg**, whose authority was undermined by increasing Nazi pressure leading to the German takeover of the country (**Anschluss**) in 1938.

Austria was separated from Germany in 1945, and was occupied by the Allies until 1955, when its independence was fully restored and the occupying armies were withdrawn. The country avoided taking sides in the Cold War and pursued generally moderate socialist policies under a succession of coalition governments. Bruno Kreisky (1911–) was chancellor from 1970 to 1983. Austria joined the European Union in 1995, and the euro monetary system in 1999. *See also* **Waldheim**.

Austro-Hungarian Empire A group of states which dominated C Europe from 1867 to 1918, including what became Czechoslovakia as well as parts of Italy, Poland,

Romania, Ukraine and Yugoslavia. There was a common monarch of the Hapsburg dynasty (founded in 1153), and joint control of the armed forces and financial policies, but each state had its own parliament.

Independence and nationalistic issues, supported by the Allies at the end of WWI, caused the Empire to break up. Its end was formally recognized by the Treaties of **Saint Germain** (1919) and **Trianon** (1920).

Autarky or **Autarchy** A nationalist policy of economic self-sufficiency aimed at removing the need for imports by producing all requirements at home. Germany adopted such a policy in the 1930s to make itself blockade-proof.

Authoritarianism A political philosophy based on strict obedience to authority, or to government by a small elite with wide powers. *Authoritarian* is used loosely to mean despotic, dictatorial or domineering.

Autocracy 1. The governing of a country by an individual with unrestricted authority (an *autocrat*).

2. The unrestricted authority of such an individual.

3. A country or society ruled by an autocrat.

Autonomy Self-government and therefore political independence. A *degree of autonomy*, or *limited autonomy*, implies the existence of a superior political authority, i.e. a federal government. The American states have limited autonomy because they are subject to the Federal authority in Washington and cannot overturn laws and decisions made by its President and Congress. Members of the British Commonwealth were once British colonies, but now have full autonomy since they have absolute political freedom and are under no obligation to accept the decisions of the Commonwealth or any other authority.

Avon, Lord *see* **Eden**.

Awami League *see* **Bangladesh**.

Axis An alliance between two states to cooperate in foreign policy or, more broadly, those two states plus any others supporting them. In WWII, the Axis (originally the *Rome–Berlin Axis*) was the collaboration between Germany and Italy, which was based on the agreement reached in October 1936 (the *October Protocols*). More broadly, the Axis powers in WWII were Germany, Italy and Japan, and their allies Hungary, Czechoslovakia, Romania and Bulgaria.

Ayub Khan, Mohammed (1908–74) A Pakistani army

Axis The axis powers.

officer and statesman. He became president in 1958 following a military coup and the declaration of martial law. He believed in encouraging democracy; he ended martial law in 1962, and achieved limited land reforms, but he became unpopular because of his repressive and militaristic government. Imprisonment of the opposition led to serious student riots in 1968, followed by his resignation in 1969. He was replaced by **Yahya Khan**.

B

Ba'ath Socialist Party A Pan-Arab movement based upon the union in 1952 of two Syrian political parties the Ba'ath ('resurrection') Party and the Socialist Party. The basic aim of the united Party is 'Freedom, unity and socialism in one Arab nation with an external mission'. The Party now rules Syria and in Iraq the Ba'ath and Communist Parties rule as the Coalition National Progressive Front.

Bad Godesberg Meeting *see* **Godesberg Meeting**

Baghdad Pact (1955) A defence and security agreement between Iraq and Turkey, subsequently joined by Pakistan, Iran and the UK. The **Suez Crisis** (1956) and the Iraqi revolution (1958) practically ended the agreement, which survived only as a basis for the **Central Treaty Organisation**.

Balance of Payments The difference over a given time between a country's total payments to and receipts from foreign countries. This is calculated from exports and imports of goods and services, and transfers of capital, interest, grants, etc.

Balance of Power The doctrine of maintaining a European system in which no single power is dominant. In the past many countries supported groupings intended to prevent one power gaining control over Europe, e.g. the German–Austro-Hungarian alliance, balanced by the entente between Britain, France and Russia before WWI.

Balance of Terror *see* **deterrence**.

Baldwin, Stanley, Earl Baldwin of Bewdley
(1867–1947) A British Conservative politician. After
serving as Chancellor of the Exchequer he became PM
(1923–4, 1924–9 and 1935–7), and was leader of the
Conservative Party (1923–37). His main success was in
uniting a divided party and in handling the **Abdication
Crisis**, but he had to deal with the problems of the
General Strike, rearmament, and mass unemployment.

Balfour, Arthur James, 1st Earl of Balfour
(1848–1930) A British Conservative politician, PM from
1902 to 1905. He became PM after holding several
ministerial offices, but his government's split over
protectionism, **free trade** and tariff reform contributed
to its defeat by the Liberals.

In the WWI coalition government he was First Lord
of the Admiralty and Foreign Secretary and was
responsible for the **Balfour Declaration**. As Lord
President of the Council he played an important part in
the postwar settlements, the establishment of the
League of Nations and the drafting of the **Statute of
Westminster** (1931).

Balfour Declaration (1917) The statement by the
British Foreign Secretary A J **Balfour** declaring British
support for a Jewish national home in **Palestine**
provided that safeguards could be reached for the
'rights of non-Jewish communities in Palestine'.

The Declaration formed the basis of the League of
Nations **mandate** for Palestine, which was given to the
UK in 1922 and lasted until 1948, when the state of
Israel was established.

Balkan Pact (1934) A defensive agreement between

Greece, Romania, Turkey and Yugoslavia by which they agreed to guarantee each other's frontiers. It was particularly aimed at Bulgaria which desired to recover territory previously lost to all four states. The signatories later formed an Entente, but this collapsed in 1940 when each state went its separate way in WWII.

Balkan Wars (1912–13) The conflicts arising from the territorial aims of various Balkan states against the **Ottoman Empire**. The wars led to the Ottoman Empire's loss of most of its European territory. The resulting tensions were an important cause of WWI.

Balkans, the A peninsula in SE Europe consisting of Albania, Bulgaria, Greece, Romania, Yugoslavia (and its successor states) and European Turkey. It was an area of political and revolutionary upheaval throughtout the last century, as shown in the **Balkan Wars** and WWI and WWII.

Baltic States Estonia, Latvia and Lithuania, territories of E Europe. Up to 1918 they were part of Russia, and were then independent republics (1919–40). In 1940 they were occupied by the USSR, and until 1990 they were republics of the Soviet Union. They declared their independence in 1990, leading to threats from Moscow and defiance from the Balts. But in 1991, with the collapse of the Soviet Union, the independence of the Baltic States was internationally recognised. The existence of large Russian minorities in all three states, particularly in Estonia and Latvia, poses potential problems.

Banda, Hastings Kamuzu (1907–97) A Malawi politician. He became leader of the Malawi National

N

ESTONIA

Baltic Sea

Riga

LATVIA

Memel

LITHUANIA

Vilna

E. PRUSSIA

to USSR 1945

POLAND

USSR

| 0 | | 200 miles |
| 0 | 200 km | |

Territory claimed by Lithuania but seized by Poland 1920. Restored to Lithuania 1945. Vilna capital of independent Lithuania, 1991

Territory seized by Hitler in March 1939

Baltic States

Congress (1958), PM of Nyasaland (1963) and led the country to independence as Malawi in 1964. He became president (1966) and subsequently followed a cautious policy in relationships with South Africa. Internally he created a one-party state on dictatorial lines. In 1992 he was forced to abandon one-party rule, and in 1994 was defeated in free elections for president by Bakili Muluzi.

Bandaranaike, Sirimavo (1916–) A Sri Lankan politician who succeeded her husband, Solomon, as leader of the Freedom Party. She became the world's first woman PM in 1960, but by following her husband's language and nationalisation policies contributed to the Party's defeat in 1965. She regained power in 1970 on a platform of social democracy and held office until 1977.

Bandaranaike, Solomon (1899–1959) A Sri Lankan politician. He became involved with the Ceylon National Congress in the 1930s. This led him to support the Sinhalese against the immigrant Tamils in the years before independence (1948). He founded the socialist Freedom Party in 1951, and on becoming PM in 1956 closed all British military and naval bases. His nationalisation programme and policy of making Sinhalese the sole official language led to serious civil disturbances and to his assassination by a Buddhist monk.

Bandung Conference (1955) The first international political conference of African and Asian states. The idea was to adopt a 'nonaligned and neutral' attitude towards the Cold War confrontations between East and West, and to create a 'united front' against colonial oppression.

The increasing rivalry of India and China within Asia, and the separate objectives of anti-colonialism in Africa and Asia, weakened the Conference's prospects of success. The Conference nonetheless helped lead to the establishment of the **Nonaligned Movement**.

Bangladesh A people's republic of S Asia. Area: 144,020 sq km. Pop: 118,700,000. Language; Bengali. Religion: Islam. Capital: Dacca.

Until 1947 the country was part of **India** but then became East Pakistan, separated from West Pakistan by a large area of Indian territory. From 1954 the Awami League sought **autonomy** for East Pakistan and the failure of talks to bring this about led to civil war, with India actively intervening to support the East in a two-week war (1971). The resulting peace established Bangladesh as an independent state (1972).

In 1975 the PM and leader of the Awami League, Mujibur **Rahman**, was assassinated in a military coup led by Brigadier Khaled Mosharraf, who himself was assassinated three months later. Civilian rule was reestablished in 1978–9, but in 1982 Lt Gen Mohammad Ershad led another military coup. The country suffered devastating monsoon floods in 1988. Ershad resigned after mass protests in 1990, and elections in 1992 were won by the Islamic, rightist Bangladesh Nationalist Party.

Barbarossa The German Supreme Command code name for the invasion of the USSR in 1941.

Basques A people of unknown origin living around the Western Pyrenees in France and Spain. Since 1973 an extreme nationalist organisation (ETA) has sought

Basque independence from Spain by a campaign of
terrorism. A limited degree of autonomy was established
in 1980.

Batista, Fulgencio (1901–73) A Cuban dictator. After
deposing President Bernadino Machado (1933) he
established a Fascist state, but in 1937 allowed
opposition political parties to be formed. Free elections
(1939) resulted in his appointment as President. He
held office until 1944 when he went voluntarily into
exile in the Dominican Republic.

As a result of another coup (1952) he returned to
power, suspended the constitution and established a
one-party state. He was forced again to flee to the
Dominican Republic (1958) following the army's refusal
to support his corrupt and repressive regime against
Castro's successful guerrilla campaign.

Bay of Pigs (1961) The site of an invasion of Cuba by
1,200 anti-Castro Cubans, trained by the CIA in the
USA and using US military supplies. Most were killed
or captured within a few days. In the same year Castro
proclaimed Cuba a socialist state.

Begin, Menachem (1913–92) A Polish-born Israeli
politician, PM (1977–83). He reached Palestine during
WWII, and became leader of **Irgun Zvai Leumi**, a
member of the Knesset (Israel's parliament) from 1948,
and from 1973 to 1983 leader of the Likud (Unity)
Party. After the 1977 general election he led a coalition
government which had to face high inflation, Arab
disturbances, the maintenance of Israeli authority on the
occupied West Bank, and PLO attacks from Lebanon.
Begin was jointly awarded with **Sadat** the 1978 Nobel

Peace Prize for efforts in achieving the **Camp David Agreement**.

Belgium A kingdom of NW Europe. Area: 30,513 sq km. Pop: 10,130,574. Languages: Flemish, French and German. Religion: Christianity (RC). Cap: Brussels.

After being ruled in turn by many western European states Belgium became an independent kingdom (1830). At the outbreak of WWI, Germany invaded Belgium the same day as declaring war on France. This disregard for Belgium's guaranteed neutrality hastened Britain's entry into the War. In WWII Belgium was again overrun by Germany.

The country occasionally suffers internal conflict between the majority Flemish population and the minority French-speaking Walloons. This division is made worse by the political separation of N and S, the former supporting mainly the conservative Christian Social Party and the nationalist Volksunie, while the latter is more radically socialist in outlook. These disagreements have led the country to be politically unstable and governed by a succession of coalitions. It is a member of the EU and NATO.

Ben Bella, Mohammed Ahmed (1916–) An Algerian national revolutionary leader. After WWII he became head of the extreme nationalist 'Special Organisation'. Imprisoned by the French in 1950, he escaped (1952) to Egypt where he founded the National Liberation Front (FLN) which played a lending role in the fight for Algerian independence. Again imprisoned by the French (1956) he was released (1962) to participate in the independence talks at Evian which also led to the

end of hostilities. He became PM and, in 1963,
President. He was overthrown (1965) in a military coup
led by Colonel Houari Boumédienne.

Benelux A customs union (1948) between Belgium,
Luxembourg and the Netherlands which developed
(1960) into an arrangement for the free movement of
capital, goods and people between each state, and for
joint commercial relations with other countries.

Ben Gurion, David (1886–1974) An Israeli politician.
In 1930 he became leader of the Mapai Party, the
strongest socialist grouping in Israel. He was PM
1948–53, 1955–63). Much of this time he led a country
at war with the Arabs, but was able to carry out
agricultural and industrial reforms.

Benes, Eduard (1884–1948) A Czech politician.
During WWI he worked hard for his country's
independence, becoming its Foreign Minister (1918–35)
and PM (1921–2). His foreign policy was based on firm
support for the League of Nations, the development of
close associations with France and the USSR, and the
strengthening of the **Little Entente**. He was president
(1935–8, 1946–8), and headed a provisional Czech
government in France and England during WWII.

Beria, Lavrenti Pavlovich (1899–1953) A Soviet
politician and chief of the secret police. In 1938 Stalin
appointed him Commissar of Internal Affairs, and he
later became head of the Soviet Security Service
(NKVD). During WWII he was vice-president of the
State Committee for Defence. On Stalin's death in 1953
he hoped to succeed him, but later the same year he was
dismissed, tried and shot as a traitor. A ruthlessly

ambitious plotter, he was a skilful organiser of espionage, forced labour and terror.

Berlin A city of N Germany, capital of united Germany 1871–1945 and again after 1990. In 1945 it was divided into two sectors. The E sector was occupied by forces of the USSR, while the W sector was occupied by US, UK and French troops.

The E sector was capital of East Germany. Area: 403 sq km. Pop: 1,145,700. The W sector formed a small independent area within East Germany, closely associated economically and politically with West Germany. Area: 480 sq km. Pop: 1,898,900.

During 1948 and 1949 the USSR placed a rail and road blockade on the W sector, in response to the introduction of currency reform in West Germany, which the Soviet authorities refused to accept in Berlin. The UK and the USA organised an airlift of supplies, the success of which convinced the USSR that the blockade could not succeed.

During this tense period two municipal authorities were established and the city administratively divided. In 1961, the East Germans built a wall dividing the sectors to halt the flow of refugees from E to W. The Berlin Wall was a symbol of the division of Germany and brought the deaths of many East Germans who tried to cross it. Political developments in the USSR and East Germany led to the demolition of the Wall in 1989, and in 1990 East and West Germany were reunited.

Berlin-Baghdad Railway The proposed railway line from the Bosporus to the Persian Gulf, which was to be engineered and financed by Germany. The Ottoman

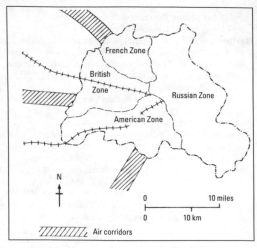

Berlin *The Blockade (1948–49).*

government agreed to the project in 1899 but only a short section of the line had been constructed by the outbreak of WWI. There was considerable British and Russian opposition to the project which would have threatened their spheres (areas) of influence.

Bevan, Aneurin (1897–1960) A British Labour politician. He was Minister of Health (1945–51) and deputy leader of the Labour Party (1959–60). He pioneered the **National Health Service**.

Beveridge Report The Report on Social Insurance and Allied Services prepared by the economist Sir William Henry (later Baron) Beveridge (1879–1963) Published in 1942, it became known popularly as a social insurance scheme 'from the cradle to the grave', which would overcome the evils of poverty and unemployment. Beveridge was a Liberal but his proposals were enthusiastically adopted by the Labour Party, which carried them out when in power (1945–51). The report outlined the basis of the National Health Service and the **welfare state**.

The five social evils	How to tackle them
1. *Disease*	A system of national health care for all
2. *Idleness*	Full employment
3. *Ignorance*	Universal secondary education
4. *Squalor*	Housing supported by Government
5. *Want*	Comprehensive social security

Beveridge Report

Bevin, Ernest (1881–1951) A British Labour politician. After a prominent career in the TUC (1921–1940), in which he united 50 unions into the Transport and General Workers Union, the largest in the world, he entered Parliament. He was Minister of Labour (1940–5), and then Foreign Secretary (1945–51). He was noted for supporting the creation of NATO, encouraging the adoption of a nuclear defence policy, and for having a sense of Commonwealth unity, which made him oppose schemes for European union.

Bhutto, Benazir (1955–) A Pakistani politician, daughter of Zulfikar Ali **Bhutto**. She became leader of the Pakistan Peoples' Party, and vigorously opposed the military regime of General Mohammed **Zia-ul-Haq**. In 1988 she was appointed Prime Minister of Pakistan, thus becoming the first woman prime minister of a Muslim country. She was dismissed from office by the President in 1990 but regained power in 1993, only to lose it again, after corruption allegations, in 1996.

Bhutto, Zulfikar Ali (1928–79) A Pakistani politician. He joined President **Ayub Khan**'s government (1958), becoming Foreign Minister in 1963. He resigned in 1966 and founded the Socialist Anti-Indian People's Party (1967). It won an Assembly majority in 1970, and in the following year Bhutto became the first non-soldier to achieve the presidency. He led his country out of the Commonwealth (1972) and initiated a new constitution under which he took office as PM with responsibility for foreign affairs, defence and atomic energy (1973). He was overthrown by a military coup in 1977 and charged with conspiracy to murder, for which he was executed.

Biafran War (1967–70) The civil war in Nigeria resulting from the secession (declaration of independence) of Biafra, the eastern region (dominated by the Ibo people) of the federal republic. The secession was led by Colonel Odumegwu **Ojukwu**, and had been preceded by heightened inter-tribal conflict. Federal government forces tried to end the rebellion, and although the main bases of Enugu and Port Harcourt were soon occupied it was not until 1970 that Biafran resistance was overcome and Ojukwu fled to the Ivory Coast.

Bin Laden, Osama (1957 –) Leader of the terrorist organisation *Al-Qaeda*, he was born in Saudi Arabia

Biafran War

from a wealthy Yemeni family. At school he joined the Muslim Brotherhood and, in 1974, when the Soviets invaded Afghanistan, he helped the Islamic fighters (mujahedin). In 1991 he was expelled from Saudi Arabia because of anti-governmental activites and by 1998 he had become so opposed to all Americans and Jews that he issued a fatwa, a religious ruling. He is considered responsible for the terrorist attacks on the US of 11 September 2001.

Bipartisanship The situation when two or more countries, organisations or political parties support each other's policies.

Black and Tans The British armed force sent to Ireland in 1920 to strengthen the Royal Irish Constabulary in its fight against republican forces. Their brutality and use of indiscriminate violence led to their withdrawal at the end of 1921. The name comes from the uniform of dark green tunics (almost black) and khaki trousers.

Black Power An economic, political and social movement of black people, especially in the USA, to obtain equality with whites. The term was invented in 1965 by radical groups discontented with the failure of the **Civil Rights** movement to secure change by nonviolent action.

Black Shirts Members of a Fascist organisation, e.g the Italian Fascist Party before and during WWII, but also of other groups, e.g. the British followers of Oswald Mosley in the 1930s (*see* **British Union of Fascists**).

Blair, Anthony (Tony) (1953–) A British Labour politician, PM (1997–), who has distanced the Labour

Party from its traditional socialist roots. He won a second landslide election in 2001, but on much-reduced turnout.

Blitz   The systematic nighttime bombing of the UK in 1940–1 by the Luftwaffe (the German air force), after its failure in the Battle of Britain. The intention was to frighten the population, cause widespread destruction and disrupt industry. Though it caused considerable damage, the Blitz failed largely because of the resilience of the civilian population.

Blitzkrieg   (*Ger.* – lightning war) A style of attack perfected by German armed forces in Poland, the Low Countries and France in 1939–40. Essential elements were speed and surprise of attack and the close cooperation of armour and dive-bombers, resulting in shock and disorganisation among enemy forces.

Bolshevism   The policy pursued by the left wing of the Social Democratic Party which seized power in the **Russian Revolution** of October 1917. In 1918 the name of the policy was changed to *Communism*. The term derives from *Bolshevik* (*Russ.* – majority) after the majority of the Social Democratic Party voted for Lenin's revolutionary policy, as opposed to the more moderate policy of the *Mensheviks* (*Russ.* – minority).

Boom   A period of high economic growth characterised by rising wages, profits and prices, full employment, and high levels of investment, trade and other economic activity. It is often followed by a **depression**.

Bosnia-Herzegovina   A region, and since 1992 a republic, of SE Europe, formerly part of **Yugoslavia**. Capital: Sarajevo.

As separate provinces Bosnia and Herzegovina belonged to the Ottoman Empire (1463–1908), but by the Treaty of Berlin 1878 were then placed under Austrian rule with the agreement of the major European powers, although technically remaining part of the Ottoman Empire. In 1908 the Austro-Hungarian Empire annexed them, and in 1910 they became a joint province. Serbia was resentful of the annexation, and anti-Austro-Hungarian agitation led to the assassination of Archduke Franz Ferdinand at **Sarajevo**, which sparked WWI. After the War they became part of Yugoslavia (1918).

Bosnia followed the example of Slovenia and Croatia and declared independence in 1992. This led to civil war between its Muslim and (Christian) Serb inhabitants. This was notable for its brutality (the prolonged siege of Sarajevo, '**ethnic cleansing**', massacres of fleeing civilians). The US-sponsored Dayton Peace Accord was signed in 1995.

Botha, Pieter Willem (1916–) A South African politician. As PM (1978–84) and President (1984–89) he pursued a policy of moderate reform, while resisting internal and external pressure for the complete dismantling of apartheid.

Bourgeoisie 1. The middle classes.

2. The ruling class (leaders and controllers) of the two basic classes of capitalist society in Marxist theory, the other being the **proletariat** (working class).
The bourgeoisie consists of bankers, capitalists, manufacturers and other employers, who exploit the workers.

Boxer Rising (1900) An outbreak of anti-foreign violence in China organized by a secret society called 'The Society of Harmonious Fists' – hence the term 'boxer'. National resentment was aroused by European powers acquiring bases and developing commercial interests. The rising was put down with severity by the Europeans who, by the Peking Protocol (1901), forced the Chinese government to pay heavy compensation.

Brandt, Willy (1913–92) A West German Social Democratic statesman. He started his political career in 1930 as an anti-Nazi socialist worker, and from 1933 to 1945 he went into voluntary exile in Norway. He entered the Bundestag (1949), was mayor of W Berlin (1951–66), and became chairman of the Social Democrats in 1964.

He was Foreign Minister in **Kiesinger**'s coalition government (1966–69), and Chancellor (1969–74) in coalition with the Free Democrats. He worked hard for reconciliation with the Communist countries (*see* **Ostpolitik**) and treaties were concluded with Poland and the USSR, acknowledging East Germany and accepting the Oder-Neisse Line (1972). He won the Nobel Peace Prize in 1971.

Brandt Report (1979) A paper prepared by the Independent Commission on International Development Issues, under the chairmanship of Willy **Brandt**. The investigation leading to the report was conducted by a group of international statesmen and leaders from 19 countries, the UK's representative being Edward Heath.

The long and complex report examined long-term reforms required by the year 2000 and priority programmes for the 1980s to avoid an imminent economic crisis. It proposed a new approach to international finance and development of the monetary system, and criticised the waste caused by the vast expenditure on armaments taking resources away from the urgent needs of **Third World** countries. Energy, food and trade were all discussed, emphasis being placed on the interests in common between the industrialised and Third World nations, and the report put forward proposals to reverse the decline in trade and the revival of the world economy.

Brazzaville Declaration (1944) The declaration that resulted from a meeting in the French Congo between members of the Fighting French (*see* **Free French**) and France's African colonies to discuss postwar relationships. It included proposals for the establishment of assemblies in each colony; the unity of the French Empire; colonial participation in elections for the French parliament; equal rights of colonial subjects as citizens of the French Republic; economic reforms; and the employment of native populations in public services.

Brest-Litovsk, Treaty of (1918) The peace agreement between the **Central Powers** and Bolshevik Russia, under which the Russians lost Finland, Poland, the Baltic States, the Caucasus, the Ukraine and White Russia (Belarus). The Treaty was cancelled later in the year by the armistice agreement.

Bretton Woods Conference (1944) An agreement reached in New Hampshire, USA, by 28 nations to establish a **World Bank** and an **International Monetary**

Treaty of Brest-Litovsk *New boundaries.*

Fund (IMF), with the object of preventing financial crises developing like those which had occurred in the interwar years. The World Bank was to grant loans for major projects in order to aid a country's development. The Fund was to operate a system of cash reserves on which member states could rely to meet balance-of-payments deficits.

Brezhnev, Leonid Ilyich (1906–82) A Soviet politician. He was president of the Supreme Soviet from 1960 to 1964 when he succeeded **Khrushchev** as First Secretary of the Communist Party, emerging as the most important member of a collective leadership. He became President again in 1977, keeping his party offices and policy-making role.

He established the principle known as the 'Brezhnev Doctrine' in defence of the Soviet invasion of **Czechoslovakia** (1968), stating that a communist state should intervene in another communist state's affairs if its Communism is threatened by internal or external attack or subversion. His period of office was notable for the growth of **détente** in the 1970s, and its decline following the Soviet invasion of **Afghanistan** (1979).

Briand, Aristide (1862–1932) A French politician, originally a socialist (*see* **socialism**) but, on entering parliament in 1902, moved towards **radicalism**. He was responsible for the separation of church and state (1905) and was eleven times PM between 1909 and 1929, but such was the instability of government in this period that his total time as PM was only 58 months.

Briand was Foreign Minister (1925–32) and was on good terms with **Stresemann**, with whom he shared the

1926 Nobel Peace prize. Their friendship helped to encourage better relations between France and Germany, especially by means of the Treaties of **Locarno**, Germany's admission to the League of Nations (1926), and the evacuation of the Rhineland (1930). He was largely responsible for the **Kellogg-Briand Pact** (1928), and put forward the idea of a federal 'United States of Europe'.

Britain *see* **United Kingdom**.

Britain, Battle of (Aug–Oct. 1940) An air campaign fought over S England by the **Luftwaffe** and the RAF. In order to destroy British defences before the planned invasion of the country, Germany launched a series of attacks against shipping, airfields and factories, using squadrons of bombers with massed fighter escorts. They were opposed by Hurricane and Spitfire fighters, and the battle ended when Germany abandoned its invasion plans after losing 1,733 aircraft to 915 RAF fighters.

British Commonwealth of Nations *see* **Commonwealth of Nations, British**.

British Empire *see* **Commonwealth of Nations, British**; and **Imperialism**.

British Union of Fascists (BUF) An amalgamation in 1932 of Sir Oswald **Mosley**'s New Party and several small Fascist groups. The Fascist salute, black shirt and extreme anti-Semitic views were adopted. Propaganda marches and meetings were deliberately used to anger left-wingers and Jews, but the Public Order Act (1936), prohibiting political uniforms and giving the police power to ban political processions, effectively put an end to the movement.

Brown Shirts *see* **SA**.

Brüning, Heinrich (1885–1970) A German politician, Chancellor from 1930 to 1932. His expertise as an economist led President Paul von Hindenburg to appoint him Chancellor in an effort to stabilise the economy and halt the rise in popular appeal of the Nazi Party. Without a Reichstag majority he governed by presidential decree, thereby undermining German democracy and encouraging the rise to power of the Nazis, who forced his resignation.

Brusilov Offensive (1916) A huge strategic offensive launched by Russia during WWI, principally intended to force Germany to withdraw troops from the hard-pressed Allied Western Front (*see* **Somme**; **Verdun**). Named after its commander, Alexei Pavelovich Brusilov, it was Russia's last, and best planned, offensive of the war, and recovered a huge swathe of territory from the Pripet Marshes to the Romanian border. It was successful in its aims, but cost Russia crippling numbers of casualties.

Buddhism One of the great religions, strongest in parts of Asia (Sri Lanka, Nepal, Burma, Indo-China, Tibet); variations of it are found in Japan and parts of China. Buddha was a man, and there is no God in the Buddhist religion. Its main teaching is to show the way, through the eight steps of the 'noble path', to inner contentment and peace, so that ultimately, after a succession of reincarnations, man can reach Nirvana – where human and nature are as one in perfect happiness and harmony. Buddhism's contemplative and almost mystical approach to life and its problems has attracted support among Westerners, especially during the 1960s and 70s.

Buffer State A smaller and usually neutral country between two rival powers, e.g. Poland before WWII acted as a buffer state between Germany and the USSR.

Bulganin, Nikolai (1895–1975) A Soviet soldier and politician. He organised Moscow's defence against the German attack (1941) and was created a Marshal of the Soviet Union at the end of WWII. In 1946 he succeeded Stalin as Minister of Defence. He was vice-premier (1953–5) and PM from 1955 to 1958, when he was deposed by Khrushchev. Later that year Bulganin was dropped from the Party Presidium and became chairman of the State Bank.

Bulgaria A republic of SE Europe. Area: 110,911 sq km. Pop: 8,992,300. Language: Bulgarian. Religion: Christianity (Eastern Orthodox). Cap: Sofia.

Under Turkish rule from 1395, Bulgaria achieved autonomy in 1878, becoming an independent kingdom in 1908 and a republic in 1946. It was allied with Germany in both world wars, and a communist regime was established by occupying Russian forces after WWII. The country was a member of the **Council for Mutual Economic Assistance** and the **Warsaw Pact**, and was a hard-line follower of Russian policy. In 1991, however, the communist regime fell, and by 1992 Bulgaria was moving cautiously towards full democracy and a market economy.

Burma A republic of SE Asia, officially known as *Myanmar*. Area: 678,030 sq km. Pop: 45,570,000. Language: Burmese. Religion: Buddhism. Cap: Rangoon.

Unified from small states in 1752, Burma became part of British India in 1885 and a British crown colony in 1937. After Japanese occupation in WWII it achieved independence (1948) followed by a period of civil war. Parliamentary democracy was abolished in a military coup and a Revolutionary Council established (1962), and in 1974 the country became a single-party state. The name was officially changed from Burma to Myanmar in 1989, though the former name is still used. The military-socialist National Unity Party follows a non-aligned policy in foreign affairs (*see* **Non-aligned Movement**), and maintains repressive rule at home. The opposition leader Aung San Suu Kyi was jailed from 1989–95.

Bush, George (1924–) A US Republican politician and statesman, and president from 1989 to 1993. He handled foreign affairs with skill – in particular during the collapse of Communism in Eastern Europe and the ending of the **Cold War** – but he was much criticised for his failure to deal with the problems of the US economy, and he was defeated in the 1992 presidential election by the Democrat Bill **Clinton**.

Bush, George W. (1946–) Son of George **Bush**, he won the US presidential election in 2001 after controversy over the vote count. He was seen as something of a novice, having only been governor of Texas for two terms beforehand. He declared war against terrorism after the attacks on America of 11 September 2001, and against the **Taliban** in Afghanistan, responsible for harbouring Osama **Bin Laden**. His main policies are about tax reduction, the military and social security.

C

Cabinet 1. The executive and policy-making body of a country, consisting of senior ministers of state.

2. The advisory council to a head of state.

Cairo Conference (1943) A meeting between Chiang Kai-shek, Churchill and Roosevelt during WWII when war aims for the Far East were approved. These included Japanese unconditional surrender and the surrender by Japan of territories acquired since 1894, which would either be restored to China or become independent. At the Conference strategic discussions also took place between Churchill and Roosevelt and these were resumed after the **Tehran Conference**.

Callaghan, James (1912–) A British Labour politician, PM from 1976 to 1979. He was Chancellor of the Exchequer (1964–7), Home Secretary (1967–70), and Foreign Secretary (1974–6). He was leader of the Labour Party (1976–81). As PM he tried to secure trade-union support for his counter-inflation policies. Lacking a parliamentary majority, he had to enter into a pact with the Liberal Party (the 'Lib Lab Pact'). He was created a life peer as Lord Callaghan of Cardiff in 1987.

Cambodia, formerly **Kampuchea** or **Khmer Republic** A republic of SE Asia. Area: 181,000 sq km. Pop: 8,055,000. Language: Khmer. Religion: Theravada Buddhism. Cap: Phnom Penh.

The country was part of **Indo-China** from 1887 until it gained independence from France in 1954. Prince Norodom Sihanouk (1922–) dominated political life until 1970 when he was deposed as a result of the country's increasing economic difficulties and intensifying indirect involvement in the Vietnam War.

After the establishment of the Khmer Republic in 1970, Marshal Lon Nol became PM and, in 1972, president. A civil war developed between the US-backed Republic and the communist **Khmer Rouge** backed by China and North Vietnam. After their victory in 1975 the Khmer Rouge, led by Pol Pot, imposed a severely regimented regime, expelled all foreigners, cut off contacts with the rest of the world and compelled the urban population to undertake agricultural work. The regime was also responsible for the massacre of almost a million people.

War with Vietnam broke out in 1977, and Vietnamese troops occupied the capital in 1979. A puppet regime was established, but Khmer Rouge forces continued to fight in remote parts of the country. In 1991 a peace agreement was signed between the various warring factions. A constitutional monarchy was established in 1993 but the Khmer Rouge continued its guerrilla activities, though with decreasing effectiveness. Pol Pot died in 1998, and the Khmer Rouge effectively ceased to exist. Cambodia joined ASEAN in 1999.

Campaign for Nuclear Disarmament (CND) An organisation founded in 1958 to agitate for the UK's unilateral abandonment of nuclear weapons. In the early years it attracted considerable, mostly youthful, support. There were frequent public demonstrations which culminated each year in a march from the Atomic Weapons Research Establishment at Aldermaston, in

Berkshire, to a rally in Trafalgar Square in London. After the signing of the **Nuclear Test-Ban Treaty** (1963) the CND's popularity weakened, although there was a revival in support in the early 1980s. *See* **disarmament**.

Campbell-Bannerman, Sir Henry (1836–1908) A British politician, Liberal PM from 1905 to 1908. His government introduced trade-union legislation (*see* **Taff Vale Case**) and land reforms, and followed a policy of reconciliation after the Boer War, granting the Boers self-government in the Transvaal and Orange Free State.

Camp David Agreement (1978) A draft peace treaty agreed at the US president's official country home in Maryland between Egypt's President **Sadat** and the Israeli PM, **Begin**. It promoted a Middle East settlement, on which was based a peace treaty signed in Washington (1979). President Jimmy Carter of the USA acted as mediator.

The agreement provided for the signing of a treaty within 3 months; the establishment of diplomatic and economic relations; for phased Israeli withdrawal from Sinai and demilitarised security zones along the frontier; and the development of a degree of Palestinian autonomy on the Jordan's **West Bank** within five years.

Capitalism An economic system based on private ownership of the means of production, distribution and exchange (capital), in which the owners of capital (capitalists) manage their property for profit. In theory, capitalism operates in a free market, but in practice monopolies and governments limit or prevent one. Capitalism leads to social inequalities and social injustices which governments have the responsibility to correct. Most capitalist states are, in fact, mixed economies where the economically weak are protected from exploitation by social laws. Communists and left-wing socialists want to see the destruction of capitalism and its replacement by a planned economy, where the state controls supply and gears its response to consumer demand according to national interest. Planned economies (e.g. the USSR) have not been a long-term success, and even China in the 1990s made significant moves back towards a capitalist economy.

Caporetto, Battle of (1917) An Italian defeat by Austro-German forces on the River Isonzo. It was one of the biggest defeats suffered by the Allied armies during WWI, with some 300,000 Italians being taken prisoner and even more deserting.

Carson, Sir Edward Henry later **Baron Carson** (1854–1935) An Irish politician. Leader of the Ulster Unionists in the House of Commons (1910–21), Carson led the opposition in 1912 to the Irish **Home Rule Bill** and raised the Ulster Volunteer Force, bringing Ireland to the verge of civil war and forcing the government to propose concessions on Ulster. *See* **Ireland**.

Carter, James (Jimmy) (1924–) A US Democratic politician, who was president from 1977 to 1981. In the presidential election he defeated Gerald Ford, but was himself defeated in 1980 by Ronald Reagan. He was successful in mediating between Egypt and Israel, resulting in the **Camp David Agreement**. He was a champion of human rights abroad, and continued the policy of détente until the Soviet invasion of **Afghanistan** (1979).

Casablanca Conference (1943) The meeting between Churchill and Roosevelt during which plans were discussed for ending the war in N Africa; the invasion of Sicily; an increase in the bombing of Germany; the transfer of UK war resources to the Far East after the surrender of the Axis powers, which was to be unconditional and not subject to negotiations; and preparation for a second front later in the year.

Casement, Sir Roger (1864–1916) An Irish nationalist, who had been a diplomat in the British consular service from 1892 to 1911. Casement went to Berlin in 1914 to seek German support for a planned uprising in Ireland, (while there trying unsuccessfully to enlist Irish prisoners of war to fight the British in Ireland). Since Germany did not give the support he hoped for, he landed by U-boat in SW Ireland shortly before the **Easter Rising** (1916) in order to persuade the leaders to postpone the uprising, which he was convinced would fail. He was arrested shortly after landing, tried and executed in London for high treason.

Castro, Fidel (1927–) A Cuban communist politician, PM from 1959 to 1976, president from 1976. He became well known when he led an unsuccessful rising against **Batista**'s oppressive regime (1953). He fled to the USA and Mexico where he organized a revolutionary movement, returning secretly to Cuba (1956) with a group that included Che **Guevara**. Waging guerrilla warfare, he became something of a legendary figure, attracting more and more followers and achieving increasing successes over Batista's forces.

After capturing Havana he became PM and Minister of the Armed Forces (1959). He introduced far-reaching reforms in agriculture, education and industry and strengthened ties with China and the USSR, as well as endeavouring to promote revolutions in Latin America and encouraging African liberation movements, notably in Angola, where thousands of Cuban troops were based during the 1980s.

CDU *see* **Christian Democrats**.

CENTO *see* **Central Treaty Organisation**.

Central African Federation *see* **Rhodesia and Nyasaland, Federation of**.

Central Intelligence Agency (CIA) The US security organisation established in 1947 to conduct and coordinate espionage and intelligence operations. Responsible to the National Security Council, it also plans secret operations for such purposes as the overthrow of governments or the downfall of persons considered to be hostile to the USA and its interests. Successes as in Guatemala, Iran (both 1953–4), and Chile (1973) have been matched by disasters, such as the **Bay of Pigs**, the failure to predict the 1973 **Arab-Israeli War** and the 1974 **Cyprus** crisis, and the Watergate Affair, which revealed that the CIA, among other government agencies, had infringed civil liberties.

Central Powers The collective term for Austria–Hungary, Germany and Italy, founder members of the Triple Alliance established in 1882. It was joined in 1883 by Romania and during WWI by Bulgaria and the Ottoman Empire, but left by Italy in 1914 and by Romania in 1916.

The term was retained to differentiate members of the Alliance from Britain, France and Russia, members of the **Triple Entente**. Italy and Romania both joined the Triple Entente against their former allies.

Before 1914 the Triple Alliance and Triple Entente had effectively divided Europe into two armed camps, thus creating an atmosphere of secrecy and suspicion that was a contributory cause of WWI.

Central Treaty Organisation (CENTO) The economic and military alliance formed by Iran, Pakistan, Turkey and the UK in 1959, with the USA as an associated member. It replaced the **Baghdad Pact**, which was dissolved following Iraq's withdrawal. Iran, Pakistan and Turkey withdrew in 1979, and the organisation was effectively dissolved.

Chamberlain, Sir Austen (1863–1937) A British Conservative politician. As Foreign Secretary (1924–9) he took part in the discussions leading to the Treaties of **Locarno** and won the Nobel Peace Prize (1925). His leadership of the Conservative Party (1921–2) ended because of dissatisfaction with his support for Lloyd George, in whose war cabinet he had served.

Chamberlain, Neville (1869–1940) A Conservative politician, PM from 1937 to 1940. He was Chancellor of the Exchequer from 1931 until he succeeded Baldwin as PM (1937). As PM he followed a policy of **appeasement** towards Nazi Germany, and signed the **Munich Agreement** (1938). The policy was unsuccessful in curbing Hitler's aggressive policies, which led to WWII. Dissatisfaction with Chamberlain's wartime leadership led to his resignation in 1940.

Chanak Crisis (1922) The situation in Anglo-Turkish relations resulting from the granting of the port of Smyrna (now Izmir) and the former Ottoman Empire's European territories to Greece by the Treaty of **Sèvres** (1920), which also established a neutral zone between Greece and Turkey on the E side of the **Dardanelles**, subject to an Anglo-French guarantee.

A revolt led by Mustapha Kemal (**Atatürk**) against the Sultan of Turkey resulted in an attempt by Greece to interfere on the Sultan's side, whereupon the rebels advanced on the Dar-Smyrna. This brought the guarantee into effect but France withdrew its troops and the outnumbered UK force had to negotiate an armistice. The Turks accepted the neutralisation of the Bosporus and Dardanelles in return for the restoration of Adrianople and E Thrace and the ending of the Allied occupation of Constantinople (now Istanbul). The agreement formed the basis of the Treaty of **Lausanne**.

Within a fortnight of the armistice the UK coalition government was out of office after the Conservative Party withdrew its support, because of what was considered Lloyd George's pro-Greek attitude during the crisis and his irresponsibility in taking the UK to the brink of war with Turkey.

Channel Tunnel The project for linking Britain and France by tunnelling under the English Channel. There was talk of such a tunnel as long ago as Napoleon's time, and a start was made early in the 20th century but was soon abandoned. A new start was made in the 1980s after much publicity and the raising of public and private funds on both sides of the Channel. After difficulties, delays and shortage of finance the tunnel was inaugurated in 1994 and services began in 1995, but a serious fire in 1996 closed the tunnel for several months and raised fears about safety. The tunnel is 50km (31 miles) long, and is for rail traffic only, road vehicles being carried through on trains.

Cheka *see* **Soviet Security Service**.

Chernenko, Konstantin Ustinovich (1911–85) A Soviet politician, general secretary of the Communist Party and president of the USSR from 1984 to 1985.

Chernobyl The site of a nuclear disaster in Ukraine in 1986, when a nuclear reactor overheated and an explosion poured large clouds of radioactive dust into the atmosphere. The disaster was played down by the Soviet authorities at first, but hundreds of square miles of land were made unfit for human habitation and agricultural use. It caused hundreds of casualties both immediately and in the long term. Its pollution affected many parts of Europe including the UK. It became powerful evidence for those who insist that all production of nuclear energy is potentially unsafe.

Chiang Kai-shek (Pinyin: **Jiang Jieshi**) (1887–1975) A Chinese general, Nationalist statesman and **Kuomintang** leader. At first he worked with **Sun Yat-sen**. Later, he commanded the army which unified China (1926–8), and was president (1928–31) and head of the executive (1935–45). His efforts to overcome army revolts, and the civil war with the communists, left little opportunity to resist the Japanese occupation of Manchuria (1931). In 1936 he was kidnapped by dissident officers and released when he agreed to call off the campaign against the communists and accept their support in resisting Japanese advances.

The Japanese launched all-out war in 1937 and caused Chiang's withdrawal to Chongqing, which remained China's capital throughout WWII, during which he became one of the 'big four' leaders with Churchill, Roosevelt and Stalin. He became president again (1948–9) but, when the split with the communists worsened and they advanced to occupy the whole country, Chiang and his Nationalist followers fled to Taiwan. There, with US military backing, the Nationalists have remained, maintaining that they are China's legitimate government and enjoying prosperity thanks to Japanese and US economic support. Chiang resumed the presidency in 1950 and held office until his death, effectively leader only of an island community.

China, People's Republic of A state of E Asia. Area: 9,597,000 sq km. Pop: 1,211,210,000. Language: Chinese. Religion: largely atheist, though Buddhism and Taoism are prominent, with elements of Christianity and Islam. Cap: Beijing (Peking).

The Manchu dynasty, which had ruled the country since 1644, was overthrown in 1911 by the **Kuomintang** led by **Sun Yat-sen**, who was succeeded by **Chiang Kai-shek**. The Communist Party, founded in 1921, opposed the Kuomintang's military dictatorship, which had shown itself indifferent to the people's wellbeing. The factions were frequently in conflict, although during the **Sino-Japanese War** they cooperated in fighting the common enemy. *See also* **Long March**.

From 1945 onwards the internal struggle was

resumed, the communists under **Mao Zedong** making such rapid progress that by 1949 the Kuomintang had been driven off the mainland to seek refuge on the island of Taiwan. On the mainland, the communists established the People's Republic, while on Taiwan a rival, US-backed government was set up by Chiang Kai-shek. Each government has since claimed its right to the other's territory.

In the People's Republic, Mao Zedong's two great efforts at radical change, the **Great Leap Forward** and the **Cultural Revolution**, badly disrupted cultural, economic and social progress and were dramatic examples of communist policy failures, as were the ideological arguments leading to the **Sino-Soviet split**. In spite of all these difficulties, however, China had the technical competence to develop the atomic bomb (1964) and the hydrogen bomb (1967), so emphasising its superpower status.

Although China's foreign policy has been opposed to the West in such matters as the **Korean** and **Vietnam Wars**, in recent years there has been considerable **détente**, commencing with **Nixon**'s visit to China, and the admission of China to the UN with a seat on the Security Council (1971). After Mao's death in 1976, **Deng Xiaoping** emerged as China's most prominent leader, and reversed or moderated many of Mao's policies. In particular, he encouraged the return of limited forms of capitalism.

In 1989 China was severely criticised internationally after the brutal suppression of a large pro-democracy protest in Tiananmen Square, Beijing. Economic reforms under the current leaders Jiang Zemin (President) and Zhu Rongji (PM) continued, however, and the release of some interned dissidents lessened international opposition.

Chou En-Lai *see* **Zhou Enlai**.

Christian Democrats The members of the Christian Democratic Union (CDU) in Germany, the Christian Democrat Party (DC) in Italy, and similar parties elsewhere.

The German CDU was founded in 1945. In some respects it is the successor of the Centre Party of the **Weimar Republic** and is politically akin to the British **Conservative Party**. In association with its Bavarian wing it is called the Christian Social Union (CSU). It held power on its own (1949–53) and in coalition (1953–7, 1961–6 and 1982–98) with the Free Democratic Party, successor of the Weimar Republic's liberal parties. The CDU's policies, based on united RC-Protestant principles, are moderately conservative, supporting maintenance of private enterprise and individual freedom, and commitment to the EC and NATO. After its loss to the Social Democrats in the 1998 election, the party's influence began to decline amid a series of financial scandals.

The Italian **DC** (Democrazia Cristiana), founded in 1943, was the successor to the Popular Party of the pre-Fascist period, which was inspired by Christian principles. Although the party was not officially tied to the RC Church, the Vatican and clergy exerted powerful influences on its anti-communist and moderate social policies, and like the CDU it was committed to the EU and NATO. It had considerable electoral success, both on its own and in coalition, dominating Italian politics until the early 1990s despite its frequent internal divisions. In 1994 the party was renamed the Italian Popular Party in the wake of serious corruption investigations, and its influence declined sharply. A centre-right faction formed a new 'United Christian Democratic Party' in 1995.

Churchill, Sir Winston (1874–1965) A British politician, PM from 1940 to 1945 and 1951 to 1955.

Churchill entered Parliament as a Conservative in 1900 but, a believer in **free trade** and laissez-faire, joined the Liberal Party (1904). He served as President of the Board of Trade (1908–10), Home Secretary (1910–11) and First Lord of the Admiralty (1911–15). The Conservative Party blamed him for the failure of the **Dardanelles** campaign and he was driven from office. He returned to the government as Minister of Munitions (1917), and was Secretary of State for War and Air (1919–21) and Colonial Secretary (1921–2).

He was out of Parliament from 1922 to 1924 and was then elected as a 'Constitutionalist' for Epping (1924), and served from then until 1929 as Chancellor of the Exchequer in the Conservative Party in 1925. From 1929 to 1939 he was out of office but consistently and forcibly warned Parliament and the country of the perils of German expansionism and the foolishness of following a policy of **appeasement**.

On the outbreak of WWII he returned to the Admiralty as First Lord and in 1940 succeeded

Chamberlain as PM of a **coalition** government. His inspired speeches and outstanding leadership qualities made him immensely popular and his 'bulldog' spirit encouraged and was felt to sum up the British people's determination to win the war whatever the cost.

The Conservative Party was defeated in the 1945 election, and Churchill did not achieve power again until 1951 when he once more became PM, finally resigning in 1955.

CIA *see* **Central Intelligence Agency**.

CIS *see* **Commonwealth of Independent States**.

Civil Defence The organising of civilians to deal with enemy attacks.

Civil Disobedience 1. A refusal to obey laws, pay taxes, etc.

2. A non-violent method of protest or attempt to achieve political aims.

Civil Liberties The rights of individuals to certain freedoms of action and speech, the most important of which are the freedoms of assembly, association, conscience, publication, speech, worship, and peaceful demonstration, petition or protest.

Civil Rights 1. The personal rights of citizens upheld by law in most countries, but especially as established by the 13th and 14th amendments to the US constitution with particular application to the black American population.

2. Equality between groups or races.

Civil Rights Acts The US laws aimed at safeguarding civil rights from being undermined by government and individuals. Several measures were passed during the

19th century, but they were largely ineffective and it was not until 1957 that more positive measures were taken.

The Civil Rights Acts of 1957, 1960, 1964 and 1968, and the Voting Rights Act (1965), provided for the creation of a Civil Rights Commission and a Civil Rights Division of the Justice Department; penalties against the use of mob action to obstruct court orders; guaranteed access to public accommodation for black Americans; strengthened and expanded voting rights; the outlawing of job discrimination; the prevention of discrimination in programmes receiving federal government funds by the threat of the withholding of such funds; the banning of discrimination in the sale and renting of houses; and for specified riot activities.

Class The grouping of people according to economic, occupational or social status. Society is commonly divided into the upper, middle and working (lower) classes, according to their wealth and position in society.

In Marxist theory, the term refers exclusively to those persons sharing the same relationship to material production (*see* **bourgeoisie** and **proletariat**).

Clemenceau, Georges (1841–1929) A French Radical politician, PM from 1906 to 1909 and 1917 to 1920. His first ministerial appointment was Minister of Home Affairs (1906) and by the year's end he was PM. He was defeated in 1909 because of his failure to expand the navy, without achieving many of the reforms he desired.

He was critical of the way the war (WWI) was being conducted and in 1917 became PM and Minister of War. He inspired the armed forces and civilian population to resist the final German onslaught in 1918 and assume the offensive, and played a major part in negotiating the Treaty of **Versailles**. His deep hatred of Germany contributed to the harshness of the terms of the Treaty, which were possibly contributory factors in the outbreak of WWII.

Clinton, William Jefferson (1946–) A US Democratic politician who became the youngest-ever governor of a US state when elected governor of Arkansas in 1978. In 1992 he was elected president of the USA, ending twelve years of Republican rule, and reelected in 1996. He was replaced as president by George W. **Bush** in 2001.

CND *see* **Campaign for Nuclear Disarmament**.

Coalition Government An alliance between two or more political parties for some specific or temporary reason, usually in order to form a government where no party has an absolute majority. *See also* **National Governments**.

Cold War The state of military tension and diplomatic and political hostility between the USA and the USSR and their respective allies from the end of WWII until the collapse of the USSR in 1991.

The Cold War involved propaganda, subversion, threats, etc., and actions with limited objectives which were not permitted to develop into direct military conflict, e.g. the invasions of **Hungary**, **Czechoslovakia** and **Afghanistan**; the **Suez Crisis**; the **Cuban Missile Crisis**; the **Berlin** blockade and wall; the **Vietnam War**; the **Arab-Israeli Wars**; and the conflict in **Lebanon**.

Collaboration The act of cooperating with an enemy, especially one occupying one's own country. Examples in WWII include the **Vichy Government** in France, and **Quisling**'s government in Norway.

Collective Security A system of maintaining world peace and security by joint action on the part of the nations of the world or, in a limited area, by members of an association of states.

Collectivisation A social system based on the principle of the ownership of the means of production by a state, e.g. a collective farm (*kolkhoz*) in a communist country. The system was opposed in the USSR in the 1930s by the *kulaks*, former peasants who had been allowed to become owners of medium-sized farms before the Revolution. In order to achieve the first **Five-Year Plan**, Stalin ordered the extermination of the kulaks and several million died or were exiled to Siberia.

Collins, Michael (1890–1922) An Irish politician who helped organise the **Easter Rising**. After WWI he organised the **Irish Republican Army** (IRA) and was a delegate to the London Conference (1921) aimed at ending the Irish War of Independence. The conference agreed to the partition of the country, and Collins became first PM of the Irish Free State. He was assassinated (1922) by anti-Treaty republicans opposed to partition.

Colombo Plan The scheme put forward at a Commonwealth ministers' meeting in 1950 in Colombo, Ceylon (now Sri Lanka) for cooperative economic development of underdeveloped Commonwealth countries in S and SE Asia. Details were agreed at a Colombo meeting of the Commonwealth Consultative Committee (1951) by which the economic advice,

financial aid and technical training provided by
Australia, Canada, New Zealand and the UK were to go
mainly to Burma, Ceylon, India, Malaya and Pakistan.

Eventually the Plan was expanded to include Japan
and the USA as contributors, and Afghanistan, Bhutan,
Cambodia, Indonesia, Iran, Laos, the Maldives, Nepal,
the Philippines, Singapore, South Korea, South Vietnam
and Thailand as beneficiaries.

Colonialism *see* **imperialism**.

COMECON *see* **Council for Mutual Economic
Assistance**.

Cominform (Communist Information Bureau)
An organisation established in 1947 for the exchange of
information and coordination of activities by the
Communist Parties of Bulgaria, Czechoslovakia, France,
Hungary, Italy, Poland, Romania, USSR and Yugoslavia,
with HQ in Belgrade. It was dissolved in 1956 as a
condition of reconciliation with the USSR demanded by
Yugoslavia, which had been expelled from the
Cominform in 1948 for following policies that were
different from those of the USSR.

Comintern The Communist or Third International, a
movement established in 1919 by Lenin to promote
revolutionary Marxist international socialism as opposed
to the reformist socialism of the Second International.
In the early years the international aims of **Trotsky** and
Zinoviev were followed but **Stalin**'s policies gradually
took their place and served only Soviet interests. The
movement was dissolved in 1943, probably to please the
Western allies of the USSR.

Common Agricultural Policy (CAP) The EU

scheme for increasing agricultural productivity, stabilising markets, and assuring the availability of supplies, reasonable consumer prices and fair living standards for the agricultural community.

The CAP is based on stable currencies, a single market structure of common prices, agreement on administrative, health and veterinary legislation, Community preference, common financing, and the stabilisation of markets against world price fluctuations by intervention measures, levies and refunds on exports and imports. By the late 1990s the CAP had become one of the main focuses of both opposition to and reform initiatives within the EU.

Common Market *see* **European Union**.

Commonwealth of Independent States (CIS) A loose union of some of the republics of the former Soviet Union. It was formed in the autumn of 1991 with the intention of ensuring cooperation in foreign and economic policies. However, several former Soviet republics refused to join, including the **Baltic States**. The two most powerful states of the CIS are Russia and Ukraine, and they have not always been able to agree, particularly on matters of defence.

Commonwealth of Nations, British An association of independent states that at some time were ruled by the UK, and which acknowledge the British sovereign as head of the Commonwealth.

Before 1931 these countries, acquired for commercial, strategic or territorial reasons, belonged to the British Empire (*see* **imperialism**), the foundations of which dated from the 17th century. The term 'British

Commonwealth' came into use during WWI to describe the relationship between Britain and the self-governing dominions (then consisting of Canada, Newfoundland, Australia, New Zealand, and South Africa), and was given force of law by the **Statute of Westminster** (1931).

The association of states was often referred to as the 'British Commonwealth and Empire', a term in general use until 1947 when, with the independence of India and Pakistan, the word 'Empire' was dropped. Since WWII most of the countries of the Empire have achieved independence and nearly all have decided to remain within the Commonwealth, exceptions being Burma, the Republic of Ireland, Pakistan and South Africa (which left in 1961 and was readmitted in 1994).

The UK's relations with its Commonwealth partners are conducted by the Foreign and Commonwealth Office, and the Commonwealth Secretariat was established in 1965 to promote relations between member states whose leaders meet periodically to discuss affairs of mutual interest.

Communism 1. The advocacy of a classless society in which private ownership has been abolished and the means of production and distribution belong to the state.

2. The economic, political or social doctrine directed towards achieving such a society.

3. A political movement that considers history as a process of **class** warfare and revolutionary upheaval, in which **capitalism** will be overthrown and the **proletariat** will emerge victorious, with public ownership of the means of production. *See also* **Marxism**.

Communist International *see* **Comintern**.

Concentration Camps The detention centres established from 1933 onwards by the Nazi regime in Germany for the imprisonment of those suspected of being enemies of the state. During WWII concentration camps were also established in several Nazi-occupied countries, and became centres of slave labour, sadistic medical experiments and mass extermination. About 6 million Jews died in the camps, the most notorious of which were **Auschwitz**, Belsen, Buchenwald, Dachau and Treblinka.

Concordat A pact or treaty, especially between the Vatican and a secular state, concerning religious matters in that state. Best known are the Lateran Treaties (1929) between the Vatican and Italy which recognised the Vatican City as an independent state and restored Roman Catholicism as Italy's official religion. Compensation was also awarded to the Vatican for papal possessions seized when Rome was occupied in 1870 during Italian unification.

Confucianism One of the main religions of China. It arose out of the teachings of Confucius, who lived in the 6th century BC. His main ideas were practical: respect for parents, respect for authority, politeness and good behaviour at all times, and an acceptance of one's lot in life. Buddha was his contemporary, but Confucius had none of Buddha's mysticism, and his ideas did not have the wider appeal of **Buddhism**. Communists in China particularly disliked Confucianism as it encouraged acceptance of things as they are, and obstructed progress. They therefore set about persecuting its followers, but they only partially succeeded in suppressing it.

Congress The US parliament, established by Article 1 of the Constitution. Its two houses are the House of Representatives and the Senate. The members of the House of Representatives, the lower chamber, are elected every two years from districts of roughly equal populations. Two senators from each state are elected to the Senate for six-year terms; every two years, a third of the Senate comes up for election.

Congress Party An Indian political organisation known before independence as the Indian National Congress. It was founded in 1885 to draw together regionally based, well-educated political groups. Between the World Wars Mahatma **Gandhi**'s doctrine of nonviolent civil disobedience as a means of achieving Indian independence dominated the Party. Its leading members were interned (1942–5) because of opposition to India's entry into WWII. After independence the Party was in power continuously apart from 1977–80 under the successive leaderships of **Nehru**, **Shastri**, Indira **Gandhi**, Rajiv **Gandhi** and P V Rao, until 1996.

Conscription or **National Service** The compulsory service in the armed forces or the direction of conscientious objectors into essential but non-military duties such as agriculture, mining, etc. It was applied in the UK during the periods 1916 to 1920 and 1939 to 1960, and is still used in a number of countries.

Conservative Party or **Conservative and Unionist Party** The British political organisation that developed from the Tories of the 1830s. It encourages property ownership, a mixed economy and strong defence based (from 1945 until about 1991) on **collective security** against communist expansion. It became known as the Conservative and Unionist Party in 1886 because of its opposition to Irish Home Rule. Until the 1980s it supported existing institutions coupled with moderate reforms, and its earlier imperialism made it a keen supporter of the Commonwealth. Under **Thatcher** the Party moved further to the right, with radical policies in favour of free enterprise and consumerism. The party suffered its heaviest electoral defeat of the century in 1997, at the hands of Tony **Blair**'s Labour Party.

Constitution 1. The system by which a state is governed, especially when it includes the rights of subjects of that state. The constitution may be written (US) or partly unwritten (British).

2. A statute embracing such principles, e.g. the US constitution.

Constitutional Monarchy The form of government in which supreme authority (usually hereditary) lies with a king or queen, who rules according to a **constitution** that defines and limits the sovereign's powers.

Consumerism A concern to satisfy the needs of consumers. It is the driving force of the consumer society, and the happiness of society and its individual members is measured by the number and quality of personal possessions. In the 1980s it came to represent a major aspect of Thatcherite Conservatism in the UK, and was open to the criticism that, in its emphasis on materialism, it neglected the true values of society.

Containment 1. The limiting of the power of a hostile country or operations of a hostile military force.

2. A principle of US foreign policy 1947–91 seeking to halt communist expansion. *See* **Truman Doctrine**.

Contras *see* **Nicaragua**.

Coolidge, Calvin (1872–1933) A US Republican politician who was vice-president (from 1921 to 1923) and president from 1923 to 1929. On President Warren Harding's mid-term death he succeeded to the presidency, and set about restoring public confidence after the scandals of Harding's administration. He was a believer in unrestricted freedom in business which led to a rapid growth in commercial monopolies, and followed a policy of conservative **isolationism**. After he left office the prosperity encouraged by his policies was destroyed in the **Wall Street Crash**.

Coral Sea, Battle of the (1942) A naval battle of WWII off the NE coast of Australia in which the Japanese, although inflicting more losses than they suffered, were forced to abandon their plans to attack the New Hebrides, Fiji and Samoa. It was, therefore, the first major check the Japanese suffered since they entered the war in December 1941. The ships in the battle made virtually no direct contact; the fighting was done by aircraft from aircraft carriers. This was to be the pattern for the subsequent battles in the Pacific.

Council for Mutual Economic Assistance (COMECON) An organisation established in 1949 to improve trade between the communist member states – Albania, Bulgaria, Czechoslovakia, Hungary, Poland, Romania and the USSR. Albania was expelled in 1961, but additional members were East Germany (1950), Mongolia (1962), Cuba (1972) and Vietnam (1978).

The USSR tried to enforce a common economic policy and trade pattern but strong opposition from Bulgaria and Romania forced a withdrawal of these proposals on the grounds that they interfered with the sovereignty of member states and would damage the less well-off members.

With the turmoil in E Europe from 1989 and the collapse of the Soviet Union in 1991, Comecon virtually ceased to operate, and most of its members sought membership of the EU.

Council of Europe An organisation established in 1949 by a decision of the Consultative Council of the **Western European Union**. Its members are Belgium, Denmark, France, the Republic of Ireland, Italy, Luxembourg, the Netherlands, Norway, Sweden and the UK. Greece and Turkey joined in 1949, Iceland in 1950, West Germany in 1951, Austria in 1956, Cyprus in 1961, Switzerland in 1963, Malta in 1965, Portugal in 1976, Spain in 1977 and Liechtenstein in 1978. Greece withdrew in 1969 because of opposition within the council to its violation of human rights.

The Council consists of a committee of ministers, and a consultative assembly of 170 members appointed or elected by the respective parliaments, usually from their own members but not necessarily so. The European Convention for the Protection of Human Rights (1950) is one of its major achievements. The Partial Agreement (1960) permits members to cooperate closely, using Council facilities, without involving all members; this has made possible group agreements on education, local government and social and public health issues.

The council's aims are the achievement of greater unity between member states and their economic and social progress; practically the only topic barred from discussion is a member state's national defence.

Council of Ministers A decision-making body of the EU, formed in 1967 by a merger of the three existing communities ECSC, EU and Euratom. It is composed of the foreign ministers of the member states who represent national as opposed to EU interests. It can make decisions with majority support, but tries to get unanimous agreement whenever possible. The presidency of the council is held in rotation for six-month periods. Since 1974, heads of state and government have met every three months to discuss Community and foreign policy affairs.

Country Party An Australian political party founded in 1920 with the objective of giving better representation to agricultural interests in a parliament dominated by MPs from the cities. By 1922 it held the balance of power between Labor and Nationalists and was a partner in coalition governments (1922–9, 1934–41 and 1949–71).

Coup d'état A sudden, violent or illegal change of government.

Cripps, Sir Stafford (1889–1952) A British Labour politician. As Chancellor of the Exchequer (1947–50), he pursued a policy of austerity, but strict taxation and a voluntary wage freeze failed to solve the problem of inflation.

Croatia A state in the northern Balkans, part of Austria-Hungary until 1918, when it joined **Yugoslavia**. Dissatisfaction with the Yugoslav Federation began almost immediately. Croat nationalists assassinated King Alexander in 1934 and some Croats, during WWII, saw collaboration with the Germans as the best way to break free from Yugoslavia. Under Tito, himself a Croat, strongly centralised communist rule held Yugoslavia together, but after his death weaker political leadership and a rapidly deteriorating economic situation gave Croatia the chance to declare independence, and to receive international recognition in 1991. The cost was a vicious war against the Serbs, who occupied considerable areas of Croatia, not all of which were ethnically Serb. However, these areas were eventually reintegrated into Croatia. During the war in **Bosnia**, Croatia tried to create and protect Croat enclaves there.

Cuba see **Batista**; **Bay of Pigs**; **Castro**; **Cuban Missile Crisis**.

Cuban Missile Crisis (1962) A sequence of events at the height of the Cold War that brought the world close to destruction by nuclear warfare. US aerial reconnaissance showed that weapons being supplied by the USSR to **Castro**'s Cuba were ballistic missiles with atomic warheads capable of reaching any part of the USA. President John F. Kennedy announced that the USA would blockade Cuba and requested the USSR to remove all weapons that had already reached the island and to order vessels carrying more to return home. In exchange for the removal of the weapons the USA pledged to lift the blockade and refrain from invading

Cuba. This firm action by the USA (and the secret US concession to remove similar missiles from Turkey), prevented an even more serious confrontation.

Cultural Revolution (1966–8) A major political upheaval in China, conceived by **Mao Zedong** as an attack on bureaucracy and privilege. The country's educational, managerial and party elite and trends towards liberalism were criticised and purged, with the result that communications were disrupted and the economy threatened. The Red Guards, a mass youth movement, led the revolutionary demonstrations by closing colleges and schools and participating in gigantic parades supported by widespread wall-poster campaigns. The revolution ended when the army stepped in to restore order. The leaders of the Cultural Revolution (the **Gang of Four**) were discredited after Mao's death in 1976.

Curragh Incident (1914) A threatened army mutiny when the British government proposed to use troops against **Ulster Loyalists** who violently opposed **Irish Home Rule**. Officers based on the Curragh plain, SW of Dublin, were informed that they could resign their commissions and be dismissed from the army if they did not wish to fire on Ulster Protestants. When a majority of the officers accordingly offered their resignations, the government agreed not to use the army in Ulster, and the situation was resolved.

Curzon, George Nathaniel, Marquis Curzon of Kedleston (1859–1925) A British Conservative politician. As Viceroy of India (1898–1905) he introduced many administrative, financial, political and social reforms, including partition of Bengal and the establishment of the NW Frontier Province. As Foreign Secretary (1919–24), his main achievement was the conclusion of the Treaty of **Lausanne** (1923).

Curzon Line The proposed border along the 'ethnic line' separating Poles and Russians, suggested by the British Foreign Secretary, Lord **Curzon**, in 1919. As a result of the Polish-Soviet War the boundary was fixed by the Treaty of Riga (1921) well to the E of the Curzon Line. Following the **Tehran Conference** in 1943, the Curzon Line became the future E border of Poland.

Cyprus A Commonwealth island republic of the E Mediterranean. Area: 9,251 sq km. Pop: 767,000. Languages: Greek and Turkish. Religions: Christianity (Greek Orthodox) and Islam. Cap: Nicosia.

The island, populated by both Greeks and Turks, was part of the **Ottoman Empire** until 1914 when Britain annexed it because of the Ottoman alliance with Germany during WWI, although Britain had held certain rights there since 1878. Cyprus became a colony in 1925, but from the 1930s the Greek population made increasing demands for union with Greece (*Enosis*). The transfer of the UK's Middle East HQ from Egypt to Cyprus in 1954 led to a terrorist campaign against the British occupation forces (and civil war with Turkish Cypriots) by extremists of the pro-Enosis underground movement (EOKA) led by General George Grivas (1898–1974), a Greek army officer.

In 1960 Cyprus became independent, and Archbishop **Makarios**, having renounced Enosis, was elected president. However, civil war broke out again between the two communities (1963), only ending with the intervention of a UN peace-keeping force in 1964. The conflict caused growing hostility between Greece and Turkey and in 1974 the Greek military junta (*see* **Greece**) backed a pro-Enosis coup which overthrew Makarios. This led to the invasion and occupation of the N part of the island by Turkey, and open war between Greece and Turkey was narrowly avoided. These events contributed to the fall of the junta in Greece, and led to the movement of 200,000 Greek Cypriot refugees to the S of the island. The island is now effectively partitioned, despite the treaties between Cyprus, Greece, Turkey and the UK which forbid partition as well as Enosis. The UK still retains its sovereign military bases of some 158 sq km.

Czechoslovakia A former federal republic of C Europe. Area: 127,871 sq km. Pop: 15,639,000 before breakup. Languages: Czech and Slovak. Religion: Christianity (RC). Cap: Prague.

The state consisted of the former Austro-Hungarian provinces of Bohemia, Moravia, Silesia and Slovakia and was established in 1918 as part of the WWI peace settlements. Tómas Masaryk (1850–1937), who had organised the Czech independence movement during the War, became president (1918–35). It was to become the most progressive and prosperous of the new European states.

After the Nazis achieved power in Germany the population of the **Sudetenland** in N Bohemia, mostly German in origin, campaigned for the area to be ceded to Germany, and this was accomplished under the terms of the **Munich Agreement** (1938). In 1939 Germany occupied the rest of Czechoslovakia, and the country remained under occupation until 1945.

Immediately after the War the coalition government was in power with Masaryk's son Jan (1886–1948) as Foreign Minister. In 1948 the communists under **Gottwald** seized control, and shortly afterwards Jan Masaryk died in suspicious circumstances. Gottwald established a hard-line and repressive communist system which was continued after his death (1953) by **Novotny**.

In 1968 pressures for change brought about the so-called 'Prague Spring', when **Dubček** attempted to introduce liberalising policies, only to see the popular support he received ruthlessly suppressed when the country was occupied by the armed forces of the Warsaw Pact states (except those of Romania). Dubček was replaced by Gustav **Husák**, under whom the country returned to its previous position as a hard-line member of the Warsaw Pact and Comecon. In 1989 the communist government collapsed in the face of popular protest it was unable to control. Under President Václav Havel, Czechoslovakia moved towards democracy and a market economy, but internal tensions led in 1992 to the break-up of the Czechoslovak state into two independent republics, Slovakia and the Czech Republic. In 1993 Havel became president of the Czech Republic; Slovakia was led after independence by Vladimír Mečiar. In 1999 a new Slovak president, Rudolf Schuster, pledged to end his country's opposition to European integration, while the Czech Republic became a full member of NATO.

D

Daladier, Edouard (1884–1970) A French Radical statesman who was PM from 1933 to 1934 and 1938 to 1940. The governments he led favoured **appeasement** and he signed the **Munich Agreement**. After the collapse of France in 1940, he tried to form a government in N Africa opposed to the **Vichy Government**, but was arrested, tried for taking France unprepared into war and imprisoned until 1945. He never held ministerial office again.

Danzig or (Polish) **Gdánsk** A Polish port at the mouth of the Vistula. Formerly belonging to Prussia, it was made a Free City by the Treaty of **Versailles** to allow Poland an outlet to the Baltic. The Treaty also granted territory to Poland to give it access to Danzig. This territory was known as the Polish Corridor, and it divided East Prussia from the main part of Germany.

In 1939 Germany demanded that Poland should return the city and allow Germany independent access routes across the Polish Corridor to East Prussia. Poland's rejection of these demands led to the country's invasion by Germany and the outbreak of WWII.

Dardanelles, formerly **the Hellespont** A strait linking the Sea of Marmara and the Aegean Sea, part of the strategic waterway connecting the Black Sea and the Mediterranean.

In 1915 an Anglo-French fleet tried to force a way through to Constantinople (Istanbul) but suffered heavy losses. The purposes of the attempt were to drive the

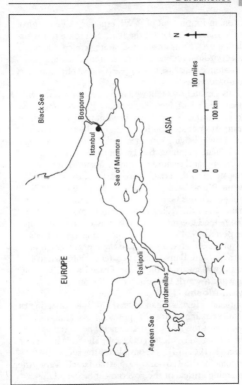

Ottoman Empire out of WWI, establish Allied control of the Balkans and open the Black Sea route to Russia. The failure of this imaginative strategic plan was due to bad coordination, inadequate planning, lack of persistence, and loss of surprise because of preliminary bombardments.

This disaster was followed immediately by another, when Australian, New Zealand and British forces landed on the Gallipoli peninsula at the S end of the strait. After eight months of fighting the troops were withdrawn, leaving Ottoman Turkey the victor yet again. Inadequate planning, bad coordination, confused leadership and high-ranking British and French opposition to the attack were causes of the failure.

Dawes Plan (1924) The scheme proposed by a US banker, Charles Gates Dawes (1865–1961), while chairman of the Allied Reparations Committee. The plan helped Germany to fulfil its treaty commitments in the period 1924–9 by permitting annual **reparations** payments on a fixed scale, and the reorganisation of the German State Bank to assist currency stabilisation. Dawes was awarded the Nobel Peace Prize (1925) for his work towards German reconciliation.

Dayan, Moshe (1915–81) An Israeli general and politician. He was Chief of Staff (1953–8), directing the Sinai campaign against Egypt (1956). As a Labour member of the Knesset (Parliament) he served as Minister of Agriculture (1959–64). He was Minister of Defence (1967–74), responsible for the successful outcome of the 1967 and 1973 **Arab-Israeli Wars**. After becoming critical of the government he joined the

opposition and became Foreign Minister (1977–9) in
Begin's coalition government.

D-Day *see* **Normandy Landings**.

Decolonisation 1. The granting of independence to a
colony.

2. The freeing of a territory from colonial status.

Britain gave independence to its larger colonies in a
gradual process starting in the 19th century. Canada
gained independence in 1867, Australia in 1901, New
Zealand in 1907 (more fully in 1931), South Africa in
1910, India and Pakistan in 1947, Sri Lanka in 1948,
Ghana in 1957, Nigeria in 1960, Tanzania in 1961,
Uganda in 1962, Kenya and Malaysia in 1963. Most of
Britain's smaller colonies have since been granted
independence, notable exceptions being Gibraltar and
the Falkland Islands.

France lost Indo-China (1954) and Algeria (1962)
after violent wars of independence, but most other
French colonies (principally in Africa) had a peaceful
transition to independence in the 1950s and 1960s.
Pressure for independence mostly came from the
growth of nationalism led by a Western-educated elite
in each country.

de Gaulle, Charles (1890–1970) A French general and
politician, president in 1945 and from 1959 to 1969.
After a distinguished military career, de Gaulle escaped
to England after the fall of France (1940) in WWII to
become leader of the **Free French** and head of the
French Committee of National Liberation (1943). His
perceived aloofness and arrogance made him a difficult
partner for Churchill and Roosevelt. He was elected

president (1945) but resigned after ten weeks in office because his proposals for the Fourth Republic were not accepted by the constituent assembly. This was after he had returned to France in 1944 and had become head of the Provisional Government when France was liberated.

De Gaulle remained in retirement until the fall of the Fourth Republic, when he formed a 'government of national safety' and a constitution for the Fifth Republic (1958). President again in 1959, he ended the Algerian War by the Evian Agreements (1962). He was determined that France should have an independent nuclear deterrent, and insisted on the UK's exclusion from the EEC. He withdrew France from NATO and insisted on the removal of NATO installations from the country because of disagreements with the USA. He was forced to make economic concessions in 1968 by serious student unrest over high taxation for military purposes at the expense of education, health and social services (*see* **Paris student demonstrations**). He resigned in 1969 after his proposals for senate and regional reforms were rejected in a referendum.

Democracy Government by the people or their elected representatives; a political or social unit governed by all its members. The term implies that free elections are held at regular intervals, with the participation of an unlimited number of political parties. The absence of democracy is variously termed **autocracy**, **dictatorship** and **totalitarianism**.

Democratic Party The more progressive of the two main political parties in the USA. Founded in 1828, its first 20th century presidential success was that of Woodrow **Wilson** (president 1913–21). The Party urged government action to stimulate industry and reduce unemployment after the interwar depression, and the proposals became part of F D Roosevelt's **New Deal**. Under Wilson, Roosevelt, Truman and Kennedy the Party displayed a sense of worldwide responsibility, in contrast to Republican isolationism. From the early 1960s, the Party has been particularly concerned with civil rights, social welfare and aid to underdeveloped countries. After **Watergate**, the Party held power under Jimmy **Carter** (1977–81), and regained the presidency in 1992 under Bill **Clinton**.

Deng Xiaoping or **Teng Hsiao-ping** (1904–97) A Chinese communist politician. Deng achieved enormous power on becoming Party Secretary in 1954. His organisational skills, moderation and dislike of uncontrolled radicalism caused him to distance himself from **Mao Zedong** and to move closer to Liu Shaoqi, the state president 1960–5. Like Liu, Deng was disgraced during the **Cultural Revolution**; he was restored to favour in 1973, dismissed again in 1976 (but only briefly), and in 1977 he was made deputy PM and Party Vice-Chairman. Although he retired from many of his official posts he remained the most powerful figure in the Chinese leadership for many years.

Depression or **slump** A decline in trade and general prosperity. The Great Depression of 1929–34 was worldwide, starting with an agricultural recession followed by financial panic and collapse, known as the **Wall Street Crash**, in the USA. This in turn affected

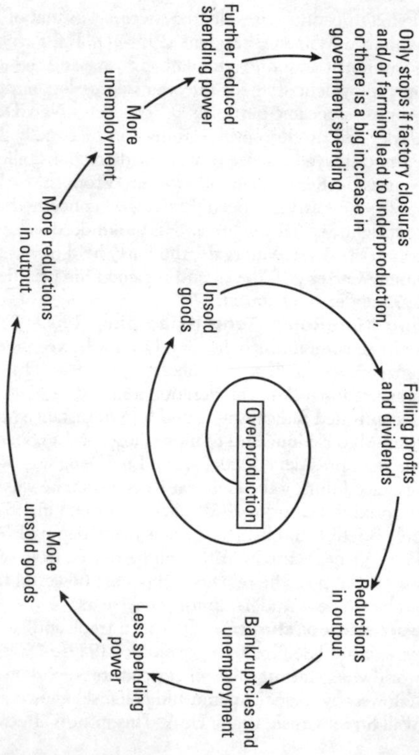
Overproduction
Unsold goods
Falling profits and dividends
Reductions in output
Bankruptcies and unemployment
Less spending power
More unsold goods
More reductions in output
More unemployment
Further reduced spending power
Only stops if factory closures and/or farming lead to underproduction, or there is a big increase in government spending

Depression *The spiral of depression.*

financial institutions and money markets in other parts of the world and caused a run on the pound in the UK. The result was a decline in internal sales and exports in industrialised countries, factory closures and massive unemployment.

Desegregation or **Integration** The policy of ending the forced separation of racial, political or religious groups within a society.

In the 1950s the US federal government ordered the end of separate schooling for blacks and whites in the southern states. This policy met with widespread white opposition, leading to race riots in Little Rock, Arkansas (1957), where federal troops were used to enforce school integration.

In South Africa, the policy of **apartheid** opposed racial desegregation.

Desert Campaign *see* **North Africa Campaign**.

Détente The easing or relaxing of tension, especially between nations. More specifically the term is used for the improvement of relations between East and West from around 1969. In 1972 the USA and the USSR started on the **Strategic Arms Limitation Talks**. East-West relations deteriorated after the Soviet invasion of **Afghanistan** (1979), although they improved to an extent when **Gorbachev** was in power. The collapse of the Soviet Union in 1991 removed the need for détente. *See also* **Cold War**.

Deterrence The prevention of hostilities by the possession by any state of a weapon or combination of weapons, especially nuclear, powerful enough to make any enemy attack unlikely to succeed. In the **Cold War**, a 'balance of terror' between the NATO (**North Atlantic Treaty Organisation**) and **Warsaw Pact** powers, which each possessed such weapons, played a major part in preventing open warfare between them.

de Valéra, Eamon (1882–1975) An Irish politician. After joining **Sinn Féin**, he took part in the **Easter Rising** (1916), afterwards avoiding execution by the British only because of his American birth. From 1917 until 1926 he was President of Sinn Féin, and was effectively leader of the Irish forces in the War of Independence (1918–22). He opposed the signing of the Anglo-Irish Treaty (1921) and led the anti-Treaty faction in the subsequent civil war (1922–3). In 1926 he formed a new political party, **Fianna Fáil**, which, with Labour, formed a coalition government (1932). He remained PM for 16 years, an office he again held from 1951 to 1954 and 1957 to 1959. He was largely responsible for the new constitution (1937) which broke the final links with the UK by creating a republic in Eire (now the Republic of Ireland), of which he was president 1959–73.

Devaluation The reduction in the foreign exchange value of a country's currency. This can be forced by excessive foreign selling of the currency, as with the British Pound in 1992, or it could be done by a government under economic and financial pressure, as in the UK in 1949 and in 1967 (*see diagram on p. 93*). The reduction in the foreign value of the devalued currency helps exports in the short term by making them cheaper for foreign buyers, but in the long term it tends to worsen inflation by making imports dearer.

Deviationism A move away from the strict following of

	Year	American Dollars to the Pound
	1925	$4.86
D	1931	$3.30
		↓ Rising value of £
	1948	$4.03
D	1949	$2.80
D	1967	$2.40
		↓ Varying value of £ but mainly a slow fall
	1991	$1.80
D	1992	$1.50 (D – year when devaluation took place)

Devaluation

an ideology or set of principles, especially from orthodox Moscow-line Communism, such as was practised by **Yugoslavia** from the 1950s and put forward by W European communist parties (*see* **Eurocommunism**).

Devolution A transfer or granting of authority, especially from a central government to regional governments or particular interests, such as the passing of certain functions and powers to Northern Irish, Scottish and Welsh authorities by the UK government.

Dictator A ruler whose power is not limited by a constitution, laws, recognised opposition, etc. Examples include Hitler, Mussolini and Stalin.

Dictatorship 1. The office, government or period of rule by a dictator.

2. A country ruled by a dictator.

3. The absolute or supreme power of authority.

Dien Bien Phu A village in North Vietnam, the scene of a decisive victory in 1954 by the **Viet Minh** over the French in the war of independence in **Indo-China**. The French defeat led to the end of French colonial rule in Indo-China and the partition of **Vietnam** following the 1954 Geneva Agreement.

Disarmament The reduction of the means of waging war, usually by a state. Before and after WWI and WWII many attempts were made to achieve meaningful disarmament on a large scale, firstly between the Fascist states and the democracies of Europe and America and, since WWII, between NATO and Warsaw Pact countries. There was no success before WWII but some progress has been made since, notably in the **Nuclear Test Ban Treaty** (1963), a **Non-Proliferation Treaty** (1968), a germ warfare agreement (1972), the **Strategic Arms Limitation Talks** (1969–72 and 1979), and the **Intermediate Nuclear Forces Treaty** (1987). Attempts to negotiate on **Star Wars** programmes were overtaken by the fall of Gorbachev and the collapse of the Soviet Union. Member states of the CIS, especially Russia, have large stockpiles of nuclear weapons, but have shown willingness to disarm and to seek economic cooperation with the West. With the end of the Cold War the problem areas for world disarmament have become the Middle East and the Far East.

Governments on both sides have generally pursued a policy of multilateralism, i.e. that no country should abandon nuclear weapons until all agree to do so. Vocal pressure groups in the West such as the **Campaign for Nuclear Disarmament** have called for a policy of unilateralism, i.e. that their own country should abandon nuclear weapons as an example to others.

Dogger Bank Incident (1904) An event during the **Russo-Japanese War** when the Russian Baltic Fleet was sent to the Far East. Steaming through the North Sea, it encountered what were thought to be Japanese torpedo boats but actually were fishing vessels from the British port of Hull. The warships sank one vessel, killing two of its crew. This caused such anger in Britain that an armed conflict was barely avoided. International arbitration and Russian acceptance of compensation claims eased tension, and long-term relations between the two countries started to improve.

Dollfuss, Engelbert (1892–1934) An Austrian politician. After WWI, Dollfuss joined the Christian Social Party, and was Chancellor from 1932 to 1934. Fearing a left-wing revolt, he suspended parliamentary government in 1933, and ordered the army to attack a housing estate in the suburbs of Vienna in order to put down a socialist demonstration there (1934). His introduction of a new and Fascist constitution in 1934 brought about his downfall. Hated by the Nazis, who wanted **Anschluss**, and by the Marxists, he was assassinated in the Chancellory by Nazis attempting to stage a **coup d'état**.

Dominion 1. A self-governing territory of the British Empire before WWII, i.e. Australia, Canada, India, New Zealand and South Africa.

   2. An area of control or sphere of influence.

3. The land governed by a government or ruler.

Domino Theory The idea that a communist takeover of one country would lead to communist takeovers in neighbouring states, just as a line of dominoes, each standing on end, will all fall when one is pushed. The theory was put forward by those in the USA who opposed withdrawal of US forces from the Vietnam War.

Dönitz, Karl (1891–1980) A German admiral and leading member of the High Command during WWII and, for three weeks in 1945, Hitler's successor. Ignoring the Treaty of **Versailles**, Dönitz helped to reorganize the U-boat fleet in the 1930s and became Commander-in-Chief of the German navy in 1943. The Allied Military Tribunal at Nuremberg sentenced him in 1946 to ten years' imprisonment for war crimes.

Douglas-Home, Sir Alec, Baron Home of the Hirsel (1903–95) A British Conservative politician, PM from 1963 to 1964. He was twice Foreign Secretary (1960–3 and 1970–4). After Macmillan's resignation (1963), Douglas-Home was elected leader of the Conservative Party, and became PM. The success of his 'caretaker' leadership probably reduced the size of Labour's majority in the 1964 election.

Dreadnought a class of big-gun battleship named after HMS *Dreadnought*, launched in 1906. The class carried ten 12-inch guns, had a speed of 21 knots, and was able to outrange and outpace any other warship. The introduction of this class of ship started a full-scale naval armaments race that reached its climax in WWI.

Dresden An industrial city of Saxony in E Germany. A beautiful city with many buildings of the 17th and 18th centuries, Dresden was almost totally destroyed by Allied bombing in 1945 with a loss of *c.*135,000 lives, an action which caused considerable criticism as being unnecessary at such a late stage in WWII.

Dreyfus, Alfred (1859–1935) A French army officer, of Jewish origin, falsely convicted for treason in 1894. Charged with passing military intelligence to Germany, he was court-martialled and imprisoned on Devil's Island. The case split French popular opinion: liberals, radicals and socialists maintained his innocence, but were opposed by the military, monarchists and RCs, who stirred up considerable anti-Semitic and anti-German feelings. Dreyfus was eventually released in 1906. Final proof of innocence was established when documents of the German military attaché were published in 1930.

Dubček, Alexander (1921–92) A Czechoslovak politician. His reforms as first secretary of the Communist Party (1968–9) led to the Warsaw Pact occupation of **Czechoslovakia** after the 'Prague Spring' (1968) and his enforced resignation. He was expelled from the Party in 1970. His fall from power was due to his desire to liberalise the economy, to widen the area of discussion within the Party without deviation from the Warsaw Pact's external policies, and to reduce the Party's totalitarian character. He was able to return to politics in 1990 after the collapse of Communism.

Dulles, John Foster (1888–1959) A US diplomat and politician. As Secretary of State from 1953 to 1959,

Dulles caused tension with America's allies, especially during the **Suez Crisis**. A firm supporter of European unity, he did much to strengthen international alliances against Communism, and his careful show of US strength was important both in safeguarding West Berlin's status, and in the retention of the Pescadores, Quemoy and Matsu islands (off the Chinese mainland) by the Chinese Nationalists in Taiwan against harassment by the People's Republic of China.

Duma The Russian elective legislative assembly established by Tsar **Nicholas II** (1905) and overthrown by the Bolsheviks (1917). The upper chamber was the Council of State and the lower chamber, the State Duma, elected on a limited **franchise**. There were four Dumas during the period 1905–17. The Tsar retained the power of dissolution and veto, and ministers were responsible to him and not to the Duma, which was allowed only limited control of the budget.

Dumbarton Oaks Conference (1944) A series of meetings held near Washington by delegates from Britain, China, the USSR and the USA to discuss proposals for the **United Nations Organisation**, with special reference to the Security Council and the individual members' use of veto powers.

Dunkirk A port of NW France, from which the British Expeditionary Force and the French 1st Army were evacuated to Britain in 1940 during WWII. About 336,000 men were rescued by a hastily collected fleet of vessels. Shortly afterwards France surrendered.

E

Easter Rising (1916) A rebellion seeking independence from Britain for **Ireland**, centred on the General Post Office in Dublin from where a provisional government of the Irish Republic was proclaimed. Hoped-for German assistance did not materialise and twelve rebel leaders, including the socialist James Connolly and Patrick Pearse of the Irish Republican Brotherhood, were executed. Others, including Eamon **de Valéra**, were imprisoned but later released under an amnesty in 1917. The general revulsion at the executions was largely responsible for turning Irish public opinion towards the idea of independence.

East Germany *see* **Germany**.

ECSC *see* **European Coal and Steel Community**.

Ecumenism The movement concerned with closer cooperation between the various Christian churches. Its first aim is to secure better understanding between the churches of each other's traditions and beliefs. It may lead to unity – the Anglicans and the Methodists have plans for eventual reunion, and the Roman Catholic and Anglican churches, despite obstacles like the ordination of women and the marriage of clergy, look to possible union in the long term. The World Council of Churches is an ecumenical body, acting on behalf of all the Christian churches. Ecumenism is also concerned with non-Christian religions, in its aim of mutual understanding and the avoidance of over-zealous missionary activity.

Eden, Anthony, 1st Earl of Avon (1897–1977)
A British Conservative politician, PM from 1955 to
1957. He was also Foreign Secretary from 1935 to 1938,
1940 to 1945 and 1951 to 1955. His administration's
handling of the **Suez Crisis** (1956) aroused widespread
opposition and this, coupled with poor health, caused
his resignation.

Education Act (1944) A reform for which R A **Butler**,
then Minister of Education, was responsible. The Act
changed the Board of Education into a ministry;
reorganised state-assisted education into primary,
secondary and further education; raised the school-
leaving age to 15; abolished fees for grammar schools;
and made compulsory daily undenominational worship.
Secondary education was split into grammar, technical
and 'modern' categories, those attending grammar
schools having been successful in the '11-plus'
examination, which resulted in these schools receiving
the more academically gifted children. Since the 1960s,
many state secondary schools have been reorganised
into comprehensive schools, which take pupils of all
abilities.

Edward VII (1841–1910) King of Great Britain and
Ireland from 1901 to 1910. The eldest son of Queen
Victoria, his playboy image earned the Queen's
disapproval, with the result that she denied him official
responsibilities. However, throughout his nine-year
reign he was a popular monarch, and he is credited with
helping to pave the way for, and make popular, the
Anglo-French Entente.

Edward VIII *see* **Abdication Crisis**.

EEC *see* **European Community**.

EFTA *see* **European Free Trade Association**.

Egypt A republic of NE Africa. Area: 1,002,000 sq km. Pop: 63,575,100. Language: Arabic. Religion: Sunni Islam. Cap: Cairo.

In 1914 Egypt was declared a British protectorate, and its independence was recognised in 1922. In 1936 an Anglo-Egyptian Treaty provided for the gradual withdrawal of British forces (except from the Suez Canal Zone), but this was delayed by WWII.

The creation of the state of Israel led to Egyptian involvement in the **Arab-Israeli Wars** (1948, 1956, 1967, 1973), and to the growth of nationalist feeling. In 1952 the monarchy was overthrown by General Muhammad Neguib, who proclaimed a republic in 1953. Neguib was in turn replaced by the radical Colonel Gamal Abdel **Nasser** in 1954. After the **Suez Crisis** (1956), Egypt increasingly depended on aid from the USSR, and formed the United Arab Republic (UAR) with Syria (1958-61). The 1967 war with Israel led to the loss of Sinai, which Egypt unsuccessfully attempted to recover in the 1973 war.

Nasser died in 1970 and was succeeded by Anwar **Sadat**, who favoured closer cooperation with the West. The **Camp David Agreement** (1978) led to a peace treaty with Israel (1979) by which Egypt recovered Sinai, but which left the country temporarily isolated in the Arab world. In 1981 Sadat was succeeded by Hosni **Mubarak**.

Eire *see* **Ireland**.

Eisenhower, Dwight D (1890–1969) A US general and

Republican president from 1953 to 1961. As Allied Commander-in-Chief, N Africa, Eisenhower directed the **North Africa Campaign** and the invasion of Italy during WWII (1942–3). As supreme commander of the Allied Expeditionary Force in W Europe he was responsible for the **Normandy Landings** (1944), the expulsion from occupied territory of the German forces, and their ultimate unconditional surrender. He was widely criticised for not allowing the Allied armies to take Berlin, Prague and Vienna before the Russians, so weakening the West's bargaining power in the postwar settlements.

As president, his honesty and willingness to compromise balanced his political inexperience. His presidency was marked by two **Civil Rights Acts**, the passing of social security laws, and efforts to achieve better understanding with the USSR while supporting mutual security programmes to combat Communism (see **Eisenhower Doctrine**).

Eisenhower Doctrine The principle recommended by President Eisenhower to Congress in 1957 that US forces should be used to protect any state in the Middle East threatened with attack by any nation 'controlled by international Communism'. Military advice and economic aid to any state in the area which considered its independence threatened was also proposed. The Doctrine was withdrawn in 1959 because those countries it was designed to assist believed it was against the principles of Arab nationalism.

Elizabeth II (1926–) Queen of the United Kingdom of Great Britain and Northern Ireland from 1952. She married Philip Mountbatten in 1947 and succeeded her father George VI in 1952. She has been less remote from her subjects both at home and overseas than previous monarchs and has maintained and developed Commonwealth ties and friendly relationships between the UK and foreign countries.

Energy Crisis *see* oil crisis.

Entente Cordiale A friendship agreement between states. The term was first used in the 1840s to denote the friendly relationship between France and Britain, although severe strains have been imposed upon that friendship from time to time.

Many differences between the countries were sorted out in 1904 in an agreement (the Anglo-French Entente) which settled outstanding colonial disputes, policy disagreements over Egypt and Morocco, and Newfoundland fishing rights. *See also* **Triple Entente**.

In 1923 there was friction between Britain and France over the **Ruhr**, and there was actual conflict in 1940 when the Royal Navy attacked the Vichy French fleet in the Mediterranean and Africa to prevent it falling into enemy hands in WWII. The Treaty of Dunkirk (1947) sought to revive the Entente's ideals but fresh strains arose, especially over EU matters, in the 1960s and 70s. Despite important political differences, Anglo-French cooperation has generally been close since that period.

Environmentalism The concern to protect the environment. This first became a major popular issue in the 1960s when there was much concern about nuclear pollution of the soil and atmosphere. Since then it has widened to include concern for the preservation of wildlife, natural habitats, equatorial forests and the world's dwindling natural resources. Excessive emissions of carbon dioxide and other gases into the atmosphere have caused alarm over the 'greenhouse effect' and its threat of global warming. Environmentalism has become a political issue, and so-called 'Green' parties in Western Europe have demanded that governments and politicians follow environmentalist policies; the most influential was that of West Germany in the 1980s.

Erhard, Ludwig (1897–1977) A West German politician. After becoming a Christian Democrat member of the Bundestag in 1949, Erhard was appointed Minister of Economic Affairs, a position he held until 1963, when he became Chancellor. As Economics Minister he presided over West Germany's transition from wartime devastation to prosperity. He was not as successful as Chancellor, and a proposal for taxation increases brought about his resignation in 1966.

Eritrea A former province of **Ethiopia** on the Red Sea. Eritrea became an Italian colony in 1890 and was a base for attacks on Ethiopia (1895–6 and 1935–6). During WWII it was occupied by British forces from 1941. Britain retained control until 1952, when Eritrea was linked with Ethiopia, which absorbed it in 1962. After 30 years of guerrilla warfare, Eritrea gained independence in 1993.

Estonia *see* **Baltic States**.

Ethiopia or **Abyssinia** A republic of NE Africa. Area: 1,221,900 sq km. Pop: 57,171,662. Language: Amharic. Religions: Christianity (Coptic) and Islam. Cap. Addis Ababa.

Menelik II (1844–1913) defeated Italy's attempt to colonise the country at the Battle of Adowa (1896), but

Italy reoccupied the country in 1935, until driven out by Allied forces in 1941. Emperor **Haile Selassie** ruled Ethiopia from 1930 (apart from a period of exile in Britain during the Italian occupation), but was an autocratic monarch, permitting parliament little real authority. He was deposed in 1974 by an army coup.

The country was then governed by a Provisional Military Administrative Council, dominated from 1977 to 1991 by Colonel Mengistu Haile Mariam. Mengistu's government had to contend with famine (particularly in 1985 and 1987), social distress, a guerrilla separatist movement in **Eritrea**, and a war over disputed territory with Somalia. Civil war led to the overthrow of Mengistu in 1991 and the creation of a new government under Menes Zenawi. A new constitution in 1994 replaced the Marxist version of 1991, and Zenawi's government won a (largely uncontested) election in 1995. Ethiopia fought a short and inconclusive, but bloody, border war with Eritrea in 1998.

Ethnic Cleansing The removal of people from an area by force or threats in order to allow the area to be inhabited or dominated by people of another religion or culture. The term was first used in 1991 and 1992 for events in the former Yugoslavia when Croats and Muslims were driven out in large numbers by Serbs, and some Serbs were expelled from predominantly Croat or Muslim areas. The 'cleansing' involves loss of homes, llivelihood, and often life, and is in direct contravention of human rights. *See* **apartheid**, **genocide**.

EU *see* **European Union**.

Euratom *see* **European Atomic Energy Community**.

Eurocommunism The liberalised form of Communism as practised by Western European communist parties from 1975, when the French and Italian parties issued a joint policy declaration, until their loss of influence following the collapse of Soviet communism in the early 1990s. Eurocommunism recognised the right of other political parties to exist, supported democratic elections, guaranteed civil liberties and the right of opposition, and abandoned the principle of the dictatorship of the proletariat (*see* **Marxism**).

European Atomic Energy Community (Euratom) An organisation established in 1957 by a treaty between the six members of the EEC. In 1967 it was absorbed into the general European Community. Its objectives are the rapid large-scale production of nuclear energy for peaceful purposes, and technical development of nuclear research. Euratom is administered by the European Commission.

European Coal and Steel Community (ECSC) An organisation that came into existence in 1952 as a result of the **Schuman Plan** of 1950 proposing a union of the Franco-German coal, iron and steel industries. Belgium, Italy, Luxembourg and the Netherlands joined France and West Germany in the union, and in 1967 the ECSC was merged with the EEC and Euratom. The objectives of the organisation were to get rid of tariffs and other restrictions and promote a free labour market.

European Commission A council of the EC whose members are appointed by agreement among the member governments for a four-year renewable term. France, Italy, the UK and Germany each have two

Commissioners and the other states have one each. The Commissioners are pledged to be independent of government, national or special interests. The Commission acts as a mediator between member governments in Community matters and has wide powers to take action on behalf of the Community.

European Economic Community *see* **European Community**.

European Free Trade Association (EFTA) An organisation formed in 1960 when Austria, Denmark, Norway, Portugal, Sweden, Switzerland and the UK joined in promoting economic expansion and trade between themselves. Finland became an associate member (1961) and Iceland joined in 1970. Denmark and the UK left to join the EC in 1972, and the remaining members negotiated an agreement with the EC which made provision for free trade in industrial products between the two organisations.

European Parliament An elected assembly which began in 1952 as part of the **European Coal and Steel Community** and was expanded by the Treaties of **Rome** (1957) to cover EEC and Euratom affairs. Until 1979 the Parliament consisted of members nominated by the national parliaments of the member states. It was then decided that every five years the electorate of each state should elect its own representatives. The membership is split on party lines similar to those in the national parliaments.

European Union (EU) An international organisation established in 1958 as the *European Economic Community* (EEC), a year after the Treaty of **Rome** was signed by Belgium, France, Italy, Luxembourg, the Netherlands and West Germany. These states were already members of the **European Coal and Steel Community**, and the EEC was an expansion of the earlier organisation based on discussions by its members at the *Messina Conference* (1955). In 1967, it was joined with the ECSC and **Euratom** to form the European Community but was popularly called the European Economic Community or Common Market until the end of the 1980s.

In 1993 the European Union, creating closer political and economic integration, was established following the *Maastricht Treaty* (1991).

The Community provided for free movement of capital and labour, joint financial and social policies, **free trade**, and the abolition of restrictive trading practices. Veto powers were available to enable a member to block proposed new entries, and France used these powers in 1963 and 1967, in defiance of the wishes of the other members, to prevent the UK joining.

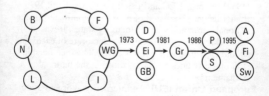

European Union *Membership.*

Denmark, the Republic of Ireland and the UK became members in 1973, Greece in 1981, Spain and Portugal in 1986, and Austria, Finland and Sweden in 1995. The EU has special links with the **European Free Trade Association** and with Third World states.

Executive The branch of government which runs a country on a day-to-day basis, making decisions about domestic and foreign policy, carrying out the laws and if necessary asking the **legislature** to pass laws. In the UK the executive consists of the Prime Minister together with the Cabinet and other ministers. In the USA the executive consists of the president and his ministers and advisers.

F

Fabian Society An association of British socialists, founded in 1884. It supported the establishment of democratic socialism by gradual reforms within the law. Notable early members were George Bernard Shaw and Sidney and Beatrice Webb.

Falange A Fascist movement founded in Spain in 1933 by José Antonio Primo de Rivera (1903–36). It was the only legal party under the **Franco** regime.

Falkland Islands (*Span.* Islas Malvinas) A crown colony of the UK, in S Atlantic Ocean. Area: 12,100 sq km. Pop: 2,400. Cap: Port Stanley

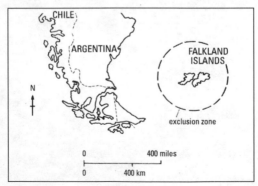

Falkland Islands

Settled by British colonists in the 19th century, the islands became an important Royal Navy coaling station. In 1914 the German heavy cruisers *Scharnhorst* and *Gneisenau* were sunk there by a Royal Navy squadron.

The Falklands have long been claimed by Argentina. In April 1982 Argentinian forces occupied the islands. Attempts by the USA and UN to bring about a diplomatic solution were unsuccessful, and the UK despatched a task force to retake the islands. After heavy fighting, the UK force eventually recaptured the islands in June 1982. Argentina has continued to claim the islands while the UK continues to refuse to negotiate on the issue.

Fascism The beliefs and political system of Benito **Mussolini**, which encouraged militarism and extreme nationalism, organising Italy along right-wing authoritarian lines directly opposed to democracy and liberalism. The term is also applied to any ideology or movement inspired by such principles, e.g. German **National Socialism** and the Spanish **Falange**.

Federation The union of several provinces, states, etc. to form a federal union; a political unit formed in such a way. The members of such a union usually keep a degree of autonomy, maintaining their own executive and legislature to govern some internal affairs, although the federal government normally deals with defence, foreign affairs, etc. Examples of federations include the USA, the USSR, Australia and Germany.

Feminism The demand by women for political and social equality with men, and for equality of opportunity with them. In the UK, women had acquired political equality and considerable legal equality before WWII, and feminism has since been mainly concerned with the battle for equality of opportunity and a change of attitude. Partly, it is a political struggle – for equal pay, for equal promotion prospects with men, for laws against any form of discrimination against women – but part of it is a struggle to change society so that women are not expected to bear an unequal share of the burden of bringing up children and running a home. Despite much lipservice to equal opportunity by politicians and others, progress in the USA and W Europe remained slow and incomplete by the end of the 20th century, and in many other parts of the world continued to be hindered by religious belief or social custom.

FGR *see* **Germany**.

Fianna Fáil The Irish political party founded in1926 by Eamon **de Valéra**, originating from the faction of **Sinn Féin** opposed to the Anglo-Irish Treaty (1921), and sympathetic towards republican ideals (*see also* **Fine Gael**).

Fianna Fáil achieved power in 1932 and has been the governing party for much of the time since. In the 1930s it took steps to remove the Irish Free State from UK influence, including the abolition of the Governor-Generalship, the introduction of high protective tariffs, the separation of Irish nationality from that of the UK, and the maintenance of claims to a united Ireland in the 1937 Constitution.

Fifth Column A group of Falangist sympathisers within Madrid during the **Spanish Civil War** who aided the four columns of rebel troops marching on the city. The term is now applied to any group of hostile or subversive infiltrators.

Fine Gael The Irish political party originating from the section of **Sinn Féin** sympathetic to the Anglo-Irish Treaty of 1921.

This faction formed the first government of the Irish Free State but lost popularity after **Fianna Fáil** achieved power in 1932. It has been unable to re-establish itself in government since 1945 except for short periods when it was supported by some of the minor parties. During the first of these periods of office, in 1949, the last connections with the UK were severed and the Republic of Ireland was created.

Finland A republic of N Europe. Area: 304,643 sq km. Pop: 5,116,826. Languages: Finnish, Swedish. Religion: Christianity (Lutheran). Cap: Helsinki.

The country was ceded to Russia by Sweden in 1809 but gained independence in 1917. Invasion by the USSR in 1939 was strongly resisted, but important land areas were ceded to the USSR in the peace treaty (1940). An alliance with Germany in WWII resulted in further Finnish territorial losses in the peace treaty (1947). Throughout the postwar and Cold War periods a series of coalition governments followed a neutral policy in international affairs.

First World War *see* World War I.

Fisher, John, Baron Fisher of Kilverstone (1841–1920) A British Admiral of the Fleet. Fisher rose to be First Sea Lord (1904–10 and 1914–15). He did much to prepare the navy for WWI, scrapping outdated ships and introducing the **dreadnought** class.

Five-Year Plan A government plan for economic development over a period of five years. In the USSR Stalin introduced a series of three such plans, starting in 1928, which involved rapid industrialisation and the **collectivisation** of agriculture.

Foot, Michael (1913–) A British politician. He was leader of the Labour Party from 1980 to 1983.

Ford, Gerald (1913–) A US politician, Republican president from 1974 to 1977. Richard **Nixon** chose him as vice-president on the resignation of the previous vice-president, Spiro Agnew, and when Nixon himself resigned over **Watergate**, Ford succeeded him as president, thus becoming the only person in US history to hold the office without ever being elected by the nation. He continued Nixon's policies of withdrawal from Vietnam and **détente**, but was defeated by the Democrat Jimmy **Carter** in 1977.

Fourteen Points A peace programme to follow the end of WWI, outlined by President Woodrow Wilson to the US Congress in 1918. The points were:

1. The ending of secret diplomacy;
2. Freedom of the seas;
3. Removal, where possible, of economic barriers;
4. Reduction in armaments;
5. Impartial adjustment of colonial claims;
6. Germany and its allies to leave Russian territory;
7. Restoration of Belgium;
8. Liberation of occupied France, and the return to France of Alsace-Lorraine;
9. Italian frontiers to be adjusted along clearly recognizable lines of nationality;

10. Separate national development for the peoples of the Austro-Hungarian Empire;
11. Occupation forces to withdraw from Romania, Montenegro and Serbia, with Serbia receiving access to the sea;
12. Self-development for non-Turkish peoples within the Ottoman Empire, and free passage of the Dardanelles;
13. Formation of an independent Poland with access to the sea;
14. The creation of a general association of nations to guarantee the political independence of all states.

The majority of these points were put into effect at the **Paris Peace Conference**, and point 14 led to the foundation of the **League of Nations**.

France A republic of W Europe. Area: 543,965 sq km. Pop: 58,317,450. Language: French. Religion: Christianity (predominantly RC). Capital: Paris.

The Third Republic (1871–1946) was established after the overthrow of the Emperor Napoleon III in the Franco-Prussian War. Because of a fear of authoritarian, anti-republican rule, its constitution favoured weak and unstable governments – for example, between WWI and WWII there were 44 governments, led by 20 different PMs. The Franco-Russian Alliance (*see* **Triple Entente**) led to France's involvement in WWI, and the instability of its governments led to near-defeat. However, with the Allied victory, France regained **Alsace-Lorraine** from Germany.

In the 1930s, France, like Britain, pursued a policy of **appeasement** towards Hitler. The instability of its governments was again a factor in its defeat (1940) and occupation by Germany in WWII, when the collaborationist **Vichy Government** came to power (1940–44). **De Gaulle** and the **Free French**, together with resistance groups in France, continued to oppose German occupation until the liberation (1944).

The Fourth Republic (1946–58) was just as unstable as the Third Republic, 23 governments holding power in 12 years. Under the Republic, the economy was effectively revived after the ravages of war, and France became a founder member of the EEC. The unsuccessful attempt to hold on to the French colonies in **Indo-China** discredited the Republic, and its plans for the independence of **Algeria** led to a threatened rebellion by French settlers in the colony and by elements in the army. The crisis led to the return to power of de Gaulle, and his establishment of the Fifth Republic (1958).

The Fifth Republic (1958–) gave extensive powers to the president, and put an end to government instability. As president, de Gaulle, having survived an army rebellion in 1961, eventually settled the Algerian problem by granting independence in 1962. In the late 1950s and early 1960s France also granted independence to most of its other colonies, principally in Africa, but it maintained close economic, political and cultural links with them.

De Gaulle's ambition was to establish France as leader of a united Europe independent of US and Soviet influence. He withdrew French forces from NATO in 1966, and twice blocked the UK's application to join the

EEC (1963 and 1967), fearing that France's dominant position might be undermined. He insisted that France develop its own nuclear deterrent, and in foreign affairs followed an independent line, e.g. by visiting Warsaw Pact countries, and by opposing Western policies in conflicts such as the Middle East and Vietnam. At home, crises developed over the value of the franc and over a lack of educational and social investment. These, combined with substantial wage demands, led to a general strike and the **Paris student demonstrations** (1968). De Gaulle resigned following a referendum defeat in 1969, and was succeeded as president by Georges **Pompidou** (1969–74), Valéry **Giscard d'Estaing** (1974–81), François **Mitterrand** (1981–95), and Jacques **Chirac** (1995–). French opposition to expansion of EC membership was dropped, and France has been more willing to cooperate with the political and economic policies of its allies and partners in Europe.

Franchise or **suffrage** The right to vote, especially for representatives in a legislative body. In the UK, following agitation for **women's suffrage**, the Representation of the People Act (1918) gave the vote to all women over 30 and all men over 21. A further Act in 1928 enabled all women over 21 to vote. In 1969, the voting age was lowered to 18.

Franco, Francisco (1892–1975) A Spanish general and politician, known as *el Caudillo*. He was Commander-in-Chief of the nationalist rebels in the **Spanish Civil War** (1936–9), defeating the republican socialist government with German and Italian military help and establishing a dictatorship. He kept Spain neutral during WWII, and afterwards made a pact with the USA for military bases in Spain in return for economic aid. He prepared the country for a return of the monarchy and the restoration of democracy after his death. *See also* **Spain**.

Franco-Russian Alliance *see* Triple Entente.

Franz Ferdinand *see* Sarajevo.

Franz Josef I (1830–1916) Emperor of Austria from 1848 to 1916 and King of Hungary from 1867 to 1916. His autocratic reaction to the 1848 revolutions led him to distrust all forms of party government. He therefore preferred to rule with the aid of a powerful bureaucracy rather than with the help of a democratically elected parliament. His reign ended during WWI.

Free French The supporters of General **de Gaulle** during WWII became known as the Free French in 1940. As well as a military contribution to the Allied war effort, they provided a political alternative to the **Vichy Government** and a rallying point for French patriots. The movement was renamed the Fighting French in 1942.

Free Trade International trade that is free of such government influence as import quotas, export subsidies, protection tariffs, etc. The opposite to free trade is **protectionism**. Free trade was the policy of 19th-century Liberalism in the UK, and was in force until **imperial preference** was introduced in 1931. Such international organisations as the EU and EFTA promote free trade between member states.

G

Gaddafi, Mu'ammar Muhammad al- (1942–)
A Libyan army officer and politician. Gadaffi held
power from the overthrow of the monarchy in 1969. His
political programme, announced in 1973, was intended
to involve the people more closely in the running of the
state, and in 1977 he renamed the country the Socialist
People's Libyan Arab Jamahiriyah ('state of the masses').

Gaddafi is a Muslim and revolutionary, who is alleged
to have supported terrorist movements worldwide with
Libyan oil wealth. His attempts to promote Arab unity
(e.g. the planned unification of Libya and Egypt in
1973) have largely failed because of his extremism,
which has antagonised a large number of other
countries.

Gaitskell, Hugh (1906–63) A British Labour politician.
As Chancellor of the Exchequer (1950–1) he became
unpopular with the left wing of the Party by introducing
prescription charges under the National Health Service.
He became leader of the Labour Party (1955–63), and
remained in conflict with the Left over unilateral
nuclear **disarmament** and **nationalisation**. He defeated
moves to oust him from the leadership in 1961.

Gallipoli *see* **Dardanelles**.

Gandhi, Indira (1917–84) An Indian politician and
Congress Party PM from 1966 to 1977 and 1980 to
1984. The daughter of Jawaharlal **Nehru**, she succeeded
Lal **Shastri** as PM. Her methods offended older Hindu
Congress members, who eventually formed a dissident

movement which charged her with corruption during the 1971 electoral campaign. She was barred for six years (1975) from public office, but retaliated by having 676 of her opponents arrested under the Maintenance of Internal Security Act, and by being granted dictatorial powers by Parliament, so bringing India to the verge of civil war (1976). She resigned after the dissidents gained overwhelming victory in the 1977 election, but was re-elected in 1980. She was assassinated by Sikh extremists in 1984.

Gandhi, Mohandas Karamchand (1869–1948) An Indian nationalist leader and social reformer, known as 'Mahatma' (Great Soul). He spent several years in South Africa opposing laws that discriminated against Indians, and on his return to India during WWI started a campaign for raising the economic and social standards of its peoples.

As leader of the Indian National Congress (*see* **Congress Party**) he adopted a non-cooperation policy of civil disobedience, supported by hunger strikes, directed against British rule in India. He spent several years in prison, but lived to see independence achieved (1947). Having opposed violence all his life, he was assassinated by a Hindu fanatic opposed to his efforts to achieve communal harmony between Hindus and Muslims.

Gandhi, Rajiv (1942–91) An Indian politician. He became PM in 1984 following the assassination of his mother Indira. He had to deal with the problems of Sikh separatists in the Punjab and the civil war in **Sri Lanka**. He also initiated a major crackdown on corruption. He was assassinated in 1991 by Sri Lankan terrorists opposed to Indian intervention in Sri Lanka.

Gang of Four 1. A radical faction within the Chinese Communist Party, consisting of Jiang Qing (Mao Zedong's widow), Zhang Chunqiao, Wang Hongwen and Yao Wenyuan. It emerged as a political force in 1976 but was denounced six months later by Party Chairman Hua Guofeng for leading the excesses of the Cultural Revolution, and was again denounced at the Party's 11th congress (1977). The members of the gang were tried and sentenced to life imprisonment.

2. The founders of the **Social Democratic Party** in the UK.

GATT *see* **General Agreement on Tariffs and Trade**.

Gaza Strip An area of about 160 sq km on the E Mediterranean coast around Gaza. Formerly part of the British Mandate for Palestine, it was administered by Egypt from 1949 to 1956, and frequently used as a base for terrorist missions against Israel. Israel occupied it during the 1956 **Arab-Israeli War**, and it was placed under UN control from 1957 to 1967. It was occupied during the 1967 War by Israel who subsequently administered it as 'occupied territory'. The territory was granted limited autonomy in 1994 as a result of the Camp David Agreement, and Israeli military forces withdrew, but tension between the Palestinian authorities and Israel remained high.

Gdánsk *see* **Danzig**.

GDR *see* **Germany**.

General Agreement on Tariffs and Trade (GATT)
A multilateral international treaty signed by 86 states in 1948. It was designed to expand international trade and promote economic development, especially by the removal or reduction of import quotas and tariffs. Eight rounds of negotiations have been concluded, and participating countries eventually accounted for some 80 per cent of world trade. In 1995 GATT was superseded by the World Trade Organisation, which has stronger powers to enforce agreed tariff cuts and can help developing countries by taking action against unfair trade practices.

General Strike (1926) The climax to several years of industrial unrest in Britain and of attempts by the miners' unions to secure sympathetic support for their grievances from workers in other major industries.

   The miners, threatened by further wage cuts, succeeded in persuading the **Trades Union Congress** to bring out all major industries – transport workers, printers, builders, workers in heavy industries, and engineers. The Government used troops to maintain food supplies. The TUC ended the strike as it felt the Government had been better prepared for the strike than had the unions. Much bitterness followed. The miners fought on without TUC support and the Government, by the Trades Disputes Act, placed restrictions on the rights and powers of trade unions.

Geneva Convention A series of four international agreements, signed as a group in 1949 by 59 governments, for the protection of war victims. The oldest agreement, of 1864, set out regulations for the care of sick and wounded. Naval combatants were covered in 1907, treatment of prisoners of war in 1929, and treatment of non-combatants in 1949.

Genocide The deliberate extermination of a nationality or ethnic group of people because of their race, colour, tribe or religion. The most horrific 20th-century example has been the Nazi mass-extermination of the Jews (*see* **Holocaust**), but tribal rivalry and wars in Africa, independence massacres in India in 1947, Stalin's treatment of the Tartars, and Serbian treatment of Bosnian Muslims in the early 1990s also have their roots in genocide.

George V (1865–1936) King of Great Britain and Ireland from 1910 to 1921, and of the United Kingdom of Great Britain and Northern Ireland from 1921 to 1936. His reign was notable for the **Parliament Act**, WWI, the Irish troubles, the **General Strike**, the Great **Depression**, the choice of **Baldwin** as PM, and the formation of a **National Government** (1931).

George VI (1894–1952) King of the United Kingdom of Great Britain and Northern Ireland from 1936 to 1952. His reign followed his brother Edward VIII's abdication, and saw WWII, the formation of the first Labour government with an overall majority, and the start of the break-up of the Empire.

George, David Lloyd *see* **Lloyd George**.

Germany A federal republic of NC Europe. Area: 356,844 sq km. Pop: 83,536,115. Language: German. Religion: Christianity Protestant and RC. Cap: Berlin. Partitioned from 1949 to 1990 between the

German Democratic Republic (GDR; *Ger.* – DDR) and the Federal German Republic (FGR; *Ger.* – BRD), also known respectively as East Germany and West Germany.

The German Empire (1871–1918) was established following the Franco-Prussian War. For centuries Germany had been divided into a large number of independent states, but in 1871 they were united into a federal system, with the King of Prussia becoming Emperor (Kaiser) of Germany. Imperial and military rivalry with Britain and France, encouraged by Kaiser **Wilhelm II**, combined with the Austro-German Dual Alliance, led to Germany's involvement in WWI. After its defeat in 1918, the Allies forced punitive terms on Germany at the Treaty of **Versailles**, including loss of territory and the obligation to pay substantial **reparations**. Attempted communist revolts, such as the **Spartacist Rising** (1919), were successfully suppressed.

The **Weimar Republic** (1919–33) was established following Wilhelm II's abdication, and was named after the town where it was established. Its constitution was democratic, but it suffered from severe economic problems caused by WWI and reparations, made worse by the Depression and mass unemployment. The economic situation paved the way for **Hitler**'s rise to power, and the Nazi Party (*see* **National Socialism**) was elected to power in 1933 and introduced a new constitution.

The **Third Reich** (1933–45) became a one-party Nazi state in 1934, with Hitler as its dictator (*Ger.* Führer).

Germany *Frontiers after World War II.*

Against the terms of the Treaty of Versailles, Hitler began a massive programme of rearmament, and ordered the occupation of the **Saarland** and the **Rhineland**. Encouraged by Britain and France's policy of **appeasement**, Germany then annexed Austria (*see* **Anschluss**) the **Sudetenland** (following the **Munich Agreement**), and then the rest of Czechoslovakia. However, Germany's invasion of Poland in 1939 in pursuit of further territorial demands caused the UK and France to declare war (*see* **World War II**). After Germany's eventual defeat by the Allies, territory was lost in the E, and the remainder, W of the **Oder-Neisse Line**, was divided from 1945 to 1949 into UK, French, US and Soviet occupation zones. The boundary between Western and Soviet zones became fixed as a national boundary in 1949 with the partition of the country into the German Democratic Republic (East Germany) and the Federal German Republic (West Germany). This partition lasted until 1990. *See also* **Berlin**.

East Germany (Area: 108,177 sq km. Pop: 16,740,000) Formed from the Soviet occupation zone, the state was Soviet-dominated, and was ruled by a hard-line Communist regime. It was a member of the **Council for Mutual Economic Assistance** and the **Warsaw Pact**. Under Walter **Ulbricht** it adopted the Soviet system of agricultural collectivisation, with poor results, and this, coupled with bad social and industrial conditions, led to an uprising which was put down with the aid of Soviet troops in 1953. Conditions failed to improve and nearly four million people emigrated to West Germany. To halt this population drain, the authorities erected the Berlin

Wall in 1961. Following the friendship treaty with the FGR in 1972 (*see* **Ostpolitik**), relations between the two German states began to improve. The East German communist regime, undermined by events elsewhere in Eastern Europe, collapsed at the end of 1989, and in November the Berlin Wall, the symbol of divided Germany, began to be torn down. In March 1990, the first free elections for nearly sixty years resulted in a massive majority for the parties demanding reunification, and in October 1990 reunion was at last achieved.

West Germany (Area: 248,667 sq km. Pop: 61,333,000 (1983)). Formed from the British, French and US occupation zones, the FGR was a parliamentary democracy. Its membership of the EU and NATO contributed towards its remarkable economic and political recovery from the destruction of WWII and its acceptance as one of the Western democracies. Like many other states in W Europe, governments frequently had to rely on coalition partners to stay in office. Chancellors since 1949 have included **Adenauer**, **Erhard**, **Kiesinger**, **Brandt**, **Schmidt**, **Kohl** and **Schröder**.

Gestapo The secret state police of Nazi Germany, headed by Heinrich **Himmler**, and notorious for its ruthless interrogation methods.

Ghana A republic of W Africa; formerly the Gold Coast. Area: 238,305 sq km. Pop: 16,904,000. Official language: English. Cap: Accra.

The original Gold Coast was established as a British colony in 1874 after being purchased from the Dutch in

1871. Ashanti and the Northern Territories were added in 1901 and the former German colony of Togoland was incorporated as a mandated territory after the WWI peace settlements. The country became independent as Ghana in 1957, with Kwame **Nkrumah** as PM. In 1960 Ghana became a republic within the Commonwealth, and in 1964 Nkrumah established a one-party state. He was overthrown by a military coup in 1966, since when the country has been ruled by a succession of civilian and military governments which have failed to deal with the problems of widespread corruption.

Gibraltar A self-governing British crown colony at the W end of the Mediterranean Sea and the S end of the Iberian Peninsula. Area: 5.5 sq km. Pop: 30,000 est. Language: English. Religion: Christianity (RC).

The 'Rock' of Gibraltar was captured from Spain by the British in 1704, possession being confirmed by the Treaties of Utrecht (1713), Paris (1763) and Versailles (1783), but Spain has constantly pressed for its return. The inhabitants voted overwhelmingly in a referendum to stay British (1967) and Spain closed its frontier and severed communications with the colony from 1969 until 1985 when Anglo-Spanish relationships improved. Gibraltar was of great strategic importance during WWII, serving as a major Royal Navy base.

Gierek, Edward (1913–) A Polish Communist politician. He replaced Wladislaw **Gomulka** as First Secretary in 1970 and led his country until 1980. From 1976 onwards he faced considerable industrial and social unrest, resulting in riots and strikes. These were caused by the raising of prices without comparable wage increases. In 1980 his government signed the 'Gdansk Agreements' with **Solidarity**, and Gierek was replaced as Party leader by Stanislaw Kania.

Giscard d'Estaing, Valéry (1926–) A French politician, president of France from 1974 to 1981. As leader of the Independent Republicans (allied to the Gaullists), he became the youngest president of France since 1848. He was faced with difficult economic circumstances, with mounting inflation and uncertain political support, especially from his Gaullist PM, Jacques Chirac. Giscard maintained a strong French position within the EC and on defence matters.

Glasnost (*Russ.* – openness) The Soviet policy of allowing more freedom of press and speech, and showing greater concern for the rights of individuals. This policy was introduced by Mikhail **Gorbachev** in 1985. *See also* **perestroika**.

Godesberg Meeting (1938) The discussion between the British PM Neville **Chamberlain** and Adolf **Hitler**, at which Chamberlain refused to agree to the German occupation of the **Sudetenland**, the German-speaking area of Czechoslovakia. A week later, Chamberlain, with **Daladier** and **Mussolini**, signed the **Munich Agreement**, agreeing to the German occupation.

Goebbels, Joseph (1897–1945) A German Nazi politician. Goebbels was an early follower of Hitler, and controlled the party propaganda machine from 1929. From 1933 to 1945 he was Minister of Enlightenment and Propaganda, and his control of press, radio and cinema contributed enormously to the establishment of

a totalitarian Nazi state. He committed suicide with his
family in 1945 in Hitler's bunker.

Goering, Herman (1893–1946) A German Nazi
politician and **Luftwaffe** officer. An early Nazi, he
joined with Hitler in the Munich **Putsch**. In 1932 he
became President of the Reichstag, and from 1933 he
was Minister of Aviation, building up the Luftwaffe into
a formidable fighting machine, used with great success
in the **Blitzkrieg** tactics of WWII. Following the
German victories in Norway, the Low Countries and
France in 1940, he was created Reichsmarshal, but
thereafter his influence declined. He committed suicide
after the Nuremberg Trials (1946) in which he had been
sentenced to death for **war crimes**.

Golan Heights The range of hills on the NE Israeli
and SW Syrian frontier N of the Sea of Galilee. This
strategic area was the scene of heavy fighting between
the two countries during the 1967 **Arab-Israeli War**,
and was finally occupied by Israel. After the 1973 War
it was occupied by UN forces.

Gold Coast *see* **Ghana**.

Gomulka, Wladyslaw (1905–82) A Polish communist
politician. He became General Secretary of the
Communist Polish Workers' Party in 1943. He was vice-
president in the first postwar government, but his
nationalist differences with orthodox Stalinist
Communism led to his dismissal from office and his
imprisonment (1951–5). He was allowed back into
public life in 1956 and, amidst growing political unrest,
later in the same year became the country's leader as
First Secretary of the Party, a position he held until

replaced by Edward **Gierek** (1970). Economic stagnation, and serious rioting which arose from substantial food price increases, contributed to his downfall.

Gorbachev, Mikhail Sergeevich (1931–) A Soviet politician. As General Secretary of the Communist Party and Soviet leader from 1985 to 1991, Gorbachev embarked on policies of social and political liberalisation (**glasnost**) and economic reform (**perestroika**). In 1987 he signed the **Intermediate Nuclear Forces Treaty** with President Ronald Reagan of the USA. He survived an attempted coup in August 1991, but resigned shortly afterwards when it became clear that the USSR could not survive as a political unit.

Gottwald, Klement (1896–1953) A Czechoslovak communist politician. Gottwald was General Secretary of the Party from 1929 to 1953. He became PM of a coalition government (1946) and established a one-party state by using the police and workers' militia to carry out a **coup d'état** (1945), which placed the country under communist control. Gottwald succeeded **Beneš** as president from 1948 to 1953.

Gowon, Yakubu (1934–) A Nigerian politician and general. Gowon emerged as head of state (1966–75) after a military coup. He introduced a new federal system of 12 states, later increased to 19. In the **Biafran War** (1967–70) Gowon successfully crushed the rebel forces. In 1975 he was removed from power by another army group.

Great Britain *see* United Kingdom.

Great Leap Forward (1958–61) The slogan used for
the massive upheaval in China aimed at transforming
the country economically and politically to the level of
advanced nations.

Inspired by **Mao Zedong**, it had radical aims: to
sweep away backwardness by getting rid of old customs
and old ways of doing things; to establish a commune
system for agriculture, education, industry, local
defence, trade and welfare; to develop new industries
and expand old ones; to reduce consumption; to
establish a truly communist society; and to make full use
of the population's talents and skills. It failed for a
variety of reasons: a series of national disasters;
managerial difficulties; withdrawal of Soviet
technological advice; bureaucratic opposition; and poor
harvests.

Great War *see* **World War I**.

Greece A republic of SE Europe. Area: 131,986 sq km.
Pop: 10,493,600. Language: Greek. Religion:
Christianity (Greek Orthodox). Cap: Athens.

The country was a monarchy until 1973 apart from
brief republican periods (1926–35, 1941–6). Greece
joined the Allied side in World War I, but only in 1917
and after much political argument and in the light of
Allied intervention against Bulgaria at Salonica. During
WWII, Greek forces defeated an Italian invasion in
1940, but the country was occupied by German and
Italian forces in 1941. Two guerrilla groups were in
action during the War, one communist-inspired and the
other a pro-monarchist organisation. They worked
together to overcome the Germans but then fought

against each other from 1945 to 1949; British troops intervened to support the monarchists, and remained in the country until 1950. The communists controlled the N of the country, receiving aid from Albania, Bulgaria and Yugoslavia, which only ceased after Yugoslavia's expulsion from the **Cominform**. The monarchists were finally victorious.

During the 1950s and 60s there were frequent changes of government and much political chaos. Fears of civil war and a left-wing takeover resulted in a right-wing army coup (1967) under Col. George Papadopoulos, after which left-wing organisations were banned, civil liberties suspended, opponents of the regime arrested, and the press censored. A dictatorial military junta ('the Colonels') lasted until 1974 when democracy was restored, partially as a result of the crisis in **Cyprus**.

Greece is a member of NATO, and became an associate member of the EU, achieving full membership in 1981. The long-standing dispute between Greece and Turkey over Cyprus and exploration rights in the Aegean Sea caused concern in NATO during the Cold War because of the danger that a vital part of the defence system against communist expansion would be in danger if war broke out between them, making either or both unable to honour their NATO obligations.

Greece elected a socialist government under Andreas Papandreou (PASOK party) in 1981, but did not proceed with the promised closure of US military bases.

Grey, Edward, Viscount Grey of Fallodon
(1862–1933) A British Liberal politician. Grey was
Foreign Secretary from 1905 to 1916, and ambassador
to the USA (1919–20). A great believer in international
dialogue, he negotiated the **Anglo-Russian Entente**
(1907), played a leading part in the peace negotiations
following the **Balkan Wars**, and was a firm supporter
of the **League of Nations**. He convinced a deeply
divided cabinet of the necessity of entering WWI, was
largely responsible for persuading Italy to join the
Allied side in 1915, and encouraged the USA to do so
as well in 1917.

Gromyko, Andrei (1909–89) A Soviet diplomat and
politician. Gromyko became deputy Foreign Minister
and permanent UN delegate (1946), Foreign Minister
(1957–85), and President of the USSR (1985–8). He
accompanied Nikolai Bulganin and Nikita Khrushchev
to the UK in 1956, and Khrushchev to Vienna for the
meeting with US President John F Kennedy in 1961.
Although closely associated with the policy of **détente**,
Gromyko was a shrewd and skilled director of the
Communist cause in the **Cold War**.

Guernica *see* **Spanish Civil War**.

Guevara, Ernesto (Che) (1928–67) An Argentinian
revolutionary. Guevara left Argentina in 1953 because
of his opposition to Juan Perón's right wing rule and
joined the exiled Cuban Fidel **Castro** in Mexico where
they planned the Cuban revolution. They fought
together in Cuba to remove the dictator Fulgencio
Batista, and Guevara became Minister of Industries in
the new regime after 1959. His revolutionary ideals

made him restless for a new cause, and he left Cuba in 1965 to rouse Bolivian tin-miners to rebellion, but was captured by the Bolivian army and executed. His guerrilla techniques influenced revolutionary movements throughout the world, and he became an icon of the 1960s counter-culture.

Gulag The Soviet central administration in charge of forced-labour camps – the camps themselves being known as gulags. These were mainly situated in Siberia, and Stalin sent millions of Soviet citizens to them during the 1930s. Forced labour had existed almost from the beginning of the communist regime, but it was Stalin who turned it into a system from 1929. Conditions in the camps were primitive and inhuman, and a sliding scale of rations was given to each labourer in direct proportion to his or her workrate. Estimates of how many were sent to the gulags vary, but the number was probably somewhere between six and ten million. Gulags remained in existence until the end of the Soviet regime. **Khrushchev** allowed the dissident Alexander Solzhenitsin's book *One Day in the Life of Ivan Denisovich* to be published in 1962, and this described the camps in detail to an astonished Soviet public. With **glasnost**, freer criticism and information were allowed, the gulag population was drastically reduced, and attempts were made to improve conditions in them.

Gulf States The collective name for the oil-producing states of the Persian Gulf: Bahrain, Iran, Iraq, Kuwait, Oman, Qatar, Saudi Arabia, and the United Arab Emirates.

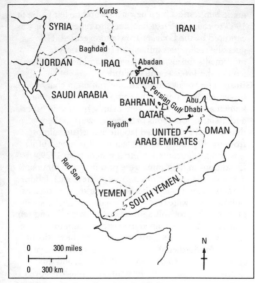

Gulf States

Gulf War 1. *see* Kuwait.
2. *see* Iran-Iraq War.

H

Haile Selassie (1892–1975) Emperor of **Ethiopia** from 1930 to 1974. One of the founders of modern Ethiopia, he westernised the country's institutions, and improved education and health. He led his country's resistance to the Italian invasion of 1935, but was forced into exile in England (1936). He returned to Ethiopia in 1941 after the Italians had been driven out during WWII, and set about rebuilding the country. However, from 1955 onwards he lost touch with the enormous social problems facing the country, and in 1974 was deposed by a group of left-wing army officers. From 1963 he took a leading part in the **Organisation of African Unity**.

Halifax, Earl of, *see* **Wood**.

Hammarskjöld, Dag (1905–61) A Swedish politician. Hammarskjöld was Secretary-General of the UN (1953–61), and was internationally respected for the impartial and skilful manner in which he carried out his duties, particularly during the Suez Crisis and the turmoil arising from the granting of independence to the Belgian Congo (Zaire). He was killed in an air crash in Zambia while dealing with the Congo Crisis, and was posthumously awarded the Nobel Peace Prize (1961).

Hapsburg Dynasty *see* **Austro-Hungarian Empire**.

Hardie, Keir (1856–1915) A Scottish Labour politician. Hardie was MP for Merthyr Tydfil from 1900 to 1915, and helped to found the **Independent Labour Party** in 1893, of which he was chairman 1893–1900 and

1913–15. An outstanding orator, he was influential in the forming of the **Labour Party** in 1906, leading it in the House of Commons after the 1906 general election. He campaigned for international socialism and against unemployment, opposed Liberal influence in the trade unions and, as a keen pacifist, opposed the Boer War and WWI.

Harriman, Averell (1891–1986) A US financier and diplomat. As a close friend of President F D Roosevelt, Harriman took part in the establishment of the **New Deal**, in which he displayed his wide business abilities. In 1941 Roosevelt sent him to London to supervise the **Lend-Lease** programme, and he played an important role as US ambassador to the USSR (1943–6). He was Secretary of Commerce (1946–8), and special assistant to President Harry Truman (1950–1), helping to organise NATO. He negotiated the **Nuclear Test Ban Treaty** (1963), and led the US delegation to the Vietnam peace talks in Paris (1968–9).

Heath, Edward (1916–) A British Conservative politician, PM from 1970 to 1974. As Lord Privy Seal (1961–3) he conducted unsuccessful negotiations for the UK's entry into the EEC (1963). He was elected leader of his party in 1965, and became PM in 1970.

Under his leadership the UK joined the EC (as it had become) in 1973, but his Industrial Relations Act and incomes policy angered the trade unions, and strike action by the miners caused the country to be placed on a three-day working week in 1974. To gain public support Heath called an election (1974) but was narrowly defeated by Harold Wilson's Labour Party, and in 1975 Margaret **Thatcher** replaced him as Conservative Party leader.

Hegemony The domination by one power or state within a group of neighbouring states, or a confederation, league, etc.; or of one social class over others.

Hellespont *see* **Dardanelles**.

Helsinki Conference A meeting attended by delegates from 35 countries to discuss security issues, with the aim of reducing international tension. The first stage of the negotiations took place in Helsinki in 1973 and the process was continued at intervals in Geneva (1973–5). Agreements were reached on economic and technological cooperation; the upholding of human rights; closer links between peoples of different states; and measures aimed at preventing accidental confrontation between opposing power blocs (including a separate section on the Mediterranean area).

Henderson, Arthur (1863–1935) A British Labour politician. He joined the Coalition cabinet in 1915 and the six-man War Cabinet as minister responsible for labour affairs (1916–17). He was Home Secretary (1924) and Foreign Secretary (1929–31), but refused to join Ramsay Macdonald's **National Government**, preferring to fight for the Labour Party's recovery from its 1931 election defeat. A crusader for disarmament, he was President of the World Disarmament Conference (1932) and was awarded the Nobel Peace Prize in 1934.

Hertzog, James Barry Munnick (1866–1942) A South African soldier and politician. Having served as a general in the Boer army in the Boer War, Hertzog founded the anti-British National Party (1913), which advocated independence for the country and opposed cooperation with Britain during WWI. He was PM from 1924 to 1939, partly in coalition with the Labour and United Parties. His support for neutrality at the start of WWII led to his electoral defeat.

Herzegovina *see* **Bosnia-Herzegovina**.

Hess, Rudolf (1894–1987) A German Nazi politician. Hess joined the Nazi Party, becoming Hitler's political secretary in 1920, and in 1923 took part in the Munich **Putsch**. He became deputy leader of the party in 1934 and was named as successor to Hitler after Goering in 1939. He flew alone to Scotland in 1941 to try to arrange a negotiated peace between Germany and Great Britain, but was imprisoned for the rest of WWII. He was sentenced to life imprisonment at the Nuremberg Trials and from 1966 until his death was the sole remaining prisoner in Spandau prison in Berlin, the Russians having consistently rejected pleas from the Americans, British and French for his release.

Himmler, Heinrich (1900–45) A German Nazi politician. Himmler became deputy leader of the **SS** in 1927 and leader in 1929. He was made commander of the unified German police forces in 1936, head of the Reich Administration in 1939, and Minister of the Interior in 1943. His ruthless direction of the secret police (Gestapo) made him a sinister figure among the Nazi leaders, and he was responsible for many atrocities, including the enforcement of Nazi extermination policies (*see* **concentration camps**). He committed suicide in 1945 shortly after being arrested by British forces.

Hindenburg, Paul von (1847–1934) A German soldier and politician. In WWI Hindenburg commanded the 8th Army, defeating superior Russian forces at Tannenberg and the Masurian Lakes (1914). He became a field marshal and Chief of the General Staff (1916), and with Erich **Ludendorff** controlled civil and military policy for the last months of the war. He advised Kaiser Wilhelm II to abdicate, and retired from the army himself in 1919.

Hindenburg was elected president of the Weimar Republic from 1925 to 1934, defeating Hitler in the 1932 presidential election. As president, Hindenburg supported **Stresemann**'s conciliatory foreign policy (1925–9) at the expense of angering extreme right-wing elements. In the early 1930s no party could achieve a Reichstag majority, with the result that during Heinrich Brüning's chancellorship Hindenburg had to rule by decree, and during that of Franz von **Papen** he had to rule through a non-party government. This political chaos helped to bring about the Nazi rise to power, and on von Papen's advice he appointed Hitler as Chancellor in 1933.

Hirohito (1901–89) Emperor of Japan from 1926 to 1989. His reign saw the growing influence of the armed forces, which was to lead to aggression against Manchuria and China, and then to Japan's involvement in WWII. Hirohito never held any real power in the government of the country, but from the 1930s to the end of WWII the cult of the emperor was a crucial factor in the growth of nationalism and Japan's aggressive territorial expansion, the emperor traditionally being worshipped as a god. After WWII the Allies allowed Hirohito to remain as a constitutional monarch, and in 1946 he renounced all claims to imperial divinity.

Hiroshima   A Japanese port on the island of Honshu. It was devastated on 6 August 1945 by a US atomic bomb, the first use of a nuclear weapon in war. A second bomb was dropped on the city of **Nagasaki** three days later. The horrific destruction caused by these bombs was partly responsible for Japan's unconditional surrender to the Allies.

Hitler, Adolf   (1889–1945)   An Austrian-born German dictator. Hitler became leader of the National Socialist German Workers' Party – the Nazi Party – in 1920 (*see* **National Socialism**). Like many of his fellow Germans, he bitterly opposed the terms of the Treaty of **Versailles**. He soon gained a growing following with his impressive public speaking, in which he put forward anti-democratic, anti-Semitic and racist policies, and demanded the return of Germany's lost territories. He also popularised the myth of the superiority of Aryan peoples, according to which the Germans were a 'master race'.

The **SA**, a brutal and intimidatory paramilitary force formed by Party members encouraged Hitler to challenge the Bavarian government; he attempted its overthrow in the so-called 'Beer Hall' **Putsch** in Munich in 1923. The Putsch failed and Hitler spent several months in jail, where he dictated to his secretary Rudolf **Hess** the first part of *Mein Kampf* ('My Struggle'), his autobiography and work of political philosophy.

The Nazi Party won twelve seats in the Reichstag election of 1928, and by 1932 had become the largest party in the country, helped to that position by the bitterness, desolation, fear and resentment caused by the mass unemployment accompanying the world **depression** of the early 1930s. Hitler became Chancellor in 1933. After the **Reichstag fire** in 1933 he moved Germany towards a one-party state, which he declared in 1934. By now he had started on the massive programme of military and territorial expansion which led to the outbreak of WWII. This policy was coupled with a ruthless elimination of all opposition and the systematic persecution of Jews, who formed the largest ethnic minority in Germany. His insistence on keeping power in his own hands meant that by 1941 he was personally directing the military campaigns of WWII, to the anxiety of his field commanders, and refused to consider the possibility of defeat even after Allied forces had crossed the German frontiers in 1945. Besieged in the Berlin Chancellory, he committed suicide surrounded by the burning ruins of the city. *See also* National Socialism; Germany; World War II; Holocaust.

Hoare-Laval Pact (1935) An agreement for ending Italo-Abyssinian hostilities (*see* **Ethiopia**) prepared by the UK Foreign Secretary Sir Samuel Hoare, Viscount Templewood (1880–1959), and the French PM Pierre Laval, at the request of the League of Nations. The proposal, if accepted, would have made substantial economic and territorial concessions to Italy based on the assumption that no state was prepared to go to war

over Abyssinia. The agreement outraged UK public
opinion and such was the uproar that the Government
rejected the plan and Hoare resigned.

Ho Chi Minh (*Vietnamese* – seeker of enlightenment)
(*orig.* Nguyen Van Thann) (1892–1969) A Vietnamese
communist politician. He founded the Communist Party
in Indo-China in 1930. After an unsuccessful uprising
against the French in 1940 he fled to S China and
founded a resistance movement of Communists and
Nationalists (**Viet Minh**) to fight the Japanese, then
occupying Vietnam.

After the Japanese surrender the French returned and
Ho then led the Viet Minh in successful operations
against them (1946–54), having managed to establish a
provisional government (1945). He continued to fight
for independence in the jungle and, after finally
succeeding, became PM from 1954 to 1955 and
president of North Vietnam (1955–69).

After his victory in the North, Ho set about gaining
control of South Vietnam by sending supplies along a
secret jungle route through Laos and Cambodia (the
'Ho Chi Minh Trail') to the **Viet Cong** guerrillas still
fighting for independence. After the US military
intervention in support of the South in 1965, he also
despatched regular army units to support the rebels. *See*
Vietnam War.

In spite of the devastation and turmoil of the war, Ho
introduced drastic land reforms, increased heavy
industrial output in the North and was a highly popular
leader among his own people.

Hohenzollern Dynasty　*see* **Wilhelm II**.

Holocaust The genocide of European Jewry by the Nazis during WWII. Hitler's hatred of the Jews had been made clear as soon as he entered politics, and after achieving power he put it into practice by the Nuremberg Laws and organised anti-Jewish rioting. It was not until 1941, however, that the systematic process began of rounding up Jews and taking them to concentration camps for extermination. The Holocaust proper lasted from 1941 to 1945, and during that time six million Jewish men, women and children, half of them from Poland, were killed, mainly by gassing or shooting. After the war, many, but not all, of those who had been responsible for the killings were punished, and West Germany agreed to pay compensation to the survivors. *See* **concentration camps**.

Home *see* **Douglas-Home**.

Home Rule Limited self-government for Ireland, the goal of the Irish Nationalists from 1870 to 1920 at a time when the whole of Ireland was part of the United Kingdom of Great Britain and Ireland. However, as a result of the Irish War of Independence (1919–21), full independence within the Commonwealth was achieved by 26 of the 32 counties with the creation of the Irish Free State under the terms of the Anglo-Irish Treaty (1921). The six northern counties (*Northern Ireland*) stayed within the framework of the United Kingdom and were granted Home Rule within that framework with a parliament at Stormont Castle (suspended from 1972 to 1999).

Hoover, Herbert (1874–1964) The US Republican president from 1929 to 1933. His administration was uneventful apart from the **Wall Street Crash** (1929). He was rejected in favour of **F D Roosevelt** at the 1932 election because of the effect the **Depression** was having on the country and because of his refusal, despite increasing hardship, to allow the government to assume responsibility for the unemployed.

Horthy [de Nagybanya], Miklós (1868–1957) A Hungarian admiral and regent. Horthy organised a counter-revolution against the communist régime of Béla Kun (1919–20), and in 1920 he became regent of Hungary, a post he held for 24 years. He followed conservative policies at home, and worked for the revision of the Treaty of **Trianon**. Although he took Hungary into WWII in 1941 (Hungarian forces assisted in the occupation of Yugoslavia and fought in the USSR), his support for Hitler was halfhearted and his attempt to negotiate a separate peace led to his overthrow and imprisonment by the Nazis in 1944. The Americans captured him at the end of WWII but refused to hand him over to the Yugoslavs to stand trial for war crimes, and he went into exile in Portugal.

'Hot Line' A direct telephone, teletype, or other communications link between heads of government for emergency use. The 'Hot Line' between the president of the USA and the leadership of the USSR was established in 1963 following the **Cuban Missile Crisis**.

House of Commons *see* **Parliament**.

House of Lords *see* **Parliament, Parliament Acts**.

House of Representatives *see* **Congress**.

Hoxha, Enver (1908–85) An Albanian communist politician. In 1943 Hoxha became Secretary-General of the Albanian Communist Party and leader of the resistance forces during WWII. After the War he led a provisional government and, with Soviet backing, established a Stalinist-style dictatorship. Disillusioned by Soviet attempts to make him an obedient puppet, he turned to China in 1968 for aid and understanding, but that association was ended by China in 1978.

Hua Guofeng or **Hua Kuo-feng** (1920–) A Chinese communist politician. Hua was severely criticised during the **Cultural Revolution** but survived to be named by **Mao Zedong** as his successor. He was PM from 1976 to 1980 and Chairman of the Central Committee from 1976 to 1981. His denunciation of the **Gang of Four** led to the arrest of its members and their subsequent imprisonment. He was succeeded as premier by Zhao Ziyang in 1980, and as Communist Party chairman by Hu Yaobang in 1981.

Huggins, Sir Godfrey, Viscount Malvern of Rhodesia and Bexley (1883–1971) A Southern Rhodesian politician. Huggins was PM of Southern Rhodesia from 1933 to 1953 and of the Federation of Rhodesia and Nyasaland (of which he was a keen supporter) from 1953 to 1956. He held a firm belief in white rule, with the result that black Africans had little involvement in the running of their country.

Hull, Cordell (1871–1955) A US Democratic statesman, Secretary of State from 1933 to 1944. Hull started the 'good neighbor' policy towards Latin America; this consisted of the idea of 'equal partnership' between the USA and the Latin American states, and a commitment to mutual assistance and joint defence, together with

renunciation of armed intervention by the USA in Latin
America. At the start of WWII, Hull was in favour of
US aid to the Allies (*see* **Lend-Lease Act**). Known as the
'father of the UN', he was awarded the Nobel Peace
Prize in 1945 for his part in its establishment.

Hungary   A republic of E Europe. Area: 93,032 sq km.
Pop: 10,225,000. Language: Hungarian (Magyar).
Religion: Christianity; of the 20 authorised
denominations the principal are RC, Calvinist and
Lutheran. Cap: Budapest.

Hungary became independent under the leadership of
Count Mihály Károlyi (1875–1955) after the collapse of
the **Austro-Hungarian Empire** in 1918. Károlyi was
overthrown by Béla **Kun**, who established a communist
system of government in 1919. This itself was replaced
with a monarchial constitution in 1920 by Miklós
Horthy, who left the throne vacant while ruling as
regent.

Between the World Wars Hungary's dissatisfaction
with the Treaty of **Trianon** resulted in close association
with Germany and ultimately an alliance during WWII.

After the War, the Smallholders' Party was in power
until it was replaced by the United Workers' Party
under Mátyás Rákosi (1892–1971). Hostility to the
Party's ultra-Communist policies resulted in the
replacement of Rákosi in 1953 by Imre Nagy
(1895–1958), whose liberalising reforms included the
freeing of political prisoners, relaxation of economic
and political controls, and the ending of compulsory
agricultural collectivisation. Less than two years later
Rákosi returned to power, only to be removed again

from office as a result of anti-Stalinist demonstrations.

In 1956 Nagy returned to power, and at the same time fighting broke out between Hungarians and Soviet forces. Nagy secured a Soviet withdrawal from Hungary, and his coalition government withdrew the country from the Warsaw Pact, tried to establish a neutral position in foreign affairs, permitted the reformation of political parties, and released the Primate of Hungary, Cardinal Jósef Mindszenty (1892–1975), who had been imprisoned in 1949 for his hostility to Communism. The government fell when Soviet forces, despite fierce resistance, reoccupied the country. János **Kádár** formed a government sympathetic to the USSR, and Nagy was executed.

In the 1980s, cautious liberalising policies, educational reforms and decentralised economic planning under Kádár's leadership made the country the most prosperous and least repressive of all the Soviet bloc states. Kádár fell from power in 1988, and the Communist Party voted to dissolve itself in 1989.

Hungary opened its border with Austria in 1989, precipitating a flow of E Germans to the West and sparking the collapse of Communist rule in E Europe. Soviet troops left the country in 1991 as Hungary moved towards a full market economy. In 1999 Hungary became a member of NATO.

Hunger Marches The demonstrations by unemployed workers in the 1920s and 30s to draw attention to the plight of the depressed areas of the UK. The first march, organised by communists and socialists, was from Glasgow to London (1922). The National

Unemployed Workers' Movement was founded in 1929 by a communist, Wal Hannington, and became the organising body for such displays of working-class solidarity. The best remembered march was from Jarrow to London in 1936, organised by the Jarrow MP, Ellen Wilkinson (1891–1947). WWII brought an end to the demonstrations, which had become a commonplace method of protest.

Husák, Gustáv (1913–91) A Czechoslovak communist politician. He was one of the organisers and leaders of the 1944 Slovak uprising against German occupation in WWII. He was imprisoned for 'bourgeois-nationalist' deviation because of his championship of Slovak rights (1951–60), and his climb to political power was slow. He was a strong supporter of Alexander **Dubček**'s proposed reforms, and was appointed deputy PM in 1968. Having deserted Dubček's policies in favour of coming to terms with the Warsaw Pact occupation of the country (1968), he became First Secretary of the Communist Party (1969–87) and president of the republic from 1975 to 1987. He resigned as demand for reform within Czechoslovakia became increasingly difficult to suppress.

Hussein [ibn Talal] (1935–99) King of Jordan from 1952. Hussein maintained a strong personal rule despite the political upheavals inside his country and in the surrounding states. He kept on good terms with other Arab states, while at the same time maintaining friendly ties with the West, particularly the UK.

His hostility to Israel resulted in Jordan signing a defence agreement with Egypt in 1967. Israel, surrounded by unfriendly states, included Jordan in its offensive action during the 1967 **Arab-Israeli War** and occupied E Jerusalem and the **West Bank**.

In addition Hussein had to contend with his country's use as a base by the **Palestine Liberation Organisation** for terrorist attacks on Israel and elsewhere. In 1970, after bitter fighting, Hussein put a stop to these activities by expelling the PLO. Iraq's seizure of Kuwait in 1990 and Jordan's sympathy with Iraq led to the country's diplomatic isolation and severe economic difficulties. In 1994 Hussein signed a peace treaty with Israel, and he was hailed internationally as a peacemaker by the time of his death.

Hussein, Saddam (1937–) Born in Baghdad, he invaded Iran in 1980 to recover the eastern half of the Shatt al Arab waterway, thus starting a war which also drew in America. He also applied his powers to root out the insurgency of the nationalist Kurds. In 1990 Saddam invaded **Kuwait**. The US President, **George Bush**, with an alliance of Western and Muslim nations, tried to stop him, but Saddam refused to comply. A bombing campaign against Iraq started then. In 1991 Saddam accepted the UN Security Council Resolution 687, but since then the economy of his country has deteriorated beyond repair due to UN-imposed sanctions.

Hydrogen Bomb *see* **nuclear warfare**.

I

Ideology A fixed set of principles, beliefs and aims belonging to a political party or other grouping. Authoritarian political movements like Communism and Fascism are more likely to have strict ideologies than democratic parties. The **Cold War** can be regarded largely as the conflict between the rival ideologies of Capitalism and Communism.

ILO *see* **International Labour Organisation**.

ILP *see* **Independent Labour Party**.

IMF *see* **International Monetary Fund**.

Imperial Conferences (1911–37) The meetings in London of the PMs of the UK and the Dominions. Under the title of Colonial Conferences, four similar meetings had taken place before 1911, and since WWII such gatherings have been called Commonwealth Conferences. The first three Imperial Conferences (1911, 1917–18 and 1921) showed the growing desire of the Dominions to control their own foreign policies free from British interference, and for the status of the Dominions to be more precisely defined. The next two conferences (1923 and 1926) drew up detailed proposals on Dominion status, and these were made law in the **Statute of Westminster** (1931). Little of consequence arose at the 1930 and 1932 conferences. The last conference (1937) was devoted to the worsening international situation.

Imperialism or **colonialism** The policy or practice of extending a state's rule over other territories, and of incorporating such colonised territories into an empire. The European powers began building empires in the Americas and Asia in the 15th century, but from *c.*1880 to 1914 there was a rush to gain previously uncolonised territory, especially in Africa, in order to satisfy the need for raw materials and for new markets for manufactured goods. Apart from such economic motives, the prestige of the imperial powers was also involved, as was the desire to prevent strategic threats (real or imagined). Imperial competition between the European powers in this period contributed to the tensions that eventually broke out in WWI.

Since WWII, the European powers have gradually granted independence to most of their colonies (*see* **decolonisation**), though the continued economic domination of the Third World by the developed countries has been called 'neo-imperialism'. The domination of Eastern Europe by the USSR for so long after WWII can also be regarded as a form of imperialism.

Imperial Preference The economic arrangement between members of the British Empire, and later the **Commonwealth**, by which preferential **tariffs** were operated between them. In the early years of the 20th century the principle was bitterly opposed by those in favour of **free trade**. These included the Liberal Party and a section of the Conservative Party, which was split on the issue, and it was not until 1932 that preferences were established on a significant scale. The **General Agreement on Tariffs and Trade** (1948) prevented any further extension of preferences and the scheme was phased out after the UK joined the EC in 1973.

Independent Labour Party (ILP) A socialist organisation founded in 1893 in Bradford by Keir **Hardie**. It was one of the groups forming the Labour Representation Committee (1900), the forerunner of the **Labour Party** (founded 1906). After WWI its influence declined, and following policy disagreements it broke away from the Labour Party in 1932. Although it is still in existence, its influence is slight.

India A federal republic of S Asia. Area: 3,159,530 sq km. Pop: 913,200,000. Official languages: Hindi and English. Religion: predominantly Hindu; also Sikh and Islam. Cap: New Delhi.

India was part of the British Empire from the 18th century. The slow progress made by Britain in the early years of the 20th century in granting India a degree of self-determination led to the organisation of a strong nationalist movement after WWI. The nationalists were strengthened by the outrage felt at the Amritsar massacre and disappointment with the Government of India Act (1919), which transferred only some powers to elected Indian officials.

Under Mahatma **Gandhi**, the Indian National Congress (*see* **Congress Party**) was reorganised into an effective protest body which started civil disobedience campaigns, and from 1930 Congress demanded complete independence. The 1935 Government of India Act established elected governments in the provinces, but the failure to grant immediate independence led to India's less than enthusiastic support for the Allied cause during WWII. Indeed, an Indian National Army

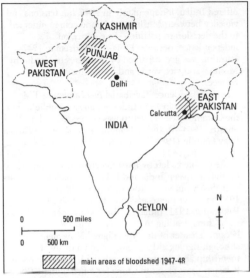

India The Partition of the Indian subcontinent, 1947.

was formed in Singapore in 1943 by Subhas Chandra Bose to fight on the Japanese side.

Meanwhile, suspicions that Congress was becoming Hindu-dominated led the Muslim League under Mohammed Ali **Jinnah** to agitate for an independent Muslim state. The postwar British Labour Government offered Indian independence in 1946, but tensions and violence between Muslim and Hindu communities led to the decision to partition the country, on independence, between India and Pakistan in 1947. Partition was accompanied by massacres of Hindus by Muslims and vice versa, and by vast movements of refugees.

On independence, Jawaharlal **Nehru** became PM (1947–64), and in 1950 India became a republic within the Commonwealth. Nehru was succeeded by Lal **Shastri** (1964–6), Indira **Gandhi** (1966–77 and 1980–4), Rajiv **Gandhi** (1984–9), N V Rao (1990–6) and Atal Bihari Vajpayee (1998–).

The problems left by Partition continued to arouse hostility between India and Pakistan, which fought wars over the disputed territory of Kashmir in 1947–9 and 1965 and over the secession of Bangladesh from Pakistan in 1971. India has also had frontier problems with China, leading to open conflict in 1962. India became a leader of the **Non-aligned Movement**, although signing aid agreements and a treaty of friendship and cooperation with the USSR. As a result, Pakistan drew closer to China for much of the 1970s. Indian involvement in the Tamil insurrection in Sri Lanka (1987–90) brought the assassination of Rajiv Gandhi, but little else.

Internally the country faced communal religious conflict, mainly sparked by militant Hindus, throughout the 1980s, with riots in 1992. Rao's Congress government from 1990 moved towards a full market economy, and in 1998, under A B Vajpayee, India confirmed its status as a nuclear power by a series of weapons tests, quickly matched by Pakistan. In 1999 a major military operation briefly cleared separatist guerillas from the disputed state of Kashmir, but military tension in the region increased again in 2002.

Indo-China A former French dependency in SE Asia which included the colonial territory of Cochin China and the protectorates of Annam, Cambodia, Laos and Tonkin. The Indo-China union lasted from 1887 until 1949 when Vietnam was established by the merger of Annam, Cochin China and Tonkin. The French connection was broken when Cambodia, Laos and Vietnam became independent states in 1954.

Inflation Increase in the general price level caused by:
  a. an increase in the amount of money in circulation, coupled with an expansion in demand for goods and services
  b. an increase in costs.
  The increase in prices means that the value of money decreases.

Integration *see* desegregation.

Intermediate Nuclear Forces Treaty (INF Treaty) A treaty signed in 1987 by the USA and the USSR banning all short- and medium-range land-based nuclear missiles.

International Bank for Reconstruction and Development (World Bank) A UN financial organisation established in 1945 to assist economic development in member states by the provision of loan capital. It supports programmes which it considers to be sound investments.

International Brigades The volunteer units organised
to fight in the **Spanish Civil War** (1936–9) against
Franco's forces. All members were anti-Fascists and
many were Communists. The volunteers totalled some
40,000 men drawn from most European countries and
the Americas.

International Court of Justice The principal
judicial body of the UN established in 1945 to judge
international disputes. The Court meets in The Hague
and comprises 15 judges, no two of whom may be
nationals of the same state. They are elected by the
General Assembly and the Security Council for a
nine-year term. If a state agrees to submit a dispute to
the Court and then refuses to accept its judgement the
Security Council has power to enforce it.

International Labour Organisation (ILO) An agency
with HQ in Geneva, established in 1919 by the Treaty of
Versailles as an agency of the League of Nations. Since
1946 it has been a specialised agency of the UN and now
has a membership of 144 states. Its aims are:

   a. the promotion of peace through social justice;
   b. the establishment of international labour standards
      for the improvement of working conditions and
      the protection of human rights;
   c. the maintenance of a technical-assistance
      programme to developing countries;
   d. the researching and publicising of information on
      aspects of economic activity in order to improve
      economic and social welfare;
   e. the provision of productive work to reduce
      unemployment.

The ILO was awarded the 1969 Nobel Peace Prize.

International Law The rules that affect or control
nations' relations with each other. In 1921 the League of
Nations established the permanent Court of
International Justice, based at The Hague, and after
WWII it was succeeded by the **International Court of
Justice** of the UN.

International Monetary Fund (IMF) A UN agency
with HQ in Washington, DC that was established in
1945. Its aims are:

  a. to support currency stability by defending
     currencies that are under pressure;
  b. to promote international monetary cooperation and
     expansion of trade;
  c. to make the Fund's resources available to reduce
imbalance in the **balance of payments** of member states,
usually subject to conditions and controls imposed by
the IMF. The Fund's assets are raised from member
states by a quota system.

International Socialism The idea of worldwide
brotherhood and solidarity between working-class
peoples, first put forward by Friedrich Engels and Karl
Marx in 1848 (*see* **Marxism**). The Second International
(founded 1889) still survives as a loose association of
social democratic parties. The Third International was
the **Comintern**.

IRA *see* **Irish Republican Army**.

Iran, formerly **Persia** A republic of SW Asia. Area:
1,648,000 sq km. Pop: 62,231,000. Language: Iranian
(Persian). Religion: Shi'a Islam. Cap: Tehran.

Despotic shahs of the Qajar dynasty ruled the country

until 1925 when the National Assembly (Majlis) deposed the dynastic ruler, Ahmed Shah, and elected Colonel Reza Khan (1878–1944) as shah. Reza Khan had led a military coup in 1921 and assumed dictatorial powers before his formal election. He adopted the dynastic name 'Pahlavi' and began the nation's modernisation, introducing European dress, breaking the power of the mullahs (Islamic clerics), abolishing the veil for women, and developing the armed forces, hospitals, railways, roads and schools. Because of his pro-German sympathies during WWII, UK and Soviet forces occupied the country (1941–6), and he was forced to abdicate in favour of his son, Mohammed Reza **Pahlavi**.

Nationalistic, anti-American and anti-British attitudes developed between 1947 and 1951, resulting in demands for the nationalisation of the oil industry, which had been controlled by the Anglo-Iranian Oil Company since 1909. An attempt was made on the Shah's life and the PM and Education Minister were assassinated in the disturbances, which were condoned, and even incited, by the fanatical Mohammed Mussadiq (1881–1967) who was PM from 1951 to 1953. Although the oil industry was nationalised, the expected economic benefits did not materialise, since most of the necessary technicians left the country following the UK's cutting of diplomatic relations, with the result that the oil installations became practically unworkable. The promised breakup and distribution of large estates also failed and civil turmoil returned to the streets, resulting in the Shah's dismissal of Mussadiq.

There followed a period of economic consolidation and expansion, the emancipation of women and a series of welfare measures, but the religious traditionalists were angered. Islamic fundamentalist and anti-Western demonstrations began in 1977 in support of the return of the Ayatollah **Khomeini**, who had been exiled for opposing the Shah's reforms. Serious rioting occurred and the Shah was forced to flee the country. In retaliation for the USA's grant of sanctuary to the Shah, student extremists occupied the US embassy and held 63 members of staff hostage (1979–81). Meanwhile Khomeini had returned to Iran in 1979 and established an Islamic republic, under which thousands of the Shah's supporters and other opponents of the new regime were killed. To add to these internal stresses, Iran became involved in war with Iraq from 1980 to 1988 (*see* **Iran–Iraq War**). After Khomeini's death in 1989, the country's strict Islamic laws were relaxed slightly under President Ali Akbar Rafsanjani, despite opposition from the new ayatollah, Sayid Ali Khamenei. Rafsanjani was re-elected in 1993. In 1995 the USA suspended its renewed trade links with Iran, citing Iranian support for international terrorism. In 1997 Mohammed Khatami, a relatively liberal cleric, was elected president in a popular reaction to the regime's repressive social policies.

Iran–Iraq War or **Gulf War** (1980–88) A conflict which started with an Iraqi attack on its neighbour Iran in pursuit of disputed territory. Enormous offensives by both sides resulted in huge numbers of casualties, and hostilities also involved attacks on neutral shipping in the Persian Gulf. Diplomatic efforts to end the war were unsuccessful, but continuing heavy losses and lack of progress led to a compromise peace in 1988.

Ireland An island of the British Isles, partitioned since 1921 into the Republic of Ireland and Northern Ireland (still part of the UK). The Norman–English conquest and subsequent colonisation of Ireland began in the 12th century. Scottish Protestant settlers were particularly numerous in the NE part of the province of Ulster, where they settled in the 16th century on land from which locals, who were RC, were evicted; thus the seeds were sown of the troubles that continue to the present day.

In an attempt to solve the 'Irish Question', UK governments in the late 19th century twice attempted to grant **Home Rule** to Ireland, but the legislation was defeated in Parliament. A new Home Rule bill in 1912 led to a threat of armed rebellion by the Protestants in the North East who feared being ruled by what would have been a Roman Catholic-dominated Irish parliament. The nationalists also began to arm, and civil war was only prevented by the outbreak of WWI, which resulted in the postponement of plans for Home Rule.

The republican nationalists rebelled unsuccessfully in the **Easter Rising** of 1916, and after this there was a swing in Irish popular opinion away from the idea of limited self-government and towards full independence. Guerrilla war broke out in 1919 and lasted until 1921, with the Irish Republican Army fighting British government forces. Meanwhile the Government of Ireland Act (1920) established separate parliaments for the six northern counties and the rest of Ireland, then the 1921 Anglo-Irish Treaty gave the 26 counties dominion status. This was followed in 1922 by the establishment of the Irish Free State.

Republic of Ireland A republic comprising all but the six northern counties of Ireland. Area: 69,893 sq km. Pop: 3,599,000. Languages: English and Irish (Gaelic). Religion: Christianity (RC). Cap: Dublin.

The establishment of the Irish Free State by the Anglo-Irish Treaty of 1921 split Irish Nationalists into those who supported the dominion status granted by the Treaty and those who wanted a fully independent republic. These two factions became respectively **Fine Gael** and **Fiánna Fail**, the latter led by Eamon **de Valéra**. De Valéra came to power in 1932 and in 1937 introduced a new constitution abolishing the Irish Free State, declaring the renamed Eire a sovereign independent state under a president, and refusing to recognise the partition of Ireland. Eire remained neutral in WWII and in 1949 left the Commonwealth and declared itself fully independent as the Republic of Ireland.

The Republic's foreign policy has remained one of neutrality, and although it joined the EC in 1973, it has refused to join NATO. An electoral system using proportional representation has meant that formation of majority governments has proved difficult, the largest party having to rely on coalition support. Meanwhile, EU development funds and relatively enlightened economic policies of successive governments in the 1980s and 90s transformed the Irish Republic from one

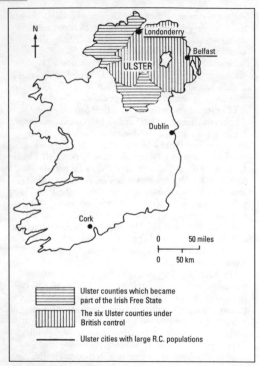

N

Londonderry

Belfast

ULSTER

Dublin

Cork

| 0 | 50 miles |
| 0 | 50 km |

Ulster counties which became
part of the Irish Free State

The six Ulster counties under
British control

Ulster cities with large R.C. populations

Ireland *The partition of Ireland, 1921.*

of the EU's poorest members to one of Europe's most successful economies. Increasingly liberalised social attitudes have also taken hold in Irish society.

Northern Ireland A part of the old province of Ulster consisting of the six north-eastern counties of Ireland, and forming part of the UK. Area: 14,146 sq km. Pop: 1,641,700. Language: English. Religion: Christianity (Protestant and RC). Cap: Belfast.

The Protestant majority in Northern Ireland results from the fact that the area was heavily settled by Scottish and English Protestants in the early 17th century. Northern Ireland achieved its own parliament (meeting at Stormont Castle) in 1920, which was dominated throughout its existence by the Ulster Unionist Party, representing Protestant interests (*see* **Ulster Loyalist**). The Stormont parliament was suspended in 1972.

In 1968 the RC minority began to demonstrate against discrimination in housing, employment and voting rights in local elections. The demonstrations led to worsening violence between Protestants and Roman Catholics, and in 1969 British troops were sent to Northern Ireland to keep the peace. The majority of the RC population, represented politically by the moderate Social Democratic and Labour Party and the militant Sinn Fein (the political wing of the IRA), sought unification with the Republic, while this aim was vigorously resisted by the Protestants.

The violence, verging on civil war, saw the IRA and armed Protestant groups carrying out numerous murders and bomb attacks. In 1972 the UK government suspended the Northern Ireland parliament and imposed direct rule from Westminster. An attempt by the UK government to introduce 'power-sharing' between Roman Catholics and Protestants in 1973–4 broke down in the face of mass strikes by Protestants, and direct rule was restored. In 1994 the IRA and the Loyalists declared ceasefires. Negotiations to find a political solution were halted by the ending of the IRA ceasefire in 1996 and revived with a new ceasefire in 1997. Sinn Féin joined the resulting talks.

Agreement was reached for a new Northern Ireland Assembly in 1998, and the Republic of Ireland renounced its territorial claims. British direct rule ended in December 1999, delayed by protracted disagreement over the timetable for IRA disarmament.

Irgun Zvai Leumi A revisionist Zionist underground organisation founded in 1937 for the defence of Jewish settlers against Arab attacks in Palestine. It was subsequently in opposition to the British mandated forces, though it declared a truce in 1939 leading to the breakaway of the **Stern Gang**. It resumed hostilities in 1944 and blew up, with the loss of 91 lives, Jerusalem's King David Hotel (1946) while it was being used as the British administrative HQ. Menachem **Begin** was its leader before it was absorbed into the Israeli Army.

Irish Free State see Ireland.

Irish Republican Army (IRA) The irregular military organisation founded in 1919 as the armed wing of the illegal Irish nationalist government created after the success of Sinn Féin in the general election of 1918. Its purpose was to carry out guerrilla operations against

British institutions and troops. Its successes contributed to the formation of the Irish Free State in 1921 but it then split into factions that either accepted or opposed the Anglo-Irish Treaty of 1921.

The anti-Treaty faction continued to agitate for the unification of the whole of Ireland. Violence in Northern Ireland flared up in 1968 and intensified after 1971, with the IRA conducting a campaign of bombing and assassinations there and later in England. A large British army presence in the province became necessary to counter the activities of the IRA. The violence, while directed mainly against members of the police force, the armed services and loyalist paramilitary organisations, was also economic and sectarian in character.

The IRA declared a ceasefire in 1997; as a result, Sinn Féin members were able to participate in all-party talks that began in that year, and in the resulting Northern Ireland Assembly. Progress towards demilitarisation of Northern Ireland and IRA decommissioning of its weapons remained slow at the end of the century.

Iron Curtain The term used by Winston Churchill in 1946 for the ideological and physical barriers that prevented interchange of people and ideas between the West and Soviet-dominated countries in E Europe, which later became members of the **Warsaw Pact**.

Isolationism A policy of nonparticipation in, or withdrawal from, international affairs, especially as practised by the USA during much of the 20th century. The sinking of the *Lusitania* by a German U-boat in 1915 strained this attitude and contributed to eventual US entry into WWI, but the policy returned in the interwar years, gradually being relaxed at the start of WWII and shattered by the Japanese attack on **Pearl Harbor**. A noisy minority urged a return to this policy of 'fortress America' in the 1980s and 90s.

Israel A republic of the Middle East, on the E coast of the Mediterranean. Area: 20,770 sq km. Pop: 5,239,000 (1992). Language: Hebrew. Religion: Judaism. Cap: Jerusalem.

From the end of the 19th century, the aim of **Zionism** was to create a homeland for the Jews in **Palestine**, from where many had been dispersed all over Europe, N Africa and the Middle East at the time of the Roman Empire. After the defeat of the Ottoman Empire in WWI, Palestine became a British **mandate** (1922–48) and the **Balfour Declaration** pledged the UK government to the eventual creation of a Jewish national home. Jewish immigration increased enormously as a result of Nazi persecution in Europe, and this led to violent opposition from the native Arab population. The UK referred the problem to the UN, which partitioned Palestine between Jews and Arabs.

The state of Israel was founded in 1948 when the British mandate ended. Immediately the neighbouring Arab states attacked the new nation, refusing to recognise its legitimacy. By the time of the 1949 armistice, Israel had increased its land area by about 25 per cent at the expense of its neighbours. The creation of the state of Israel led to the exodus of large numbers of Palestinian Arabs, and it was their desire for a homeland, coupled with the unwillingness of Arab nations to accept a non-Arab state in the region, that was at the root of much of the subsequent conflict in the Middle East (*see* **Arab-Israeli Wars** and **Palestine Liberation Organisation**).

In the 1967 war, Israel further increased its territory to include the **Gaza Strip**, the **West Bank** of the River Jordan, the **Golan Heights**, and **Sinai**. Israel has had to rely heavily on US economic and military aid, and it was through US pressure that the **Camp David Agreement** (1978) was signed with Egypt, following which Sinai was returned to Egypt. The agreement's provision for a degree of Palestinian autonomy on the West Bank and in the Gaza Strip finally materialised in 1994, but relations between Israel and the devolved Palestinian authority led by Yasser **Arafat** have remained difficult. Israel also became involved between 1982 and 1985 in the civil war in Lebanon.

Internally, Israel established many modern industries and irrigation schemes that transformed what was once desert into productive agricultural land, though severe ecological problems remain to be solved. Because of the enormous cost of defence, the country suffers from high inflation and balance of payments problems. Israel is governed by a single-chamber legislative assembly (the Knesset), elected by proportional representation, which has meant that most governments have had to rely on coalition support to remain in power.

Italy A republic of SC Europe. Area: 301,245 sq km. Pop: 57,517,000. Language: Italian. Religion: Christianity (RC). Cap: Rome. After the collapse of the Roman Empire, Italy was divided into numerous independent states and areas ruled by foreign powers.

The nationalist movement of the 19th century eventually unified the country as a monarchy in 1870, although Italy continued to claim other territories in the Balkans and S Austria. By the **Treaty of London** (1915), Italy joined the Allied side in WWI on the understanding that it would gain these territories following an Allied victory. At the peace settlement, only some of the promised territories were granted to Italy, and the resulting disappointment, combined with social unrest, parliamentary instability and fear of Communism, assisted the rise of Fascism and the appointment of Benito **Mussolini** as PM in 1922.

By manipulating electoral laws and with the help of King Victor Emmanuel III, Mussolini crushed parliamentary opposition and established a Fascist dictatorship, which lasted from 1925 to 1943. Mussolini's ideas of colonial expansion led Italy into the conquest of Abyssinia (*see* **Ethiopia**) and support for the nationalist rebels in the Spanish Civil War. Italy formed the **Axis** alliance with Germany in 1936, joined the **Anti-Comintern Pact** in 1937, and in 1940 entered WWII on the German side, again in the hope of territorial gains. In 1943 the Allies invaded Italy, resulting in Mussolini's forced resignation, Italy's surrender, and its declaration of war on Germany. German forces immediately occupied much of the country and put up a stubborn resistance until 1945.

In 1946 a referendum decided in favour of the establishment of a republic, and parliament now consists of a Chamber of Deputies and a Senate. Since the War until 1995, Italy was ruled by a succession of unstable coalition governments. Economic difficulties, financial crises, unemployment and the poverty of S Italy contributed to the growth of the Communist Party, which was the largest in Western Europe. However, it failed to overcome the dominance of the Christian Democrats in national government, and both parties declined in influence during the 1980s and 90s, amid a series of bribery scandals. The late 20th century saw the rise of the centrist parties, but also of neo-Fascists and the so-called Northern League, a grouping of parties dedicated to the secession of N Italy from Rome and the remainder of the country. Changes in electoral laws led to the election of the first government with a stable majority in 1995.

Italy is a founder member of the EU and NATO.

Iwo Jima An island in the Pacific on which Japan built a major air base in WWII. Its capture by US forces in February 1945 gave them an airfield within reach of the Japanese mainland, but the enormous cost in casualties – more than 7,000 Americans died – raised doubts as to whether island-hopping was the best way to defeat Japan, and influenced the decision to drop atomic bombs on Japan six months later. *See also* **Okinawa**.

J

Japan An island monarchy of E Asia. Area: 369,660 sq km. Pop: 124,310,000 (1992). Language: Japanese. Religions: Buddhism and Shintoism. Cap: Tokyo.

Japan was rapidly industrialised in the last quarter of the 19th century, and by the early 20th century was able to defeat Russia in the **Russo-Japanese War** (1904–5). In WWI Japan fought on the Allied side.

Between the Wars, extreme nationalists in the army increasingly controlled political life, reviving traditional beliefs, such as the divinity of the Emperor **Hirohito**, to create an autocratic state. The military, backed by nationalist sentiment at home, started a policy of colonial expansion to relieve pressure on the overpopulated country. This led to the conquest of Manchuria (1931), the invasion of China (1937), and the **Sino-Japanese War**. Japan withdrew from the League of Nations in 1933, and, wary of the USSR, joined Germany in the **Anti-Comintern Pact,** which was strengthened by the Tripartite Pact (1940).

Japan entered WWII as one of the Axis powers in 1941 with its attack on the US navy at Pearl Harbor. This was followed by the rapid conquest of large parts of SE Asia and the Pacific. Japan was eventually forced to surrender following the dropping of atomic bombs on Hiroshima and Nagasaki, and was occupied until 1952 by Allied forces. Japan made a remarkable recovery from the effects of WWII, and became one of the world's principal industrialised nations, developing close ties with the West, especially the USA. The country is now a parliamentary democracy, having in the 1946 constitution abandoned the belief in the Emperor's divinity. The constitution also renounced war, and the country's defence is guaranteed by the US-Japan Security Treaty (1960).

Jarrow Marchers *see* **Hunger Marches**.

Jaruzelski, Wojciech (1923–) A Polish general and statesman. He became First Secretary in 1981, PM (1981–5) and head of state (1985–90). He imposed martial law (1981–3), banning **Solidarity** and imprisoning many of its leaders, but he was eventually forced to recognise the organisation and allow it a share in government in 1989.

Jinnah, Mohammed Ali (1876–1948) A Pakistani politician. Jinnah joined the Indian National Congress, the Indian Muslim League and the Viceroy's Legislative Council before WWI. He resigned from Congress because of dislike of **Gandhi**'s disobedience campaign and Hindu domination of the independence movement. He was president of the **Muslim League** from 1934. He gave support to the UK during WWII when Congress refused to do so and from 1940 was a leading supporter of the partition of the subcontinent into separate Hindu and Muslim states. When this happened, in 1947, he became his country's first Governor General, having to cope with problems of fighting, rioting and refugees, and the difficult relationship with India.

Johnson, Lyndon Baines (1908–73) A US politician and Democratic president from 1963 to 1969. Johnson became vice-president in 1961 and after John F

Kennedy's assassination succeeded him as president in 1963, retaining the position after the 1964 election. During his administration Congress approved legislation making limited improvements to the position of black Americans (*see* **Civil Rights Acts**), together with other social reforms. However, Johnson's increasing involvement of the USA in the **Vietnam War** led to growing opposition, which caused him to decide not to stand for re-election in 1968.

Judiciary A country's courts and judges. In the UK the judiciary carries out the law as laid down by the legislature (Parliament). In the USA the judiciary (the Supreme Court) has the power to decide whether the laws are in accordance with the constitution, and if it decides they are not it declares them invalid.

Junta A ruling group of officers in a military government, especially after a coup d'état or revolutionary seizure of power. The term is also applied to an executive or legislative council in several Latin American states.

Jutland, Battle of (1916) The only major naval engagement of WWI between the Royal Navy and the German High Seas Fleet. The British lost 14 vessels to Germany's 11. As the Germans were able to return to port, despite British dominance in ships and firepower, the battle was tactically indecisive. However, Jutland was regarded as a strategic victory for Britain since the High Seas Fleet never again ventured to seek out the British fleet.

K

Kádár, János (1912–89) A Hungarian communist politician. Kádár became Minister of the Interior in 1948 but was imprisoned from 1951 to 1953 for displaying 'Titoist' sympathies, i.e. independence from hard-line Stalinist principles. He had been First Secretary of the Party since 1956.

    When the anti-Soviet revolution commenced in 1956 he was a member of Nagy's 'national' anti-Stalinist government but a few days later formed a counter-government with Soviet support. He took control of the post-revolutionary regime as PM (1956–8) and instituted a period of severe repression. He again became PM in 1961, and pursued a policy of gradual liberalisation and national reconciliation that ultimately made Hungary the most Westernised of the Soviet Bloc countries. Demands for increased political freedom and economic change led to Kádár's resignation in 1988.

Kaiser *see* **Wilhelm II**.

Kampuchea *see* **Cambodia**.

Kashmir Dispute A dispute between India and Pakistan concerning ownership of the northernmost region of the Indian subcontinent. It is a major cause of disagreement between the two countries. At the time of the partition of India and Pakistan in 1947, Kashmir had a largely Muslim population but was ruled by a Hindu Maharajah who decided to permit the state to be merged with India. Fighting broke out between Hindus and Muslims, with the result that Pakistani troops moved into the state to support the Muslim population and came into conflict with the Indian army.

India branded Pakistan as an aggressor and appealed to the UN, which appointed a peace commission to establish a provisional boundary line. This left most of the state under Indian control, but when arbitration was suggested as a means of achieving a final settlement, India opposed it. India feared that, as the majority of

Kashmir Dispute

the population was Muslim, most of the region would be absorbed by Pakistan if the issue depended on the principle of self-determination.

Kashmir has continued to be the cause of hostilities between India and Pakistan, e.g. in 1965 (*See* **Tashkent Conference**), and in 1971. The dispute remains unresolved, despite the Simla Agreement (1972), which drew a new demarcation line. India continues to accuse Pakistan of supporting Kashmiri separatist guerrillas.

Kaunda, Kenneth (1924–) A Zambian politician. Kaunda joined the Northern Rhodesia National Congress in 1949 to promote African independence. He founded the Zambia National Congress in 1958; it was later banned because of its opposition to colonial rule and the Federation of Rhodesia and Nyasaland. He became leader of the United Nationalist Independence Party in 1960 and PM of Northern Rhodesia in 1964 and, after independence, president of Zambia (1964–91), establishing a one-party state and assuming autocratic powers (1972).

Kellogg-Briand Pact (1928) An agreement aimed at avoiding war. In 1927 the French Foreign Minister, Aristide **Briand**, proposed that France and the USA should sign a pact renouncing war. Frank Kellogg (1856–1937), the American Secretary of State, wanted the whole world to be involved. Eventually 65 states signed, agreeing to renounce war as an instrument of national policy. The signatories included Germany, the USA and the USSR, even though the latter two were not members of the League of Nations. The Pact made no provision for punishing aggressors, and therefore had no power; by the end of the 1930s it had become more or less meaningless.

Kennedy, John Fitzgerald (1917–63) A US politician and Democratic president from 1961 to 1963. His youthful appearance, effective organisation and political style made him the most popular president of the century. Foreign affairs dominated his administration. They included the **Bay of Pigs** fiasco; discussions with **Khrushchev** in Vienna; the building of the **Berlin** Wall; the launching of the Peace Corps, the purpose of which was to develop assistance to underdeveloped countries, and of the Alliance for Progress, an aid programme for Latin America (1961); the **Cuban Missile Crisis**; and the conclusion of the **Nuclear Test Ban Treaty** (1963).

Domestically his civil-rights (*see* **Civil Rights Act**s) and social-reform programmes (the New Frontier) met opposition in Congress but eventually became law some three years after he had proposed them. Lee Harvey Oswald was accused of his assassination in November 1963 in Dallas, Texas.

Kenyatta, Jomo (1892–1978) A Kenyan politician. He was an early supporter of African nationalism and a campaigner for African rights and land reform. In 1947 he became president of the Kenya African Union which advocated extreme nationalism and was a screen for **Mau Mau** terrorist activities. Although Kenyatta eventually denounced these excesses, he was distrusted by the UK government and sentenced to imprisonment (1953–61). In 1960, while still in jail, he was elected president of the Kenya Africa National Union (KANU) and when it came to power in 1963 he became PM, playing a prominent part in negotiations towards independence (1963). He was president of Kenya from 1964 to 1978.

Kerensky, Alexander (1881–1970) A Russian politician. A democratic socialist, Kerensky became War Minister and weeks later PM in the Provisional Government following the February Revolution of 1917. He was determined to keep Russia in WWI, but his attempts to launch a powerful offensive in the summer were unpopular with the Russian people who were anxious for peace. He was pushed out of office by the Bolsheviks in the October Revolution of 1917. *See also* **Russian Revolutions**.

Keynes, John Maynard (1883–1946) A British economist who challenged much of the accepted economic theory of his time. He criticised reparations as damaging not only to Germany but also to the world's economy. Although not a socialist, he did not believe in allowing free market forces to go unchecked, and believed that government action was often necessary, especially to deal with a slump. Thus he urged governments to tackle unemployment by increased government spending, and to finance extra government expenditure by increasing government borrowing. For a long time after WWII, Keynes's ideas were widely accepted, but they came increasingly under attack from monetarists, especially during the 1980s. Keynesianism made something of a comeback in the 1990s.

KGB *see* **Soviet Security Service**.

Khan *see* **Ayub Khan; Yahya Khan**.

Khmer Rouge The Cambodian Communist Party. It

seized power following its victory in the civil war
(1970–5), and under Pol Pot instituted a harsh,
regimented regime, expelled all foreigners, and cut off
the country from contact with the rest of the world.
Cities and towns were forcibly evacuated, much of their
populations massacred and the rest made to take up
agricultural work. After the country's invasion by
Vietnam in support of an uprising by the Kampuchean
National United Front (1978) and the fall of the capital
Phnom Penh (1979), the Khmer Rouge went
underground and waged a guerrilla war. The
organisation only ceased to pose a threat to Cambodia
in 1998, after the death of Pol Pot.

Khomeini, Ruhollah (1900–89) An Iranian Islamic
fundamentalist leader. As an ayatollah of the Shi'ite sect,
Khomeini came into prominence when he condemned
the Shah's Western-type reforms, especially women's
emancipation (1963). He was sent into exile, from
where he called on Iranians to overthrow the Shah and
establish an Islamic republic. This was achieved after
the Shah fled the country in 1979, Khomeini returning
in triumph to Tehran shortly afterwards. There followed
a period of drastic repression and terror when
thousands of the Shah's followers and others opposed to
Khomeini's radical fundamentalist reforms were
executed or imprisoned. Khomeini effectively became
head of state with a government organised by a
Revolutionary Committee of Shi'ite clergymen, and links
with the West were severed. The **Iran-Iraq War** was
entered into for religious as well as territorial reasons.
Khomeini set himself up as the defender of Islam and it

was he who proclaimed a death sentence on the British writer Salman Rushdie in 1989.

Khrushchev, Nikita (1894–1971) A Soviet politician. Khrushchev was First Secretary of the Party from 1953 to 1964 following Stalin's death. At the 20th Party Congress (1955) he made a remarkable attack on Stalin's 'personality cult' and other misdeeds. He was PM from 1958 to 1964 while remaining First Secretary, and undertook a series of overseas visits, talking much about peaceful intentions yet accompanying them with threats. In 1963, however, he signed the **Nuclear Test Ban Treaty.**

He was largely responsible for the **Cuban Missile Crisis**, allowed relations with China to deteriorate (*see* **Sino-Soviet split**), and disrupted the economy by encouraging agricultural decentralisation and the production of consumer goods at the expense of heavy industrial output. His responsibility for these crises, together with accusations of nepotism (favouring family members), the revival of a personality cult, and authoritarian and unruly handling of state and Party affairs, resulted in his sacking and enforced retirement (1964). He was succeeded as First Secretary by Leonid **Brezhnev** and as PM by Alexei **Kosygin.**

Kibbutz An Israeli collective agricultural settlement, worked and owned by its members and on which children are collectively raised. The first was established by Jewish settlers in Palestine in 1910.

Kiesinger, Kurt Georg (1904–88) The West German Christian Democrat Chancellor from 1966 to 1969. His government was a coalition of the Christian and Social Democrats. It succeeded in halting the recession which had led to the downfall of **Erhard**'s government and reestablished diplomatic relations with Romania (1967) and Yugoslavia (1968) which had been broken off during WWII. Kiesinger was a believer in better relations with the Warsaw Pact countries (*see* **Ostpolitik**) and a keen supporter of European unity.

Kim Il Sung (1912–94) A North Korean Communist marshal and politician. He joined the Communist Party (1931) and organised and led the Korean People's Revolutionary Army against the Japanese (1932–45). He was put in charge of administration by the Soviet army of occupation (1945), quickly established himself, and became PM on the formation of the Democratic People's Republic (1948–72).

He was supreme commander of the army in the **Korean War**, though his position was insecure. However, he managed to remove his rivals in a 'cultural revolution' and became the focus of a personality cult, aiming to centre the country on himself and to make it completely self-reliant. He was succeeded as president by his son, Kim Jong Il.

King, Martin Luther (1929–68) A US Baptist minister and civil-rights leader. King supported nonviolent confrontation as a weapon of social protest. In Montgomery, Alabama, he organised a boycott of buses by the black American community in protest at racial segregation, which eventually produced a federal-court desegregation order in 1955. This success encouraged him to extend the campaign, and in many parts of the country peaceful demonstrations were held opposing racial discrimination in matters such as employment, housing and schooling. This agitation contributed towards the passing of several **Civil Rights Acts**, and in 1964 King was awarded the Nobel Peace Prize. He was assassinated in Memphis, Tennessee, supposedly by James Earl Ray.

Kinnock, Neil (1942–) A British politician, leader of the Labour Party from 1983 to 1992. Despite his left-wing origins, Kinnock's main achievement was to wean the Labour Party away from traditional left-wing policies, such as nuclear disarmament. The electoral victory of the Conservatives in 1992 led to his resignation, and replacement by John Smith.

Kissinger, Henry (1923–) A US diplomat, born in Germany. Kissinger was Richard **Nixon**'s Special Adviser on National Security from 1969 to 1973, visiting China and the USSR in efforts to obtain some form of détente and the easing of tension between East and West. For his efforts to secure peace in the **Vietnam War** he was awarded the Nobel Peace Prize in 1973. He was Secretary of State from 1973 to 1977, practising a conservative and pragmatic style of diplomacy. (*Pragmatism* is the doing of what is possible rather than of what may be desirable.) He became particularly well known for his 'shuttle diplomacy' in the Middle East where on several visits he flew from country to country in efforts to secure peace between Israel and its Arab neighbours, notably helping to negotiate a ceasefire in the 1973 Arab-Israeli War.

Kitchener, Horatio Herbert, Earl Kitchener of Khartoum (1850–1916) A British field marshal. Kitchener was commander-in-chief from 1900 to 1902 in the Boer War, and became Secretary for War in WWI (1914–16). He raised an army of 70 divisions with the aid of the famous recruiting poster carrying the slogan, 'Your country needs you', accompanied by his portrait. He was drowned on his way to Russia when HMS *Hampshire* was mined and sank off Orkney.

Kohl, Helmut (1930–) A West German politician. As leader of the Christian Democratic Party from 1976 Kohl was elected Chancellor in 1982 and became the first Chancellor of the reunited Germany in 1990. His government was defeated in the 1998 election, and he was investigated for involvement in a financial scandal.

Korea A peninsula of NE Asia, now divided into North Korea and South Korea.

Korea was annexed by Japan in 1910, and after Japan's defeat at the end of WWI, forces of the USSR and the USA occupied the country. For mutual military convenience the occupiers divided the territory into two regions along the 38th parallel of latitude, in accordance with terms agreed at the **Yalta Conference**. The ultimate objective was a unified democratic country, but it soon became evident that North and South had different loyalties, the former towards the USSR and the latter towards the USA, and so it has remained since negotiations between the Americans and Russians broke down (1946). In 1950 North Korea invaded the South, marking the start of the **Korean War** (1950–3).

North Korea Area: 122,370 sq km. Pop: 23,904,000. Language: Korean. Religions: all repressed since 1945; formerly Buddhism, Confucianism, Chondokyo and Shamanism. Cap: Pyongyang.

The People's Democratic Republic of North Korea was proclaimed in 1948 under the leadership of **Kim Il**

Korea

Sung, who remained in power until his death (1994).

South Korea Area: 98,447 sq km. Pop: 45,545,280. Language: Korean. Religions: Animism, Buddhism, Christianity and Confucianism. Cap: Seoul.

The Republic of South Korea was proclaimed in 1948 with Syngman Rhee (1875–1965) as president. This right-wing nationalist ran a corrupt regime which was overthrown in 1960, being replaced in 1962, after a period of instability, by an administration headed by Major General Park Chung Hee (1917–79), who was assassinated by the head of the Korean Central Intelligence Agency. South Korea's first fully democratic presidential elections were held in 1987, although there were widespread accusations of corruption. In the 1980s and 1990s South Korea's economy was one of the most dynamic in Asia.

Korean War (1950–53) A conflict resulting from the partition of **Korea** into the Soviet-occupied North and the US-occupied South along the 38th parallel of latitude in 1945. After both occupying forces were withdrawn in 1948, border clashes occurred and eventually there was a full-scale invasion of the South by eight North Korean divisions. Within three days the South Korean capital, Seoul, fell and the UN Security Council, which at the time was boycotted by the USSR, approved the despatch of armed forces to drive out the North Koreans. Contingents were sent from 15 nations, under the command of the US Commander-in-Chief, Far East, General Douglas MacArthur. Within a fortnight the North Koreans were back on their own side of the partition line, but then China warned that it would enter the war should the UN forces approach the Yalu river (the North Korean-Chinese border). This warning was ignored, and China intervened with such force that the UN forces were compelled to retreat. Counter-offensives finally forced back the Chinese and the partition line was restored. Peace talks commenced in 1951, but an armistice agreement was not reached for two years (*see* **Panmunjom Armistice**). All attempts at peaceful reunification of Korea have failed and the country remains divided.

Kosygin, Alexei Nikolayevich (1904–80) A Soviet politician. Kosygin held many state and party appointments before becoming chairman of the Council of Ministers (1964–80), effectively sharing power with **Brezhnev**. He concentrated on internal matters rather than foreign affairs, being concerned with economic development and reform, and particularly the decentralisation of agriculture and industry. In foreign affairs, however, he did succeed in mediating between India and Pakistan at the **Tashkent Conference**.

Kremlin (*Russ.* – citadel) The former imperial palace in Moscow, which became the administrative HQ of the USSR government. The term was also used for the central government of the USSR.

Kronstadt Mutiny (1921) A revolt by the Soviet garrison (consisting largely of peasant recruits) of the Kronstadt naval base on Kotlin Island in the Gulf of Finland. The mutineers were concerned by rural disturbances taking place all over the USSR during the period of **War Communism**, and they issued a variety of demands: fresh elections to the soviets by secret ballot;

freedom of assembly for peasant and trade-union
movements; of speech and press for all left-wing parties;
reestablishment of a free market for the peasants; and
the disbanding of grain-requisitioning squads.

Although eventually the mutiny was savagely put
down by loyal troops it was not unsuccessful since some
policy changes (e.g. the **New Economic Policy**) were
made in line with the mutineers' demands.

Krupp A German industrial combine founded in 1811
for steel manufacture but later expanding into
armaments, mining, shipbuilding and agricultural and
railway machinery. It remained a family concern for five
generations. It was vitally important to Germany's
ability to wage both World Wars, and was notorious for
its exploitation of occupied countries and the use of
slave labour.

Ku Klux Klan A US secret society of white Southern
men formed after the Civil War to fight Northern
domination and black emancipation. Largely a
Protestant organisation, it has shown hatred towards
blacks, RCs, Communists, Jews and alien or foreign
minorities. Its symbol is a fiery cross and its members
disguise themselves in white masks and robes, their
leaders being given fanciful names such as Grand
Wizard, Grand Dragon, etc. Murder, lynch law and
intimidation were practised, but the society's influence
has declined in recent years.

Kulaks *see* **Collectivisation**.

Kun, Béla (1886–1937) A Hungarian Communist
dictator. Kun was captured in WWI by the Bolsheviks,
who after indoctrination returned him to Hungary as an

agitator. He succeeded in overthrowing the liberal government and in 1919 establishing a regime noted for its cruelty and ruthlessness, although it only survived a few months. The country was invaded by Czechoslovakia and Romania, and a counter-revolutionary government was established by Miklós **Horthy**, causing Kun to flee to the USSR, where he was later killed in the **purges**.

Kuomintang A Chinese nationalist political movement. Under **Sun Yat-sen** it helped in the overthrow of the Manchu dynasty (1911). **Chiang Kai-Shek** took over as leader (1925–75) and set out to reunify China by extending the movement's political influence and military domination. Superficially this objective was achieved in 1928 and the Kuomintang was China's ruling party until 1949.

However, the movement became increasingly army-dominated, right-wing and authoritarian, and the economic, political and social reforms proposed by Sun Yat-sen were not carried out. This was in some degree owing to the Japanese invasion of China (1937–45).

Chiang had purged the communists from the movement in 1927, and engaged in an intermittent civil war with them until 1949, when the Communists under **Mao Zedong** drove the Kuomintang from the mainland. The chief causes of the Kuomintang's downfall were its blatant corruption and inefficiency, the devastation caused by years of war, and the resulting inflation. Since 1949 it has been the ruling party of Taiwan.

Kursk (1943) A huge tank battle of WWII in which Soviet forces defeated the last major German offensive on Russian soil. German losses were crippling, partly owing to superior Russian air power, and the battle is often regarded as the point at which German defeat in WWII became certain.

Kuwait An important oil state on the Persian Gulf which was effectively a British protectorate from 1899 and which gained independence in 1961. Western support for the rulers of Kuwait has been part of the West's policy for stability in the area in order to safeguard oil supplies. However, in 1990, Iraq seized Kuwait and refused to obey a UN order to withdraw. A UN armed force, mainly drawn from the USA, Britain, France and Saudi Arabia recaptured the country in 1991 after an intense aerial bombardment of Iraq (the *Gulf War*). Kuwait was left devastated, but had made great progress towards recovery by the end of the 1990s.

L

Labour Party The name of the British and New Zealand socialist parties; the Australian equivalent uses the spelling 'Labor'.

The British Labour Party was founded in 1900 as the Labour Representation Committee, a combination of various socialist bodies. The Committee became the Labour Party in 1906 and its supporters grew rapidly in number as a result of unemployment and the **Taff Vale Case** judgement. The Party's policies of industrial reform, **women's suffrage**, slum clearance and old-age pensions steadily won it by-elections and local government elections, so building on the successes of the 1906 general election.

Labour members' first experience of office was in the WWI coalition government. In 1922 the party became the official Opposition, and in 1924 formed a short-lived minority government, with Ramsay **MacDonald** as PM. The party regained power in 1929 but was unable to deal with the financial crisis and unemployment caused by the Depression. When a **National Government** was formed in 1931, the party split over MacDonald's decision to serve as PM.

The party was represented in the WWII coalition government but its first real taste of power was after the 1945 general election when it obtained an overwhelming majority. With Clement **Attlee** as PM, Labour brought in extensive nationalisation measures, established the National Health Service and many other features of the modern **welfare state**, and granted independence to India, Pakistan, Ceylon and Burma. The party was in opposition from 1951 to 1964, a period marked again by internal stresses. When it returned to office with Harold **Wilson** as PM (1964–70) it faced rising inflation, **balance of payments** problems and industrial unrest, problems that also confronted the Labour government of 1974–9, in which Wilson, and then James **Callaghan**, served as PM. This period was also marked by a widening gulf between the left and right within the party. It was led in opposition by Michael **Foot**, Neil **Kinnock** and John Smith; 1997 the reinvigorated party achieved a landslide victory under Tony **Blair**.

The *Australian Labor Party* was founded in 1891, and formed coalition governments with the Liberal Party in 1904 and 1908–9, before being able to form majority governments (1910 and 1914). These started the construction of the transcontinental railway and the development of land, established the Commonwealth Bank, and introduced income tax. During WWI the party was split over conscription and thereafter was out of office from 1916 to 1941 except for 1929–31 when its policies were disrupted by the **Depression**.

It was again in power from 1941 to 1949 under John Curtin and Joseph Chifley, and launched postwar economic, immigration and reconstruction programmes designed to achieve full employment and social security. Labor was defeated in 1949 and did not regain power until 1972, under Gough Whitlam. This period of office (1972–5) was marked by internal dissension and parliamentary upheavals. Finally the Governor General intervened and dismissed the government, an episode that strengthened the republican cause. Labor came to power again in 1983 under Bob Hawke.

The *New Zealand Labour Party* first returned MPs in 1890, but first achieved office in 1935, under Michael Joseph Savage, when it introduced sweeping social reforms. It was defeated in 1949, but held power again in 1957–60 and 1972–5 and 1984–90. In 1999, under Helen Clark, Labour formed a minority government after a very close election.

Lateran Treaties *see* **Concordat**.

Latvia *see* **Baltic States**.

Lausanne, Treaty of (1923) The final peace settlement between Turkey and the Allies after WWI, following the refusal of the Turkish Republic to consider the Treaty of **Sèvres** binding.

Turkey surrendered all claim to former territories of the **Ottoman Empire** occupied by non-Turks. Greeks were confirmed in possession of all Aegean Islands, but they surrendered the Turkish port of Izmir (Smyrna). Italy kept the islands of the Dodecanese, and the UK kept Cyprus. The Bosporus and **Dardanelles** were demilitarised, and Turkey recovered E Thrace. As a result of the territorial changes required by the treaty, considerable exchanges of population occurred.

Laval, Pierre (1883–1945) A French politician. A socialist until 1920, Laval moved further and further to the right. He was PM from 1931 to 1932 and 1935 to 1936, and Foreign Minister from 1934 to 1936, but public anger over the **Hoare-Laval Pact** forced him to resign. He subsequently supported the ideas of **Pétain**, and joined his **Vichy Government** in 1940, later becoming PM (1942–4). He avoided any military commitment to the Nazis, and in trying to convene a National Assembly in 1944 he was arrested by the Germans. Laval fled to Spain but returned to France in 1945 to be tried for treason, and was shot.

Law, Andrew Bonar (1858–1923) A British Conservative politician, PM from 1922 to 1923. He became leader of the Conservative Party in 1911. In the WWI coalition government, Law was Chancellor of the Exchequer (1916–18). His brief premiership set the fashion for cautiousness ('safety first') which was to mark British Conservatism in the interwar period.

Lawrence, Thomas Edward (1888–1935) A British soldier who became known as Lawrence of Arabia because of his leadership of the Arabs in the revolt (1917–18) against the **Ottoman Empire** in WWI. During the revolt Lawrence led raids on the Hejaz railway, took part in the capture of Aqaba and Damascus and maintained close Arab liaison with General Sir Edmund Allenby's army in Palestine. He was trusted by the Arabs, opposed the **Balfour Declaration**, and supported the Arab cause at the **Paris Peace Conference**.

League of Nations An international organisation created in 1920 to preserve the peace and settle disputes by discussion and agreement. Its Covenant was incorporated into the Treaty of **Versailles** and other post-WWI treaties, the **mandates** created by these treaties becoming the League's responsibility.

Though the creation of the League had been urged by US President Woodrow **Wilson** (among others), the USA was never a member. The League's only weapon against wayward members was **sanctions**, and it failed to prevent aggression among member states: Japan in Manchuria and **China**, Italy in Abyssinia (**Ethiopia**), the USSR in Finland. Brazil left the League in 1926, Germany and Japan in 1933, Italy in 1937, and the USSR was expelled in 1940. The League did however succeed in resolving international disputes in the Balkans and South America. It was dissolved in 1946, transferring its services and property to the **United Nations Organisation**.

Lebanon A republic of the Middle East, on the E coast of the Mediterranean. Area: 10,400 sq km. Pop: 2,897,000. Language: Arabic. Religions: Christianity and Islam. Cap: Beirut.

Until 1918 the country was part of the **Ottoman Empire**. It was captured by Britain and France in WWI and then mandated to France in 1920 by the League of Nations (*see* **mandate**). Lebanon became a fully independent state in 1946, having achieved degrees of independence in 1926 and 1941. Postwar economic and political instability was caused by the high cost of living, rising unemployment, loss of wartime trade, and increasing hostility between the Christian and Muslim communities. These problems resulted in rioting and near civil war, so that in 1958 the government requested US assistance to restore order.

The country has tried to avoid taking sides in disputes between Arab groups and avoided involvement in wars against Israel. This has succeeded only partially since large numbers of Palestinians sought refuge there after being driven out of Jordan in 1970, and immediately the PLO began using Lebanon as a base for terrorist activity across the frontier into Israel. The arrival of the Palestinians aggravated the tensions between Lebanese Christians and Muslims and the fighting that followed provoked Syria into sending in troops to oppose the Christians. The Israelis reacted by giving support to the Christians and occupied Lebanon S of the Litani river (1978). In 1982–5 Israel extended its military involvement as far north as Beirut, forcing the PLO leadership to leave the country.

Lebanon was once the Middle East's banking and commercial centre but large parts of it were ruined in the prolonged civil war. A UN force tried to keep the peace between 1978 and 1992, when an uneasy cease-fire was agreed and the pro-Syrian Muslim government was confirmed in power. In 1996 fighting broke out again between the Islamic Hizbollah movement and Israeli forces in S Lebanon. In May 1999 Israel announced its intention of withdrawing its troops.

Lebensraum (*Ger.* – living space) The Nazis' name for the non-German-speaking territories to the E of Germany which they thought the German people should settle. Hitler attempted to carry out this policy in his invasions of Poland (1939) and the USSR (1941). This was in addition to Hitler's claims to countries already settled by Germans.

Lee Kuan Yew (1923–) A Singaporean politician. He founded the People's Action Party in 1954 and was elected to the Legislative Assembly in 1955 after campaigning for 'an independent, democratic, and non-Communist Malaya' that would include Singapore. He became first PM of Singapore in 1959 after separation from Malaya and then led it into the Federation of Malaysia in 1963 and out again in 1965. He encouraged foreign industrial development, and in foreign affairs pursued a policy of nonalignment and regional cooperation. He resigned as PM in 1990.

Legislation 1. The act or process of passing laws. 2. The laws so made.

Legislature A country's law-making body, with the power to make, amend or repeal (cancel) laws. In the UK this is Parliament, in the USA it is Congress. In the UK the legislature has power to change the executive, in the USA the legislature, executive and judiciary are kept rigidly separate with clearly defined separate powers. *See* **separation of powers**.

Lend-Lease Act (1941) The US legislation authorising the lease, loan, transfer or exchange of equipment required by any state recognised as being of vital importance to the defence and security of the USA. In practice, this meant the immediate release of vast quantities of war materials to the UK, and later to China and the USSR, and placed US industry on a war footing even before the country entered WWII. Lend-Lease ended in 1945 after some $50 billion worth of aid had been granted.

Lenin, Vladimir Ilyich (*orig.* Vladimir Ilyich Yulianov) (1870–1924) A Russian politician. Lenin studied **Marx** as a student, and during a spell in W Europe he became recognised as the leader of the Bolsheviks, the militant wing of the Russian Social Democrats (*see* **Bolshevism**).

Returning to Russia in 1917 he led the October Revolution (*see* **Russian Revolutions**), becoming head of the new government, the Council of People's Commissars. He agreed an armistice with Germany in 1918. followed by the Treaty of **Brest-Litovsk**. His attempt to achieve a communist economic revolution while waging civil war led to the virtual collapse of the economy, but by 1920 he had successfully defeated Russia's enemies at home and abroad and prepared the way for the creation of the Soviet Union. In 1921 he introduced the **New Economic Policy** in reaction to economic difficulties and internal unrest.

Leningrad, Siege of (1941–4) The heroic defence of the USSR's second city (now St Petersburg) during WWII when Finnish and German armies encircled the city and practically cut it off from the rest of the country. About 11.5 million civilians and troops perished from cold and hunger even though a counter-offensive in 1943 partially relieved the city. The complete lifting of the siege occurred after the Germans were forced to retreat by massive Soviet counter-attacks.

Liberalism A loose term for political views favouring progress, reform and individual freedom.

Liberal Party The name of British, Australian and Canadian political parties.

The *British Liberal Party* is the successor of the 18th- and 19th-century Whigs, and until it was overtaken by the Labour Party in 1922, was one of the two major political parties, a position it has never been able to regain. Its greatest period in office was from 1906 to 1916, when Sir Henry **Campbell-Bannerman** and Herbert **Asquith** were PMs. During this period the foundations of the welfare state were laid by the introduction of minimum wages, old-age pensions and national insurance. The Liberal government was also responsible for legislation legalising trade-unions and for the **Parliament Act** of 1911.

The decline in the party's popularity started with the WWI split between the Asquith and **Lloyd George** factions, the abandonment of **free trade policies**, and the rise of the **Labour Party**. Since WWII it has campaigned, with limited success, for a change in the voting system, for the decentralisation of government from London to the N and W of England and to Scotland and Wales, for the prevention of the growth of monopolies, for individual liberties, civil rights and racial and religious tolerance, and for employees to be awarded shares in the decision-making and profits of the firms where they are employed.

In 1977 the so-called 'Lib-Lab Pact' was concluded with the Labour Party which helped to keep the minority Labour Government in power in return for consultation over acts of government policy. This effectively split the Liberal Party and the arrangement was abandoned at the time of the 1979 election. In 1981 the Liberals joined the **Social Democratic Party** in a political alliance, fighting the 1983 and 1987 elections on this basis. The parties merged in 1988. The Liberal Democrats grew in strength under Paddy Ashdown, and in the 1997 general election achieved the largest Liberal parliamentary representation since Lloyd George's time. Charles Kennedy became leader of the party in 1999.

The *Australian Liberal Party* was founded in 1944 by Robert Menzies out of the United Australia Party which evolved in 1931 from the Nationalist Party established in 1917. In coalition with the **Country Party** it was in power from 1949 to 1972 and 1975 to 1983, its policies in many ways resembling those of the British Conservative Party. Under PM John Howard they have held power since 1996.

The *Canadian Liberal Party* has held power for much of last century (1896–1911, 1935–57, 1963–79, 1980–4, and 1993–). In coalition with the Progressive Party it was also in office from 1921 to 1930. Its policies are in line in many ways with those of the British party. It split into two factions because of policy disagreements in the period from 1911 to the end of WWI. It campaigns on Commonwealth interdependence and minority rights, especially those affecting the French-speaking population of the country.

Libya A Socialist People's republic of N Africa. Area: 1,759,540 sq km. Pop: 4,385,000. Language: Arabic. Religion: Islam. Cap: Tripoli.

Formerly an Italian colony, Libya became a battleground during WWII and gained independence in 1951. From then until 1969 the country was ruled by King Idris I (1890–1983). He was overthrown by a coup led by Col. Mu'ammar **Gaddafi**, who formed a Revolutionary Command Council which declared the country a republic with Gaddafi as head of state.

At first the republic relied on the UK and the USA for

financial assistance in return for the use of military bases, but the agreements were terminated by Libya because it considered the UK and the USA to have shown a pro-Israeli bias during the 1967 Arab-Israeli War. The Anglo-Libyan Treaty of Friendship (1953) negotiated during the monarchy was ended in 1972 and UK oil interests were nationalised.

After this Libya developed friendly relationships with **Warsaw Pact** countries, but Gaddafi's aggressively pan-Arabist outlook isolated it from all but a few Arab states. Egypt in particular received threats from Libya following the **Camp David Agreement**, and other Arab states have also been targets of propaganda attacks and attempts at internal interference. Libya has actively supported the PLO, and has provided money, arms and refuge for various terrorist organisations, though in the 1990s Gaddafi began to distance himself from such links.

Lie, Trygve (1896–1968) A Norwegian socialist politician, first Secretary-General of the UN from 1946 to 1953. His period as Secretary-General was notable for his unsuccessful support of the admission of China to the UN and his organisation of UN forces to check North Korea's attack on South Korea (1950–3).

Liebknecht, Karl *see* **Spartacist Rising**.

Lin Biao or **Lin Piao** (1908–71) A Chinese communist soldier and politician. Lin was appointed Minister of Defence in 1959, setting himself the task of strengthening political control of the army, taking the unusual step of abolishing ranks. During the **Cultural Revolution** he emerged as Mao Zedong's principal supporter and was named as his successor in 1969. He disappeared in mysterious circumstances, supposedly dying in an air crash while fleeing to the USSR after organising an unsuccessful coup against Mao in Beijing.

Lithuania *see* **Baltic States.**

Little Entente (1921) An alliance formed with French encouragement by Czechoslovakia, Romania and Yugoslavia to resist any attempt by Hungary to recover territory lost after WWI. In the same year France itself concluded an alliance of mutual guarantee with Poland. The alliances were intended to maintain the post-war political divisions of Central Europe and to prevent a restoration of the **Austro-Hungarian Empire** or any change in the frontiers. In 1933 the Little Entente was converted into a formal organisation with a Permanent Council and Secretariat. It was dissolved in 1939.

Litvinov, Maxim (1876–1951) A Soviet diplomat and politician. In the 1930s he was strongly in favour of Soviet support for the League of Nations, better relations with the West, and collective security against the rising tide of Fascism. During this period he was Commissar for Foreign Affairs (1930–9); he negotiated the Franco-Soviet Pact (1935) and generally worked for the acceptance of his country abroad. He was ambassador to the USA from 1941 to 1943 and Vice-Minister of Foreign Affairs from 1943 to 1946.

Lloyd George, David, Earl of Dwyfor (1863–1945) A British Liberal politician, PM of coalition governments from 1916 to 1922. He was President of the Board of Trade (1905–08) and Chancellor of the Exchequer (1908–15). On the radical wing of his party,

he supported social reforms such as old-age pensions
and national health insurance. He introduced the
'People's Budget' (1909) by which such social reforms,
and a large defence programme, were to be financed by
higher death duties, an extra tax on high incomes and a
land tax. The Budget's rejection by the House of Lords
led to the 1911 **Parliament Act**. As PM from 1916 he
proved an energetic war leader. He modified some of
the harsher proposals leading to the Treaty of **Versailles**,
but fell from power following his handling of the
Chanak Crisis.

Locarno, Treaties of (1925) Agreements between
various groups of nations made in an attempt to settle
problems arising from WWI.

   The principal treaty was signed by Belgium, France
and Germany, agreeing to the maintenance of their
existing frontiers, settlement of disputes by arbitration
without resort to force and acceptance of the
demilitarisation of the **Rhineland**. This treaty was
guaranteed by Italy and the UK, but neither they nor
Belgium and France took action, other than making
formal protest, when Germany reoccupied the
Rhineland in 1936.

   The other Treaties concerned France, which agreed
mutual security guarantees with Czechoslovakia and
Poland; and Germany, which concluded agreements to
settle disputes by arbitration with Belgium,
Czechoslovakia, France and Poland.

Lomé Conventions (1975 and 1979) Trade
agreements between the **EU** and various developing
countries, the first of which permitted 46 developing

countries (known as the African, Caribbean and Pacific States) free access for exports to the EU. Provision was also made for aid and investment to be supplied by the EU. The second convention (1979) provided for a £3.6 billion aid from the EU to developing countries in the period 1980–5.

London, Treaty of (1915) A secret agreement between Britain, France, Russia and Italy, guaranteeing Italy territorial gains if it entered WWI on the Allied side within a month of signing, which it duly did.

The Treaty's terms were made public by the USSR in 1918 when the Bolsheviks denounced all pre-revolutionary international commitments. At the **Paris Peace Conference** (1919), Britain and France refused to honour the treaty, and Italy received considerably less territory than it had been promised. This caused much resentment in Italy and was a factor in the rise of Italian **Fascism**.

Long March (1934–35) An epic migration of Chinese Communists in the course of the civil war with the **Kuomintang**. In 1931 the Communists had established a Chinese Soviet Republic in Jiangxi, but the successes of Chiang Kai-shek's armies forced the Communists to evacuate and march 13,000 km (8,000 miles), heading NW for a year to Yenan. Of the 100,000 who set out, fewer than half survived, but they regrouped in stronger positions against the Kuomintang until 1937, when a truce was declared in order to fight the common enemy, Japan. **Mao Zedong** established himself as the Communist leader during the march.

Ludendorff, Erich (1865–1937) A German general

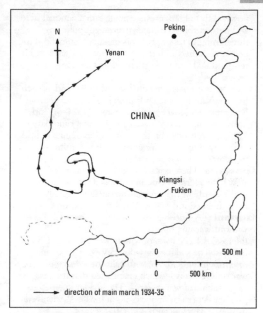

N

Peking

Yenan

CHINA

Kiangsi
Fukien

0   500 ml

0   500 km

→ direction of main march 1934-35

Long March

and politician. Ludendorff became famous in WWI
when he captured Liège and was successful in the
battles of **Tannenberg** and the Masurian Lakes (1914),
victories on which he subsequently built his political

power. His military prestige made him a national hero and he was able to dictate government policy by threatening to resign from his military command. His power collapsed with the 1918 Allied successes and he resigned and fled to Sweden before Germany capitulated.

Ludendorff was a nationalist and racist, and as such took part in the Munich **Putsch** in 1923. He became a Reichstag National Socialist member (1924–8), and unsuccessfully stood as Nazi presidential candidate in 1925. He remained on the fringes of extremist politics, even founding his own right-wing anti-Semitic movement, the Tannenbergerbund.

Luftwaffe The German air force. Commanded in WWII by Herman **Goering**, it was defeated by the RAF in the **Battle of Britain** and the **Blitz**, and finally overwhelmed in 1944 by Allied air attacks on Germany.

Lusitania A British passenger liner torpedoed and sunk without warning by a U-boat off Ireland in 1915, with the loss of 1,200 lives, of whom over 100 were US citizens. The sinking caused widespread anger and resentment in the USA, with calls for a declaration of war on Germany – which maintained that the vessel's cargo included war material. The incident helped to prepare American public opinion for USA's involvement in WWI, which occurred in 1917.

Luthuli, Albert John (1898–1967) A South African political leader, president of the African National Congress from 1952 to 1967. He openly opposed **apartheid**, advocating nonviolent resistance. He was kept under restriction after 1952 and was arrested for treason in 1956 but acquitted in 1959. He was awarded the Nobel Peace Prize in 1960.

Luxembourg A grand duchy of NW Europe. Area: 2,586 sq km. Pop: 378,400. Languages: French and Letzebürgesch (German dialect). Religion: Christianity (RC). Cap: Luxembourg.

A duchy from 1354, Luxembourg became a grand duchy within the Netherlands in 1815 and an independent country in 1890. It was invaded by Germany in both World Wars. It formed the Benelux customs union with Belgium and the Netherlands in 1948 and is now a member of the EU and NATO. It houses the headquarters of the European Court of Justice and the secretariat of the European Parliament.

Luxemburg, Rosa (1871–1919) A Polish born German revolutionary. A Marxist, she founded the Spartacus League (1916) with Karl Liebknecht. She was arrested and killed after leading the **Spartacist Rising**.

M

Maastricht Treaty *see* **European Union**.

MacArthur, Douglas (1880–1964) An American general who was recalled from retirement in WWII to help in the defence of SE Asia from the Japanese. Driven from the Philippines in 1942, he returned to liberate them by 1945, by which time he was Allied commander-in-chief in the SW Pacific. He commanded the occupation forces in Japan from 1945 to 1951 and was largely responsible for the political reform and economic revival in Japan. In 1950–1 he commanded UN forces in Korea but was dismissed by President Harry Truman for suggesting the use of nuclear weapons against China.

McCarthyism The practice of accusing people of being connected with Communist organisations, with little evidence to support the claim. It was named after Joseph McCarthy (1908–67), Republican senator for Wisconsin. At the height of the **Cold War** in 1950, McCarthy alleged that the US State Department had on its staff 205 employees known to be communist sympathisers and 57 who were Communist Party members. This revelation was followed by a campaign to discredit prominent Democrats, including such respected figures as Dean **Acheson** and George Marshall. On becoming chairman of the Permanent Sub-committee on Investigation (1953), his attacks intensified, with accusations against Robert Stevens, Secretary of the Army, and many intellectuals and officials. His activities led to the establishment of 'black-lists', and many people's careers were ruined. Finally, after being condemned by the Senate in 1954, McCarthy attacked President Eisenhower, but by then his campaign was thoroughly discredited.

MacDonald, Ramsay (1866–1937) A British Labour politician, PM in 1924 and from 1929 to 1935. He was leader of the Labour Party (1911–14), resigning over his opposition to WWI, but became Leader again after the war (1922–31). He was the first Labour PM and Foreign Minister (1924), but his government lost the 1924 general election, partly because of the **Zinoviev Letter**. He became PM again in 1929, but his desire for a 'responsible party of government' led to the 1931 cabinet split over his plan to cut unemployment benefit. This in turn led to his decision to form a **National Government** and to campaign against the Labour Party, which immediately expelled him. He later served in Stanley **Baldwin**'s government (1935–7).

Macmillan, Harold, 1st Earl of Stockton (1894–1986) A British Conservative politician, PM from 1957 to 1963. He was in turn (1951–7) Minister of Housing and Local Government, Minister of Defence, Foreign Secretary, and Chancellor of the Exchequer, before becoming PM.

His government was marked by stable prices and economic prosperity (illustrated by his famous declaration, 'You've never had it so good'), followed by **balance of payments** problems and rising unemployment. In 1961 his government established the National Economic Development Council ('Neddy'), which aimed to improve Britain's economic performance. It was abolished in 1992.

In foreign affairs, his government strengthened Anglo-American cooperation, and tried to act as mediator between the superpowers. The colonial policy of his government, which involved ending the Federation of Rhodesia and Nyasaland, the granting of independence to many African states, and opposition to **apartheid**, was summed up in his 'Wind of Change' speech to the South African parliament (1960). An attempt to take Britain into the EEC was vetoed by France in 1963, largely because de Gaulle regarded the **Nassau Agreement** (1962) as a sign that the UK was too closely allied to the USA to assume a role in Europe. In 1963 Macmillan was forced to resign because of ill health.

Maginot Line A series of French fortifications built between 1929 and 1934 from Longwy (on the Luxembourg border) to the Swiss frontier and named after the Minister of War, André Maginot (1877–1932). Belgian opposition prevented the line being continued along the Franco-Belgian frontier to the North Sea, and it was this weakness that Germany exploited in WWII by advancing into France from S Belgium in 1940. The line was practically intact when France capitulated.

Major, John (1943–) A British Conservative politician. Major entered parliament in 1979 and after serving as Chancellor of the Exchequer, he succeeded Margaret **Thatcher** as Conservative PM in 1990. He won the general election of 1992, but was defeated in 1997 by Tony **Blair**.

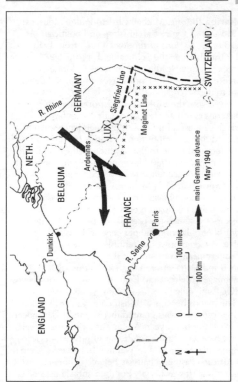

Maginot Line

Makarios III (*orig.* Mikhail Christodoulou Mouskos) (1913–77) A Cypriot archbishop and politician. As head of the Cypriot Orthodox Church from 1950, Makarios became the political and spiritual leader of the Greek Cypriots, leading the movement for union with Greece (Enosis). The British arrested him and deported him to the Seychelles (1956–7) believing he was involved with the EOKA terrorist organisation. Makarios eventually renounced Enosis in favour of British proposals for Cypriot independence when he realized that the opposition to Enosis by Turkish Cypriots could lead to the partition of the island. On independence in 1960 Makarios was elected president, but independence failed to stop intercommunal violence (*see* **Cyprus**). In 1974 Makarios was overthrown by a pro-Enosis coup backed by Greece, which led to the invasion and occupation of N Cyprus by Turkey. Makarios resumed the presidency, but was left in control of only about 60 per cent of the island.

Malta A Commonwealth republic of the C Mediterranean, consisting of the islands of Comino, Gozo and Malta. Area: 316 sq km. Pop: 352,430. Languages: Maltese and English. Religion: Christianity (RC). Cap: Valletta.

The islands became a British colony in 1814. Internal self-government was granted in 1947 and independence in 1964. For many years Malta was a principal Royal Navy base and during WWI was of great strategic importance because of its position between Italy and the N African coast, and halfway between Gibraltar and the Suez Canal. It was heavily bombed and almost starved into submission, but convoys managed to get through, frequently suffering heavy losses in the process. The courage of its inhabitants was recognised by the award of the George Cross to the entire population in 1942.

From independence to 1971 the Nationalist Party of Dr Borg Olivier (1911–) was in power. From 1971 until 1987 the Labour Party, led by Dominic Mintoff, formed the government. Immediately after his electoral victory Mintoff ended the defence agreement made with the UK on independence, forbade US naval vessels from visiting the country, and refused to co-operate with NATO.

Since the withdrawal of the British garrison and the closure of the Royal Naval Dockyard, unemployment has been a major problem, and to prop up an ailing economy Mintoff turned to China and Libya for support, the important tourist industry not providing sufficient income to sustain prosperity. Another domestic issue which has troubled the islands from time to time is the government's differences with the RC Church on political and religious issues.

Manchuria A region of NE China. It was developed by Russia, but after the **Russo-Japanese War** Japan gained concessions in the region under the Treaty of Peking (1905). These included the right to maintain troops to guard the South Manchurian Railway which connected Port Arthur with the Trans-Siberian Railway. Japan occupied the whole region in 1932 after accusing the Chinese of destroying part of the line at Mukden.

The area was named Manchukuo and placed under the nominal control of a puppet regime headed by

Hsuan T'ung (Henry Pu-Yi) (1906–67) who had been deposed as the last emperor of China (1908–12) while still a child. China protested to the League of Nations which responded by sending a five-man Commission of Inquiry headed by Lord Lytton and representing France, Germany, Italy, the UK and the USA. Its report rejected the excuse made by Japan for its occupation, refused to recognise the establishment of Manchukuo, and recommended the creation of a self-governing Manchuria under Chinese sovereignty. Japan refused to accept the Commission's report and left the League in 1933. The territory was regained by China at the end of WWII in accordance with the terms of the **Cairo Conference**, but was controlled by the Communists who used it as a base against Kuomintang forces.

Mandates or **mandated territories** The former German colonies and non-Turkish areas of the **Ottoman Empire** ceded (given) to the Allies after WWI but remaining the ultimate responsibility of the League of Nations. The UN took over responsibility from the League in 1946 and mandates were renamed 'trust territories'. Mandated territories included the Cameroons, Iraq, Lebanon, New Guinea, Palestine, Samoa, South West Africa, Syria, Tanganyika, Togoland and Transjordan. The administering countries included Australia, Belgium, France, New Zealand, South Africa and the UK.

Mandela, Nelson Rolihlahla (1918–) A South African nationalist politician. Mandela trained as a lawyer, and joined the **African National Congress** (ANC), campaigning against **apartheid** and demanding a

democratic multiracial South Africa. The ANC was
banned in 1960 and Mandela was arrested in 1962,
eventually being sentenced to life imprisonment
following a widely publicised trial in which he
conducted his own defence. He was not released until
1990 when he began the delicate and difficult task of
negotiating with the white South African government
for the ending of apartheid and the establishment of a
multiracial government. Despite tribal rivalry and white
fears, this was eventually achieved in 1994, and Mandela
became president of the republic. He was succeeded as
president in 1999 by Thabo M'Beki.

Mannerheim, Carl Gustav Emil, Friherr von
(1867–1951) A Finnish soldier and statesman. After
Finland gained independence in 1917, civil war broke
out between Finnish Bolsheviks and nationalists led by
Mannerheim. The Bolsheviks were defeated and
Mannerheim became supreme commander and regent,
but was defeated in the 1919 presidential election. He
was responsible for the construction of the system of
fortification known as the 'Mannerheim Line' close to
the Russian frontier near Leningrad, and when the
USSR attacked Finland at the beginning of WWII he
was appointed commander-in-chief; he later allied the
country with Germany. He was elected president
(1944–6) and made peace with the USSR (1944), joining
the war against Germany (1945).

Maoism Marxism and the ideas of **Lenin** as interpreted
by **Mao Zedong**, based on a revolutionary peasantry and
guerrilla warfare.

Mao Zedong or **Mao Tse-tung** (1893–1976)

A Chinese revolutionary and politician. Mao was a founder of the Chinese Communist Party in 1921. In its formative years the party cooperated with the **Kuomintang**, but after the break between the parties Mao organised the unsuccessful Autumn Harvest Uprising (1927). He fled to the mountains, where he established a guerrilla base on the Hunan-Jiangxi border. This became the main centre of communist activity until it was disbanded before the **Long March**, during which Mao was elected party chairman by the politburo. During the **Sino-Japanese War** the communists once more collaborated with the Kuomintang (1937–45) but then resumed their struggle against **Chiang Kai-Shek**'s forces. After the Communist victory, Mao became Chairman of the People's Republic (1949–59), and remained as party chairman until his death. He started the **Great Leap Forward** and the **Cultural Revolution**, believing always in peasant supremacy over urban proletarianism. For the last five years of his life illness prevented him from being active in politics; he remained the figurehead, but **Zhou Enlai** was effectively in control of China.

Maquis The French underground resistance movement that fought against the German occupying forces in WWII.

March on Rome (1922) A Fascist-inspired legend about Benito **Mussolini**'s rise to power in Italy. Throughout 1922 there was a danger of civil war in Italy, with the Fascists seizing control of several cities. Mussolini demanded a Fascist government and concentrated his supporters on the approaches to the capital. King Victor Emmanuel III gave way before this overt threat, dismissed the PM, and invited Mussolini to return from Milan to Rome to form a government.

Marne, Battles of the The two engagements fought at the beginning and end of WWI. The first battle, in 1914, halted Germany's advance into France. The over-extended enemy armies had come within a few miles of Paris before the French commander-in-chief, Joseph Joffre, judged the moment right for a counter-attack. Troops that Joffre had steadily withdrawn from Alsace, supported by the British Expeditionary Force, were able to force the Germans back from the River Marne to the Aisne, to positions they were to hold until the second battle (1918). This was the last German offensive of the War and brought them again within striking distance of Paris, but again French counter-attacks drove them back, the initiative passed to the Allies, and within four months the War was over.

Marshall Plan (1948) The proposal drawn up by the US Secretary of State George Marshall (1880–1959) offering US economic and financial help wherever it was needed to fight the hunger, poverty, desperation and chaos that followed WWII. The plan led to the establishment of the European Recovery Programme by which 16 W European countries (but not the USSR or other communist states) accepted US aid. Some $13 billion flowed into W Europe, helping the recovery of agriculture and industry. The USSR saw the programme, based as it was on the **Truman Doctrine**, as an attempt at political indoctrination and bribery by the USA, rather than as an economic necessity.

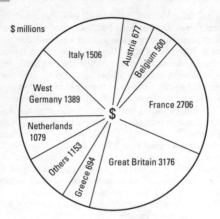

$ millions

Austria 677

Belgium 500

Italy 1506

West
Germany 1389

France 2706

Netherlands
1079

Others 1153

Greece 694

Great Britain 3176

$

Marshall Plan *Marshall Aid 1948–52.*
Total $12,880,000,000.

Marxism The political theory and doctrine based on the
writings of Karl Marx (1818–83).

Marx saw history as a struggle between one **class** and
another to control the means of production (i.e.
agriculture, industry, banking, etc.). The old feudal
society ruled by the aristocracy had by this time been
largely overthrown (e.g. in the French Revolution) by
the **bourgeoisie** (the middle class), who controlled the
economic system known as capitalism. According to
Marx, capitalism, although increasing the sum of human

wealth through industrial expansion, relied on the exploitation of the **proletariat** (the industrial working class), whose material wealth and social conditions were not improved.

Although Marx believed that capitalism contained the seeds of its own destruction, he saw the inevitability of its revolutionary overthrow by the proletariat (leading to the 'dictatorship of the proletariat') followed by the establishment of **Communism**. Under Communism, social classes would be abolished, the means of production would be owned in common by all members of society, and all citizens would be freed from exploitation by others to develop their full potential.

Since the 19th century, Marx's followers have been divided into social democrats and socialists on the one hand (who range from advocates of the manipulation of the capitalist system for the benefit of weaker members of society, to believers in the gradual and non-violent end of capitalism) and on the other hand Communists such as **Lenin** and **Mao Zedong** who believe in the need for immediate and violent revolution.

Many of the specific points that Marx proposed – such as the **nationalisation** of industry and transport, a state bank, a graded income-tax system, universal state education, and the abolition of child labour – have been established in various degrees in many democracies without the tight and often repressive controls of many Communist countries. However, the redistribution of land and the abolition of private property, which Marx also proposed, in most cases took place only in those Communist states.

Masaryk *see* **Czechoslovakia.**

Mau Mau A Kenyan secret terrorist society based in the Kikuyu tribal area. It considered itself to be a national liberation movement, and was committed to the expulsion from the country of white settlers. The organisation was operative between 1952 and 1959, but its worst excesses – also committed against Africans who opposed them – were committed in 1952 to 1954. Some 11,000 Mau Mau members were killed by the defence forces and about 2,000 white settlers and Africans were killed by Mau Mau. After the society was stamped out, rapid constitutional change took place in Kenya, leading to independence in 1963.

Means Test The practice of using the level of a person's income to work out how much financial or social assistance should be given by the state. It was imposed in the UK in 1931 as part of government spending cuts arising from the international economic crisis (1929–31) and its resulting long-term unemployment problem, which made inadequate the existing national insurance provision. The government refused to meet the deficiency by additional borrowing or increased taxation so applicants for relief had to prove their need. The system was ended in 1948, but many non-contributory state benefits are still means tested.

Meir, Golda (1898–1978) A Russian-born Israeli politician who was PM from 1969 to 1974. She settled in Palestine in 1921 and became a founder member of the Zionist Socialist Party (Mapai). She held various ministerial posts from the 1950s onwards, including Foreign Minister (1955–66). She was secretary-general of Mapai (1966–8), and PM of a series of coalition governments, and she successfully led the country during the 1973 **Arab-Israeli War**.

Menshevik *see* Bolshevism.

Menzies, Sir Robert (1894–1978) An Australian Liberal politician, Menzies entered the Federal Parliament as a United Australian Party (UAP) member in 1934, serving as Attorney General (1935–9) and PM (1939–41 and 1949–66). Between 1943 and 1945 he reorganised the UAP into the broader-based Liberal Party, which became the official opposition and which he led from 1943 to 1949. He was a supporter of close links with the UK and of Commonwealth interests.

   In office from 1949, he concluded the **Anzus Pact** and participated in the establishment of the **South-East Asia Treaty Organisation**. After WWII he encouraged British and European immigration, university expansion and large-scale industrial enterprises as part of national development and reconstruction, together with an imaginative social-security programme.

Mercenary A person hired to fight for a foreign army.

Messina Conference *see* European Union.

Ministerial Responsibility The British constitutional principle that government ministers are responsible to Parliament for their actions and those of their departments. If a minister or the department's actions are condemned by Parliament, then the minister may have to resign, even though the department may have acted without the minister's knowledge or approval.

Mitterand, François (1916–96) A French politician. As leader of the Socialist Party from 1971, he became the first socialist in 35 years to be elected president (1981–95).

Molotov, Vyacheslav Mikhailovich (*orig. surname* Skriabin) (1890–1986) A Soviet politician. Molotov was Foreign Minister from 1939 to 1949 and 1953 to 1956. He negotiated the **Nazi-Soviet Pact** (1939), the 20-year Treaty of Alliance with the UK (1942), and the Austrian State Treaty (1955), and he attended the San Francisco Conference (1945) as USSR representative at the founding of the UN. He was a vigorous defender of his country's interests in the **Cold War**. Having opposed the rise of **Khrushchev**, he was relieved of his posts in 1957.

Monnet, Jean (1888–1979) A French economist. He put forward the Monnet Plan (1947–53), a programme for the modernisation and re-equipment of French industry, based on transport and a few key industries. He became first president of the **European Coal and Steel Community** (1952–55) and in 1956 founded the Action Committee for the United States of Europe, the ideals of which were opposed to those of **de Gaulle**. Subsequently Monnet became a severe critic of de Gaulle's foreign policy.

Monroe Doctrine The principle of US foreign policy put forward in 1823 by President James Monroe (1758–1831), which stated that 'the American continents. . . are henceforth not to be considered as subjects for future colonisation by any European power'. In 1904 President Theodore Roosevelt extended the principle to justify any future US intervention to stop European interference in the Americas (the 'Roosevelt Corollary'). Eventually this unilateral US policy was adopted by all the republics of the W hemisphere, acting on the theory that aggression against one would be considered an attack against all. After WWII, the spread of communism in the area gave added significance to the Doctrine. and the USA supplied vast amounts of economic and military aid to neighbouring countries (or to right-wing rebel groups) to oppose what it saw as the communist threat. The actions of the USA over Cuba, such as the **Bay of Pigs** and the **Cuban Missile Crisis**, were examples of the Doctrine in action.

Montenegro (*Serbo-Croat*: Crna Gora) A republic of SW Yugoslavia. As a kingdom it fought against the Ottoman Empire in the **Balkan Wars** and joined Serbia against the German alliance (1914). In 1918 it became part of a newly constituted Yugoslavia. It remained closely tied to Serbia during the upheavals of the 1990s and the break-up of the rest of the Yugoslav Federation, but tensions between the two states began to emerge at the end of the century.

Mosley, Sir Oswald (1896–1980) A British politician. Mosley was in turn a Conservative, Independent and Labour MP (1918–31). In 1931 he founded the New Party, and in 1932 the **British Union of Fascists**. He was interned between 1940 and 1943, and afterwards lived in Paris.

Mountbatten, Louis, Earl Mountbatten of Burma (1900–79) A British admiral of the fleet and administrator. During WWII he was Supreme Allied Commander, SE Asia (1943–6). He became viceroy of India in 1947 and supervised the granting of independence and the transfer of power. Because of communal strife and mounting disorder, he decided on the partition of the subcontinent into India and Pakistan, and was India's first governor-general (1947–8). He was Commander-in-Chief, Mediterranean (1952–5), First Sea Lord (1955–9) and Chief of the Defence Staff (1959–65). He was assassinated by an IRA bomb.

Mubarak, Hosni (1929–) An Egyptian politician. Mubarak succeeded Anwar **Sadat** as president in 1981, and continued Sadat's moderate, pro-Western policies.

Mugabe, Robert (1924–) A Zimbabwean nationalist leader and socialist politician. In 1961 he became deputy secretary-general of the Zimbabwe African People's Union (ZAPU), but left it to found the Zimbabwe African National Union (ZANU) in 1963. After being a political prisoner (1964–75) he became joint leader with Joshua **Nkomo** of the Patriotic Front and leader of the guerrilla organisation, the Zimbabwe African Liberation Army, that fought the illegal régime of Ian **Smith** in what was then Rhodesia. He attended the London talks (1979) with Nkomo and Smith that eventually led to the independence of Zimbabwe in 1980. ZANU won the following election and Mugabe became PM, subsequently dismissing his rival Nkomo from the government in 1982. By 1990 Mugabe had established a one-party state, and although he announced the abandonment of Marxism-Leninism in 1991, he embarked on a major programme of compulsory land purchase and redistribution.

Munich Agreement (1938) The settlement agreed

between **Hitler**, **Daladier**, **Chamberlain** and **Mussolini** on behalf of Germany, France, Britain and Italy.

The agreement compelled Czechoslovakia to cede (hand over) the **Sudetenland** to Germany, and smaller amounts of territory to Hungary and Poland. In return the signatories to the agreement guaranteed Czechoslovakia's revised frontiers. France had previous treaty obligations with Czechoslovakia, but these were ignored at Munich in the hope that the agreement would put an end to Hitler's territorial demands.

Chamberlain claimed the agreement represented 'peace for our time . . . peace with honour', and at the time it was widely felt that Britain and France's policy of **appeasement** had avoided another world war. However, there were many who saw the agreement as a betrayal of democracy and a victory of 'might over right'; **Churchill** noted, 'We have sustained a defeat without a war.'

In 1939 Germany occupied the remainder of Czechoslovakia, ignoring the territorial guarantees made at Munich.

Muslim League A Pakistani political party that developed from the religious organisation established to protect Islamic interests in British India. Under Mohammed Ali **Jinnah**'s leadership, the League proposed the partition of India and the foundation of an Islamic state (Pakistan). After Jinnah's death the League's authority and power declined, its parliamentary majority disappeared, and it fragmented into opposing factions.

Mussolini, Benito (1883–1945) The Italian dictator who founded Fascism in 1919.

In his early years Mussolini was a revolutionary socialist but after serving in WWI decided to promote his nationalist ambitions by establishing Fascism, the system that is most closely associated with his name. He developed the movement into an anti-communist, conservative, middle-class organisation.

After WWI Italy was practically in a state of civil war and King Victor Emmanuel III appointed Mussolini as PM in an effort to stop the rioting that was widespread in the major cities (*see* **March on Rome**) and to prevent a communist takeover. Mussolini assumed the title *Duce* (leader) and headed a Fascist and nationalist coalition.

Mussolini assumed dictatorial powers in 1925, restricting civil liberties, stepping up attacks on the opposition and creating a one-party state that ruled by decree with the aid of the secret police. His desire for military glory led to Italy's conquest of Abyssinia (see **Ethiopia**) and **Albania**, support for **Franco** in the **Spanish Civil War**, the **Axis** ties with Germany and Japan, and entry into WWII in 1940.

The disasters of WWII caused his followers to desert him and he resigned in 1943 and was arrested. He was rescued by German paratroopers and placed at the head of a puppet regime in German-occupied N Italy where he arranged the execution of some of his principal opponents, including his son-in-law, Galeazzo Ciano. He himself was executed by partisans after being captured near Lake Como in 1945.

Muzorewa *see* **Zimbabwe**.

Myanmar *see* **Burma**.

N

Nagasaki A Japanese port on the island of Kyushu destroyed in 1945 by the USA by an atomic bomb, the second wartime use of a nuclear weapon. This event and the earlier devastation of **Hiroshima** helped bring about Japan's unconditional surrender.

Nagy *see* Hungary.

Nassau Agreement (1962) A settlement reached at Nassau in the Bahamas, by which the USA agreed to supply the UK with Polaris missiles for its nuclear submarines. The outcome of this meeting between **Kennedy** and **Macmillan** displeased **de Gaulle**, who considered Anglo-American nuclear collaboration an indication that the UK was not sufficiently committed to Europe to deserve admission to the EEC, and accordingly he vetoed the British application in 1963.

Nasser, Gamal Abdel (1918–70) An Egyptian soldier and politician. After the first **Arab-Israeli War** Nasser and other officers saw a need for radical change and in 1952 organised a coup d'état. He then became PM (1954) and president (1956), with virtually dictatorial powers. His social and economic policies were dominated by the need to improve agriculture, establish industries and introduce improved social-welfare schemes. In 1956 he nationalised the Suez Canal, an act which subsequently led to the **Suez Crisis** Nasser united Syria and Egypt as the United Arab Republic (1958–61), and he concentrated on closer relations with the USSR in order to receive aid. His offer to resign

after the Egyptian defeat in the 1967 Arab-Israeli War
was not accepted, and he remained in office until his
death.

National Governments (1931–5 and 1935–45)

The governments formed from members of several
parties with the objectives of unifying the UK in the
national interest in times of crisis.

The first of these governments, initially consisting of
members of the Conservative, Labour and Liberal
parties, was formed by the Labour PM Ramsay
Macdonald, to tackle the economic crisis of the
Depression and the problem of growing unemployment.

The government was formed when a number of
important ministers in the previous Labour government
refused to support reductions in unemployment benefit.
These reductions were part of heavy expenditure cuts
required by the French and US money markets before
they would provide financial assistance to support the
pound. With the Labour government divided,
MacDonald formed a coalition to restore confidence
and impose the cuts, to which was soon added the
abandonment of the gold standard for sterling.

The Labour Party went into opposition and
MacDonald and other ministers who supported him
were expelled from the party; they subsequently called
themselves the National Labour Party. In practical terms
the coalition became a Conservative government when
the Liberal Party split in 1932, some Liberals
supporting the opposition, and others, calling
themselves the Liberal National Party, supporting the
government.

The 1935 election resulted in a landslide victory for the National Government, again dominated by the Conservatives. Its PMs were Stanley **Baldwin** (1935-7), Neville **Chamberlain** (1937-40) and Winston **Churchill** (1940-5). This government faced the Depression and high unemployment, and eventually WWII, which resulted in the postponement of the following election until 1945.

National Health Service (NHS) The British system of health care for all, funded out of taxation. The main proposals of the **Beveridge Report** were adopted by the Labour government in the Act of 1946, which came into effect in 1948. All British citizens now had access to general and specialist medical services, to treatment by dentists and opticians, and to maternity care and child welfare services. Medicines, dentures and glasses were provided for all who needed them. It had been originally intended that the service should be absolutely free, but unexpectedly high costs and the rapidly rising demand for expensive drugs and treatment led to the imposition of limited charges as early as 1951, and charges have continued to rise and to be applied more widely ever since. Even so, although NHS costs rise at a rate significantly above that of inflation, most of its benefits are still provided free of charge to children and to people with low incomes.

Aneurin **Bevan**, the Minister of Health, met much opposition from the medical profession in introducing the National Health Service, but it was successful from the start. By the 1990s its administration had been the subject of two major reorganisations, which resulted in some degree of decentralisation.

Nationalism **1.** Devotion or loyalty to one's country; patriotism.

2. The sentiment founded on common cultural characteristics (e.g. language, religion, race, history) that unites a population, frequently producing a desire for separatism or national independence. **Fascism** contains elements of extreme nationalism (*see also* **National Socialism**).

Nationalisation The placing of an industry or resource under state control or ownership, a policy required by communist and socialist doctrine. Nationalisation measures in the UK were carried out by Labour governments, and included the Bank of England, most hospitals, and coal (1946), railways and electricity (1947), gas (1948), iron and steel (1949, denationalised in 1953 by the Conservatives, nationalised again in 1967), and aircraft manufacture and shipbuilding (1977). These measures have traditionally been opposed and reversed by the Conservative Party; *see* **privatisation**.

National Socialism (Nazism) An extreme right-wing political ideology similar to Italian Fascism, adopted by the National Socialist German Workers' Party (NSDAP), successor of the German Workers' Party of which Adolf **Hitler** was a founder member in 1919. Hitler soon gained control of the German Workers' Party and renamed it the NSDAP (1920). Membership grew rapidly and by the time Hitler achieved power it was some two million strong, its representation in the Reichstag rising from 12 in 1928 to 288 in 1933.

Nazi doctrine included the principle that the individual was subservient to the state and the state subservient to the Party, which in turn was controlled by a single leader – Hitler himself. It also included the idea of Aryan superiority, the Germans being considered the 'master race'; a policy of anti-Communism, anti-Semitism and racism; the building up of armed forces; and a determination to regain territory lost at the Treaty of **Versailles** and to create a German empire in E Europe (*see* **Lebensraum**).

These were Hitler's own beliefs, which he successfully imposed on the party, aided by the discontent and frustration in the country after the German defeat in WWI and the unemployment resulting from the **Depression**. After WWII the party was dissolved and its re-establishment became an offence.

Nation-state An independent sovereign state inhabited by all the people of one nation, and of one nation only. The term does not necessarily imply a racist policy, but could indicate opposition to foreign domination.

NATO *see* **North Atlantic Treaty Organisation**.

Nazism *see* **National Socialism**.

Nazi-Soviet Pact, Molotov-Ribbentrop Pact or **Non-aggression Pact** (1939) A treaty signed in Moscow by Joachim von **Ribbentrop** and Vyacheslav **Molotov** on behalf of Germany and the USSR.

The published section of the treaty covered a ten-year non-aggression period, and agreement by each party to remain neutral should the other be involved in war. Secret clauses set out spheres of influence in the Baltic States, Finland and Poland. In 1939 Germany invaded

W Poland, an action that led to the outbreak of WWII; two weeks later the USSR invaded E Poland, and the country was divided between the two occupying nations. The pact was ended by the German attack on the USSR in 1941.

Nehru, Jawaharlal (1889–1964) An Indian Congress Party politician, PM from 1947 to 1964. He became a leader of the nationalist movement and follower of Mahatma **Gandhi** in the 1920s. For this he was imprisoned several times between 1921 and 1945; his imprisonment during WWII was largely due to his opposition to Indian aid to the UK unless immediate independence was granted. When independence was achieved he became PM and Foreign Minister.

Nehru attempted to solve India's poverty problem by adopting a series of **Five-Year Plans**, and, by equality of educational opportunities, to eliminate restrictions imposed by Hindu religious and social customs, he himself having no religious beliefs. He committed the country to industrialisation but a population explosion ruined efforts at economic reform.

His foreign policy was one of non-alignment and he became a leader of uncommitted Afro-Asian nations. He cultivated relationships with China and the USSR while maintaining firm Commonwealth connections. He was an anti-colonialist and an opponent of the use of force, although he did not shrink from using it when India annexed Goa, a Portuguese territory, in 1961. However, he showed commendable restraint in dealing with Pakistan over the complicated problem of Kashmir.

NEP *see* **New Economic Policy**.

Neuilly, Treaty of (1919) The post-WWI peace
settlement between Bulgaria and the Allies, resulting
from the Paris Peace Conference. The treaty restricted
the Bulgarian army to 20,000; made the country liable
for **reparations**; and compelled it to cede territory to
Greece and Yugoslavia. The loss of W Thrace to Greece
deprived Bulgaria of access to the Aegean Sea.

Neutrality The state of being impartial or neutral,
especially in a dispute, war, etc., thereby avoiding
involvement in hostilities, or in diplomatic or political
exchanges.

New Deal The economic and social programme
launched to help the USA recover from the **Depression**.
'A new deal for the American people' was the phrase
used by F D Roosevelt in his presidential nomination
acceptance speech (1932).

There were two programmes (1933–5 and 1935–9)
and they included measures to meet the immediate
economic and financial crises; to assist the large
numbers of unemployed; to increase economic and
social security for the aged and those in ill-health; to
provide agricultural and industrial aid; to permit the
re-financing of mortgages at low interest rates; and to
start large-scale federal industrial developments which
included forestation schemes, the construction of
hydroelectric power stations, dams and other public-
works projects (*see* **Tennessee Valley Authority**). *See
diagram on p.234.*

New Economic Policy (NEP) A modification in
Communist practice introduced in the USSR by **Lenin**
in 1921, following peasant disturbances and riots in

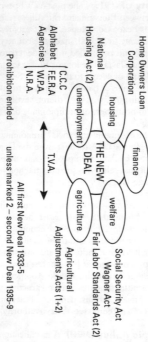

Emergency Banking Act
Securities and Exchange Commission
Economy Act

Home Owners Loan
Corporation

National
Housing Act (2)

Alphabet
Agencies
{ C.C.C
F.E.R.A
W.P.A.
N.R.A.

Prohibition ended

THE NEW DEAL

unemployment

housing

finance

welfare

agriculture

T.V.A.

Social Security Act
Wagner Act
Fair Labor Standards Act (2)

Agricultural
Adjustments Acts (1+2)

All first New Deal 1933-5
unless marked 2 – second New Deal 1935-9

New Deal

Petrograd (later Leningrad, now St Petersburg) and Kronstadt. The NEP allowed some freedom of internal trade, re-introducing limited private commerce and re-establishing state banks. It was abolished by the Bolshevik Party Congress in 1929, which gave full support to the first of the **Five-Year Plans**.

Nicaragua A republic of Central America. Area: 128,000 sq km. Pop: 4,272,000. Language: Spanish. Religion: Christianity (RC). Cap: Managua.

From the 1930s the government of Nicaragua was dominated by the Somoza family, whose corrupt and dictatorial rule was finally ended in 1979 after a civil war with the Sandinista National Liberation Front. The Sandinista government subsequently pursued socialist policies. The US government alleged that the Sandinistas were arming rebels in neighbouring El Salvador, and supported the right-wing 'Contra' rebels that were attempting to oust the Sandinistas. The Sandinistas lost power in elections in 1990.

Nicholas II (1868–1918) Tsar of Russia from 1894 to 1917. His reign saw the **Russo-Japanese War**, alliance with Britain and France against the Central Powers in WWI, food shortages because of bad harvests, and the **Russian Revolutions** of 1905 and 1917.

He opposed badly needed political reforms, although the 1905 Revolution forced him to introduce the **Duma**, and from 1911 was unduly influenced in his choice of ministers by the unscrupulous **Rasputin**. He was forced to abdicate in 1917, and he and his family were executed by the Bolsheviks in 1918.

Nigeria A Commonwealth republic of W Africa. Area:

923,773 sq km. Pop: 105,470,000. Official language: English. Religions: Islam, Christianity. Cap: Abuja.

Formerly a British colony, Nigeria achieved independence in 1960 and was declared a republic in 1963. A federal structure of twelve states was created in 1967, and seven new states were added in 1976. Its recent history has been one of regional and tribal rivalry, of civil war (*see* **Biafran War**), and a succession of military coups. The country has never exploited its economic potential, including its great natural wealth, including oil, to the full, because of its government by a series of corrupt and unstable regimes.

Night of the Long Knives *see* SA.

Nixon, Richard (1913–94) A US Republican politician, vice-president from 1953 to 1960, and president from 1969 to 1974. At home Nixon introduced his 'new economic policy' in 1971, designed to reduce unemployment, stimulate the economy, contain inflation, and correct the balance of payments deficit.

In foreign affairs he followed a policy of **détente** with Communist states. He gradually reduced US commitments in the **Vietnam War**; sought normal relations with China, in the course of which he paid the first-ever visit there by a US president (1972); reached an agreement at the **Strategic Arms Limitation Talks** with the USSR (1972); and began peace moves in the Middle East which proved to be unsuccessful.

Nixon became the first US president to resign from office when he was in danger of impeachment for his involvement in the **Watergate affair**.

Nkomo, Joshua (1917–99) A Zimbabwean nationalist

leader. He founded the Zimbabwe African People's Union (ZAPU) in 1961, which was banned in 1962. Nkomo spent ten years in detention as a political prisoner and then joined Robert **Mugabe** as joint-leader of the Patriotic Front, promoting guerrilla activities to achieve independence and black majority rule. With Ian **Smith** and Mugabe, he took part in the London talks in 1979 which eventually led to independence in 1980. Nkomo lost the ensuing election to Mugabe, in whose government he served until his dismissal in 1982.

Nkrumah, Kwame (1909–72) A Ghanaian politician. In 1949 Nkrumah founded the Convention People's Party with the slogan 'self-government now'. When Ghana gained independence in 1957 he became PM after the party's election victory. In foreign affairs he pursued a non-aligned policy in the **Cold War** but was pro-Arab, Pan-African, and opposed to South Africa. In domestic affairs his drastic economic reforms, interference with the judiciary and the introduction of a one-party state aroused considerable opposition. He was overthrown by a military coup in 1966.

NKVD *see* Soviet Security Service.

Non-aggression Pact *see* Nazi-Soviet Pact.

Non-aligned Movement A grouping of nations established at the Belgrade Conference of 1961 which consisted for the most part of African and Asian states. The movement was pledged to follow foreign policies independent of the East and West superpower blocs, and to use its influence to reduce antagonism between the USSR and the USA and their respective allies. India and Yugoslavia were the principal members of the movement, which held regular meetings in the capitals of the associated states.

Nonviolence **1.** A policy of passive resistance or peaceful demonstration for political purposes.

2. The refraining from violence on moral grounds to achieve objectives; pacifism.

Normandy Landings (1944) The start of the Allied invasion of W Europe in WWII, when British, Canadian and US troops landed on five beaches in Normandy. They were transported from S England by an armada of ships, heavily protected by air and naval forces. D-Day was 6 June and the operation was code-named Overlord. After heavy fighting, particularly around the Norman towns of Caen and Falaise, German forces evacuated most of France.

North African Campaigns or **Desert Campaigns** (1940–3) A series of defensive and offensive operations in WWII, in which Allied forces fought those of Germany and Italy in efforts to control the S coast of the Mediterranean. The Axis objective was to capture Alexandria, Cairo and the Suez Canal, and ultimately to advance into the Middle East and secure the oilfields. The Allied purpose was, defensively, to protect Egypt and thus the oilfields, and later, offensively, to secure the area from Egypt through Libya to Tunisia as a springboard for the invasion of S Europe, and which would also relieve pressure on Malta.

Major engagements included those fought at El Alamein (in 1942 – the first major British victory over German forces in WWII), Tobruk, Benghazi and Tripoli, attack and counter-attack resulting in frequent

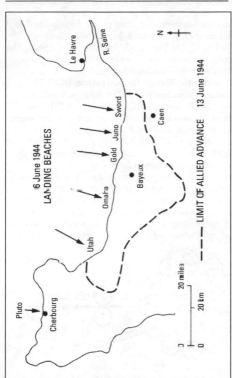

Normandy Landings

changes in occupation of many places. Finally the Allied forces advancing from the E joined those that had landed in Algeria (the 'Torch' landings, Nov. 1942). The meeting of the two Allied armies took place in Tunisia where the Axis forces finally surrendered.

North Atlantic Treaty Organisation (NATO)

A military alliance established by the North Atlantic Treaty (1949). The original members were Belgium, Canada, Denmark, France, Iceland, Italy, Luxembourg, the Netherlands, Norway, Portugal, the UK and the USA. Greece and Turkey joined in 1952, West Germany in 1954, and Spain in 1982. France withdrew from the joint military command in 1966.

The organisation's policy-making body is the Council of Ministers consisting of the PMs or departmental ministers of member nations according to the matters under consideration. It normally meets twice yearly, its chief administrative officer being the Secretary-General. There are Defence and Military Committees on which

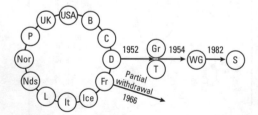

North Atlantic Treaty Organisation Membership.

chiefs-of-staff and other high-ranking officers serve, the Supreme Allied Commander Europe being in overall charge of the multinational armed forces.

  The treaty provides that should any of the participating states be subject to armed aggression then such attacks will be considered as being made against them all, and collectively and individually they will provide all possible aid considered necessary to restore and maintain the security of the North Atlantic area. Since the demise of the the **Warsaw Pact**, NATO has undertaken international peacekeeping, and several ex-Warsaw Pact states have been admitted to membership.

Northern Ireland *see* **Ireland**.

Northern Rhodesia *see* **Zambia** *and* **Rhodesia and Nyasaland, Federation of**.

Novotný, Antonin (1904–75) A Czechoslovak Communist politician. He was First Secretary of the party 1953–68, and was president of the republic from 1957 to 1968. He was a hard-line Stalinist and as such became increasingly unpopular as the liberalisation demanded by intellectuals and students spread through the civilian population and armed forces, eventually forcing his retirement. His efforts to remain in power included a limited number of political concessions and the abandonment of the third **Five-Year Plan**, but these were of no use against the growing opposition. He was succeeded as First Secretary by Alexander **Dubček**.

Nuclear Test Ban Treaty (1963) An agreement between the UK, the USA and USSR by which nuclear testing in the atmosphere, outer space or under water is prohibited. Many other nations subsequently signed the treaty, but China, France, India and South Africa refused to do so.

Nuclear Warfare A potential form of conflict employing either *atomic bombs* (weapons based on the fission of a heavy atomic nucleus), or *hydrogen bombs* (weapons based on the fusion of two light nuclei) – both of which cause vast thermonuclear explosions and the release of large amounts of highly radioactive fallout. The theory behind the possession of such horrific weapons is that they act as a deterrent, no nation daring to use them for fear of retaliation. *See also* **disarmament**; **deterrence**.

Nuremberg Rallies The annual convention of the Nazi party held in the 1930s in Nuremberg, Bavaria. They consisted of vast open-air gatherings, impressive marches, torchlight processions and speeches by Party leaders, all designed to spread propaganda and rouse the assembled multitude to near-hysteria. They also served to demonstrate the party faithful's devotion to Adolf **Hitler** who used the occasions to deliver major policy speeches.

Nuremberg Trials *see* **war crimes**.

Nyerere, Julius (1922–99) A Tanzanian politician. Nyerere became president of the Tanganyika African National Union after completely reorganising it between 1954 and 1955. He entered the Legislative Council in 1958 and became chief minister in 1960 after the Union's electoral successes. He was PM in 1961, before resigning to establish the Union as a Christian Socialist movement. He became president of Tanganyika on independence (1962) and president of Tanzania when

Tanganyika and Zanzibar merged in 1964. He retired in 1985 and died in 1999. Nyerere adopted a non-aligned policy in foreign affairs for his one-party state but was a keen supporter of Pan-Africanism and made his country a leading member of the Organisation of African Unity.

O

OAS *see* **Organisation of American States**.

OAU *see* **Organisation of African Unity**.

Obote, Milton (1924–) A Ugandan politician. Obote was leader in the independence negotiations with the UK and was PM from 1962 to 1966. The first president of Uganda, the Kabaka (prince) of Buganda, opposed Obote's wish to establish a one-party state so Obote deposed him in a coup. He assumed the presidency but was overthrown himself by Idi **Amin** in 1971. He fled to Tanzania and regained the presidency in 1980, following Amin's downfall. He was deposed again in 1985.

Oder-Neisse Line The post-WWII frontier between Germany and Poland agreed at the **Potsdam Conference** in 1945. The line follows the course of the River Oder south to its confluence with the River Neisse, and then along the Neisse to the Czech border.

OECD *see* **Organisation for Economic Cooperation and Development**.

OEEC *see* **Organisation for European Economic Cooperation**.

OGPU *see* **Soviet Security Service**.

Oil Crisis An economic crisis arising in the late 1960s and early 1970s caused by rising demand for oil and political action by Arab oil-producing nations against Israel and those countries they considered to be aiding or sympathising with Israel.

The Arab oil producers imposed price increases of some 70 per cent, and this increased inflation and caused **balance of payments** difficulties for the consumer nations of the West. The situation was made worse by interruptions in the oil supply (amounting to a loss of 15 per cent) owing to the **Arab-Israeli Wars** and the closing of the Suez Canal, which forced tankers to make a long detour around the Cape of Good Hope. The attitude of the Arab producers was criticised by non-Arab members of the **Organisation of Petroleum-Exporting Countries** and the crisis gradually faded, although not before it had become of such concern to the UK government that it considered introducing a petrol-rationing system.

In the UK the oil crisis developed into a wider energy crisis with the miners' strikes of 1972 and 1974. In 1974 a state of emergency was declared by Edward **Heath**'s Conservative Government with a three-day working week for industry. Heath called a general election and was defeated by Labour.

Ojukwu *see* **Biafran War**.

Okinawa An island in the China Seas between Taiwan and Japan. US forces captured the island in June 1945 after two months' fighting at a cost of 13,000 American and 100,000 Japanese lives. It gave the Allies a base from which to prepare a final assault on Japan, and the heavy American losses, along with those suffered in the capture of **Iwo Jima**, provided the senior Allied commanders with a reason for trying to end the war by the use of a nuclear weapon.

OPEC *see* **Organisation of Petroleum-Exporting Countries**.

Orange Order The largest Protestant organisation in

Northern Ireland, founded in 1795. It was named after William III (William of Orange) who reigned 1689–1702, and who defeated the RC ex-king James II (reigned 1685–8) at the Battle of the Boyne in 1690. In the 20th century, the Order fiercely opposed home rule and wished Ulster to remain part of the UK.

Organisation for African Unity (OAU) A body of 48 African states established in 1963 with HQ in Addis Ababa, Ethiopia. The founding membership was 31 nations but 17 more have since joined.

The OAU's objectives are the ending of colonialism (now achieved); the encouragement of common objectives among the membership; the raising of living standards by increasing progress in the fields of education, health and social welfare; the expansion of cultural, economic, scientific and technical affairs; the promotion of international cooperation; and the defence of independence, sovereignty and territory.

Heads of state meet annually and the Council of Ministers six-monthly, but the organisation's purposes are at times frustrated by the different stages of development of its member countries, and by their cultural, economic, political and religious differences.

Organisation for Economic Cooperation and Development (OECD) The international agency with HQ in Paris that replaced the Organisation for European Economic Cooperation in 1961, when Canada and the USA joined the 18 W European members. Japan joined in 1964, and Finland in 1968. Australia, New Zealand and Yugoslavia are associate members. The organisation consists of the West's leading industrial states, its objectives being to contribute to the expansion of world trade, provide aid for developing countries, achieve financial stability, and promote economic growth.

Organisation for European Economic Cooperation (OEEC) An international agency established in 1948 with HQ in Paris. Its members were Austria, Belgium, France, Greece, Iceland, Ireland, Italy, Luxembourg, the Netherlands, Norway, Portugal, Sweden, Switzerland, Turkey and the UK. West Germany joined in 1955 and Spain in 1959. Canada and the USA were associate members, and Yugoslavia was permitted limited participation. Its objective was to attack the economic problems resulting from WWII by making best use of aid supplied through the **Marshall Plan**. It was replaced by the **Organisation for Economic Cooperation and Development** in 1961 as a result of US pressure to broaden its objectives to include responsibilities to developing countries worldwide.

Organisation of American States (OAS) A body of 21 American states established in 1948 by the Ninth International Conference of American States at Bogota, Colombia. Its HQ is in Washington, DC. Cuba was expelled in 1962, but recent admissions, particularly among the new small island states of the Caribbean, increased its membership to 32.

The objectives of the OAS include promotion of economic and social development; peaceful settlement of disputes; strengthening of security, including military aid; and opposition to communist subversion. Policy arrangements are made by a council on which every state is represented, by meetings of foreign ministers, and by a 5-yearly Inter-American Conference.

Organisation of Petroleum-Exporting Countries (OPEC) A body of 13 states established in 1961 in Caracas, Venezuela, to agree a common policy for oil pricing. The founder-members were Iran, Iraq, Kuwait, Qatar, Saudi Arabia and Venezuela, but seven more have joined at various times since: Abu Dhabi, Algeria, Egypt, Indonesia, Libya, Nigeria and Syria. These nations dominated the oil market, although other producers (e.g. North Sea oil in the 1970s to 1990s, or Russia) weakened OPEC's monopoly position.

OPEC's aims include the maintenance of stable price structures by the regulation of production, so avoiding price variations that might affect the economies of both producing and purchasing nations.

Ostpolitik The attempt by West Germany to improve relations with the **Warsaw Pact** countries, started by Willi **Brandt** when Foreign Minister in Kurt **Kiesinger**'s government during the years 1966 to 1969, and pursued later when he was Chancellor from 1969 to 1974. Agreements were reached on posts and telecommunications, traffic, and visits by relatives between E and W Berlin. West Germany recognised East Germany and the **Oder-Neisse Line**, and peace treaties were signed with Poland and the USSR (1972).

Ottawa Conference (1932) A meeting to discuss economic problems affecting the UK and the Dominions, India, and Southern Rhodesia. It established an **imperial preference** system based on quotas and tariffs, following the introduction by the UK of protective **tariffs** to deal with the effects of the **Depression**.

Ottoman Empire The former Turkish empire in Africa, Asia and Europe, dating from *c.*1300 to 1922 when the Sultanate was abolished and replaced by the Republic of **Turkey**.

Overlord Operation *see* **Normandy Landings**.

P

Pahlavi, Mohammad Reza (1919–80) The Shah of **Iran** from 1941 to 1979. He was a popular monarch early in his reign when he set up a liberal Westernised system of government, but lost favour when he imposed a series of autocratic reforms, including the social emancipation of women. This offended the Islamic authorities and the most outspoken Muslim critic, Ayatollah Ruhollah **Khomeini,** was arrested and exiled.

For some time the Shah appeared to have silenced the opposition but eventually high inflation, a series of repressive measures, excessive spending on royal occasions and his lack of sympathy with Arab opposition to Israel roused uncontrollable opposition from fundamentalist students and puritanical religious leaders, leading to massive street demonstrations and violence. The Shah left the country in 1979 and two months later he was deposed, dying in exile in Cairo.

Pakistan A republic of SC Asia. Area: 803,943 sq km. Pop: 129,808,000. Language: Urdu. Religion: Islam. Cap: Islamabad.

Pakistan came into existence as a result of the Indian Independence Act (1947). Following pressure from Mohammed Ali **Jinnah** and the **Muslim League** for an independent state for Muslims, the Act partitioned Pakistan from India, dividing the new state into two geographically separate parts, East and West Pakistan, which became a republic in 1956.

The bloodshed accompanying Partition left much

bitterness between Pakistan and India, and the two
countries have fought wars over the disputed territory of
Kashmir (1947–9 and 1965). Tension also developed
between the two parts of Pakistan, separated by 1,750
km of Indian territory. In 1971 East Pakistan declared
itself independent as **Bangladesh**. The Pakistan army
put down the secession with much bloodshed, causing
millions of refugees to flee to India. India then
intervened militarily in support of Bangladesh and its
own claims to **Kashmir**, defeated the Pakistan army, and
ensured Bangladeshi independence. Pakistan left the
Commonwealth in 1972 when Bangladesh applied to
join, but rejoined in 1990.

Politically, Pakistan's history has been turbulent, with
military coups and periods of martial law interrupting
democratic rule. The country's leaders have included
Ayub Khan (1958–69), **Yahya Khan** (1969–71), **Zulfikar
Ali Bhutto** (1971–7), **Zia Ul-Haq** (1977–88) and
Benazir Bhutto (1988–90, 1993–6). In 1990, President
Ghulam Ishaq Khan dismissed the government of
Benazir Bhutto, initiating a struggle between parliament
and the president that also brought the dismissal of
Bhutto's rival Narwaz Sharif. Bhutto was dismissed
again by President Farooq Leghari in 1996 and charged
with corruption. Under Sharif's government of 1997–9
Pakistan conducted nuclear weapons tests in response
to tests by India, and the two clashed in Kashmir. In
1999 a bloodless coup by General Pervez Musharraf
removed Sharif and he was exiled.

Palestine A territory on the E coast of the
Mediterranean. It was part of the **Ottoman Empire** until

after WWI, and is now occupied by the state of Israel. After the Turks had been expelled (1917–18) and following the **Balfour Declaration**, Palestine was a British mandated territory (1922–48). During this period, hostility between Arabs and Jews grew rapidly, with the British army struggling to maintain peace and stability.

The Arabs resented the huge influx of Jews caused by Nazi persecution in Europe and the Jews resented immigration quotas imposed by the British, so that many entered the country by illegal means. Jewish opposition to the British grew and extremists launched terrorist attacks which only ceased during WWII. Afterwards these were resumed by **Irgun Zvai Leumi** and the **Stern Gang**, and eventually, in 1947, the UK referred the problem to the UN which partitioned the land between Jews and Arabs, the UK being relieved of the mandate.

As a result of the **Arab-Israeli Wars** Israel occupied the Palestinian lands given to the Arabs by the partition settlement. Following the Camp David Agreement (1978), Israel allowed these territories (the Gaza Strip and West Bank) limited autonomy in 1994, but retained control over all security matters. Tension between Israelis and Palestinians remained high, despite formal Palestinian acceptance of the existence of the Israeli state. Fighting broke out again from late 2000 onwards.

Palestine Liberation Organisation (PLO) The body formed in 1964 in Jordan, uniting various Palestinian Arab groups and representing c.1.5 million Palestinian refugees who lived in Palestine until the creation of Israel. Originally its intention was to destroy the state of Israel, but its aims by the late 1990s were to secure full Palestinian independence and to end Israeli encroachment into the autonomous Palestinian areas.

The most important group is **Al Fatah**, led by Yasser Arafat, who committed the organisation after the **Camp David Agreement** to achieving its objectives by political means rather than terrorism. This has resulted in various extremist groups breaking away from Al Fatah and persisting with terrorist operations, carried out largely in Israel itself. In the 1970s and 80s the PLO carried out terrorist attacks in various parts of Europe and the Middle East, including the hijacking of aircraft, hostage-taking and assassination.

Pankhurst, Emmoline (1857-1928) A British campaigner for **Women's Suffrage**. Pankhurst founded the Women's Franchise League in 1889 and the more militant Women's Social and Political Union in 1903, with its slogan of 'Votes for Women'. She served eight prison sentences for taking part in acts of vandalism. Her objective of women's suffrage on the same terms as that for men was achieved during the month of her death. Her daughters, Christabel (1880–1958) and Estelle Sylvia (1882–1960) also campaigned for women's suffrage.

Panmunjom Armistice (1953) A peace agreement between North and South Korea ending the **Korean War**, signed at the village of Panmunjom in the demilitarised zone separating the two states. Talks had been in progress for over two years, the obstacles to peace being political rather than military, and it was

Stalin's death that finally modified the previously inflexible Communist position, opening the way to agreement and a general relaxation of international tension.

Pan-Slavism A movement of opinion in E Europe in the 19th century which emphasised the unity of Slavonic peoples through their common culture and related languages. It was strong in Russia, supporting the country's historic aim of gaining Constantinople (Istanbul) and freeing the southern Slavs from Austrian and Ottoman rule. The movement was at its peak between the 1860s and 1880s, and it was revived during the **Balkan Wars** and WWI, although in a more moderate form.

Papen, Franz von (1879–1969) A German diplomat and politician. Papen was a Centre Party deputy from 1921 to 1932 and Chancellor in 1932. He tried to solve the country's political problems by making concessions to the Nazis, and calling fresh elections.

However, the elections only strengthened Nazi representation in the Reichstag and increased the violence. Adolf **Hitler**'s insistence on being appointed Chancellor spoiled von Papen's efforts to form a Centre-Nazi coalition and he resigned under pressure from the army, which feared a civil war. After Hitler became Chancellor, von Papen was appointed Vice-Chancellor, a post he held from 1933 to 1934.

Paris Peace Conference (1919–20) The assembly held after WWI during which the **League of Nations** was set up and the peace agreements between the Allied and Central Powers were worked out and ultimately concluded by the Treaties of **Versailles**, **Saint Germain**, **Neuilly**, **Trianon** and **Sèvres**. Proceedings were dominated by Britain, France, Italy, Japan and the USA, although 32 nations took part.

Paris Peace Talks (1968–73) A series of meetings aimed at ending the **Vietnam War**. These lengthy negotiations between representatives of North and South Vietnam and the USA were political as well as military, and much time was wasted in wrangling over such trivialities as the shape of the conference table. Within a fortnight of the signing of the ceasefire agreement in 1973, the first US troops left Vietnam, which remained partitioned until the North finally overran the South and unified the country in 1975.

Paris Student Demonstrations (1968) Massive street disturbances caused by what many considered excessive defence expenditure, especially on an independent nuclear deterrent, at the expense of France's educational and social services.

   The demonstrations, organised by a loose alliance of left-wing, intellectual and anarchist groups (*see* **anarchism**), rapidly developed into riots, and the police responded with great severity. The demonstrations and riots were followed by a general strike, workers taking the opportunity to protest at the policies of the Fifth Republic under **de Gaulle**. The government was forced to give the workers considerable concessions, including wage increases of 33 $\frac{1}{3}$ per cent, and the students were granted many of the reforms they were seeking.

Parliament The law-making body of the UK, consisting of the House of Commons, the House of Lords, and the monarch. The Commons is the lower chamber and consists of members elected at general elections or by-elections. The Lords is the upper chamber and consists of the lords spiritual (two Archbishops and 24 senior Church of England bishops), and the lords temporal (hereditary and life peers). The life peers include certain judges, the Lords of Appeal, who form the highest UK appeal court.

Parliament Acts (1911 and 1949) Acts that reformed the way Parliament was organised. Both acts limited the powers of the House of Lords.

The *1911 Act* arose out of the rejection by the Lords of Lloyd George's 1909 budget, and abolished the Lords' delaying powers over money bills (and also bills to extend the length of a parliament). It restricted the Upper House's delaying powers over other bills passed by the Commons to three parliamentary sessions spread over two years.

In addition, the act reduced the maximum duration of a Parliament from seven years to five.

The Lords only approved these measures, introduced by **Asquith**'s Liberal government, because of King George V's threat to create 250 Liberal peers in order to end the Conservative Party's majority in the Lords.

The *1949 Act* was introduced by Clement **Attlee**'s Labour Government to reduce the Lords' delaying powers to two sessions, i.e. one year. The act arose from Labour's fear that its nationalisation programme, especially of the iron and steel industry, would be held up by the delaying power of the Lords, which was dominated by Conservatives.

Partisan A member of an armed resistance group within occupied territory. During WWII such guerrilla groups were often Communist-led, Stalin having encouraged their formation. They operated successfully in parts of the USSR, Albania, Czechoslovakia, Greece, Italy, and in particular, Yugoslavia under the leadership of **Tito**. They lived off the land where possible, but also on supplies dropped by Allied air forces or captured from the enemy. *See also* **resistance movements**.

Partition *see* **Cyprus**; **India**; **Ireland**; **Pakistan**.

Passchendaele *see* **Ypres, Battles of**.

Patriotism A proclaimed love of one's country, loyalty to the ruler or government of a state. Often indistinguishable from **nationalism**, it may differ from it in that loyalty to a state sometimes cuts across national differences. Thus patriots might show loyalty to Prussia rather than to Germany, or to the Austro-Hungarian Empire rather than to a Slav nation within it. One Basque might be a patriotic Spaniard, another might be a strong Basque nationalist.

Pearl Harbor The main US naval base in Hawaii. Although there had been no declaration of war, Japanese carrier-borne aircraft attacked Pearl Harbor early on 7 December 1941, sinking or disabling 19 ships (including 8 battleships), destroying 188 planes and killing 2,400 people. The US Congress declared war on Japan on 8 December, and within days Germany and Italy, Japan's allies, declared war on the USA. American naval losses at Pearl Harbor gave an advantage to Japanese sea power in the early months after the attack. However, the strategically important aircraft carriers were undamaged as they were not in the harbour at the time.

Pentagon The main offices of the US Department of Defense and HQ of the US armed forces in Arlington, Virginia – hence the term is also used for the military leadership of the USA.

Perestroika (*Russ.* – restructuring) The Soviet policy of economic reform begun under Mikhail **Gorbachev** in 1985. *See also* **glasnost**.

Perón *see* **Argentina**.

Pétain, Henri Phillipe (1856–1951) A French soldier and politician. As a WWI general Pétain won fame by his defence of **Verdun** in 1916. He was appointed commander-in-chief of the French forces (1917), promoted to marshal (1918) and was the leading military figure in France in the 1920s and 1930s.

In WWII he was appointed PM in 1940 and within a week had concluded an armistice with the invading Germans. He then took the position of head of state and between 1940 and 1942 adopted a policy of cooperation with the Germans (*see* **Vichy Government**). His government became a puppet regime, passing anti-Semitic laws, doing nothing to prevent the transfer of $c.\frac{3}{4}$ million workers to Germany for forced labour, and doing little to oppose other German demands.

Replaced by Pierre **Laval**, Pétain was eventually forced by the Germans to retreat with them into Germany. After the war he returned voluntarily to France where he was tried for treason and condemned to death, although his sentence was commuted to life imprisonment.

Phoney War The period between the start of WWII in 1939 and the German onslaught in the West (1940). During these months little hostile action occurred, except in Poland and at sea, the period being used for the spreading of propaganda and the mutual probing of enemy positions on land and in the air.

Pilsudski, Josef (1867–1935) A Polish marshal and politician. After WWI Pilsudski was made head of state until 1921, and commander-in-chief of the armed forces fighting the Bolsheviks, a position he held until 1923. In 1926 he led a military coup, and effectively became dictator of Poland until his death. He was PM from 1926 to 1928 and in 1930, and Minister of War from 1926 to 1935. He signed a non-aggression pact with Germany (1934) in a vain attempt to reduce the growing threat of Nazism against his country.

Plebiscite *see* **referendum**.

PLO *see* **Palestine Liberation Organisation**.

Pogrom 1. The organised persecution of a religious or racial group, especially Jews.

2. The anti-Semitic violence and stirring up of hatred practised by Communist and Fascist regimes before and during WWII.

Poincaré, Raymond Nicolas Landry (1860–1934) A French politician. Poincaré was PM of a coalition government (1912–13), and as president of the Third Republic from 1913 to 1920 he was an inspiring leader during WWI. When he again became PM (1922–4), he followed a severe reparations policy towards Germany. When Germany fell behind with the payments, his government, jointly with Belgium, ordered the occupation of the **Ruhr** (1923–5). His conservative and nationalist policies and the decision to occupy the Ruhr brought about his government's downfall (1924), but he became PM again from 1926 to 1929.

Poland A republic of E Europe. Area: 312,683 sq km. Pop: 38,612,000. Language: Polish. Religion: Christianity (RC). Cap: Warsaw.

Poland became an independent state in 1918, having previously been partitioned between Austria, Prussia and Russia since the 18th century. In 1919 to 1920 Poland conducted a successful war against the Bolsheviks, gaining territory to the E of the **Curzon Line**. Between the Wars Poland was largely ruled by right-wing dictatorial governments, notably those of Josef **Pilsudski**.

In 1938, Germany pressed for the return of **Danzig** and for special rights across the Polish Corridor to E Prussia, demands which were resisted by Poland. Following the **Nazi-Soviet Pact**, Germany invaded Poland in 1939, bringing the UK and France (which had earlier guaranteed Polish security) into WWII. The USSR invaded two weeks later and occupied E Poland until the German attack on Russia in 1941. Poland was conquered in six weeks in 1939, but again became a battleground in 1944. During the German occupation (1939–44), the civilian population suffered severely, and three million of Poland's Jewish population were wiped out (*see* **Holocaust**). Poland was liberated by Soviet forces in 1945.

After WWII Poland lost territory in the E to the USSR, the new frontier following the Curzon Line, but

SWEDEN

LATVIA

Baltic Sea

LITHUANIA

Danzig

Vilna

Berlin

USSR

EAST
GERMANY

Warsaw

POLAND

R. Vistula

N

CZECHOSLOVAKIA

| 0 | 200 miles |

| 0 | 200 km |

Territories gained by Poland in 1945

Territories lost by Poland in 1945

Poland

gained territory in the W from Germany, the new
frontier being the **Oder-Neisse Line**. The country fell
under the political influence of the USSR, became a
Communist state, and joined the **Council for Mutual**

Economic Assistance and the **Warsaw Pact**.

The lack of political liberty, rising food prices and shortage of consumer goods led to periods of rioting, strikes and demonstrations of anti-Soviet feelings from 1956 onwards. Nationalist sentiment and the unifying force of the strongly supported RC church gave extra impetus to the disturbances, which led to the fall of Wladislaw **Gomulka** in 1970 and Edward **Giereck** in 1980. In 1980 the independent trade union **Solidarity** openly demanded reform, and its defiance led the government, under Wojciech **Jaruzelski**, to declare martial law (1981–3). Continued economic and political difficulties forced the government to allow partially free elections in 1989, and in 1990 Lech Walesa, the leader of **Solidarity**, became Poland's president. The country had eight PMs between 1990 and 1996, including Hanna Suchocka, its first woman PM (1992). Walesa was defeated in the 1995 presidential election by Aleksander Kwásniewski of the Democratic Left Alliance (SLD), which included the reformed Communists. Solidarity again won power in the 1997 elections, and a new constitution reduced the power of the president. Poland joined NATO in 1999.

Polish Corridor *see* **Danzig**.

Politburo The political bureau of the central committee of the Communist Party, which was the governing and policy-making committee, especially in the USSR, where the name was first used in 1917. Stalin replaced the Politburo with the Presidium in 1952, but the name was restored in 1966.

Pompidou, Georges (1911–74) A French Gaullist

politician. After WWII service with the French resistance he served **de Gaulle** as an adviser, and played an important part in the Evian Agreements which ended the Algerian War (1962). He was PM from 1962 to 1968, and succeeded de Gaulle as president from 1969 to 1974, following similar policies.

Popular Front The name of various coalitions of centre and left-wing parties opposed to Fascism in the 1930s, especially those that formed the governments in France, Spain and Chile. Their programmes included social reforms and economic improvements for the working classes. In Spain, right-wing opposition to the Popular Front government resulted in increasing disturbances and eventually the outbreak of the **Spanish Civil War**.

Potsdam Conference (1945) The meeting following Germany's defeat attended by the Allied leaders **Stalin**, **Truman** and **Churchill** (replaced during the conference by **Attlee**) to decide the fate of postwar Germany and to carry out the agreement reached at the **Yalta Conference**. The main decisions were:

a. to partition Germany into four zones occupied by French, US, UK, and Russian forces;
b. to initiate a programme of de-Nazification;
c. to appoint local administrations and central authorities run by Germans in each of the zones, supervised by an Allied Control Council;
d. to control German industry and dismantle certain industrial plants as a form of reparations to the Allies;
e. to redistribute certain German territories to Poland and the USSR.

Privatisation The policy of transferring industries and services from public to private ownership; the opposite of **nationalisation**. Between 1979 and 1997, the UK Conservative government privatised a number of state-owned companies (including British Telecom, Britoil, British Gas, British Airways, British Petroleum, the electricity industry and British Rail) by selling shares in them to the public.

Prohibition The banning of the manufacture and sale of alcoholic drinks. It came into force in the USA in 1920 and lasted until 1933. During that time illegal making of alcohol – bootlegging – and illegal drinking places – speakeasies – flourished. Organised crime, based on satisfying the demand for alcohol, reached record heights, and enormous untaxed illegal profits were made.

The US Federal government committed vast sums of money and many staff to the impossible task of trying to enforce Prohibition. F D **Roosevelt**, with the words 'I think now would be a good time for beer', brought Prohibition to an end.

Proletariat The class of wage-earners, in **Marxist** philosophy, especially industrial workers in a capitalist society whose only possession of value is their labour and who are exploited by the ruling class (the **bourgeoisie**).

Propaganda 1. The organised spreading of allegations, information, etc. to assist or damage the cause of a government, movement, etc.

2. The actual allegations, information, etc. so spread. The technique was the principal ideological instrument

of Hitler, Mussolini and Stalin to influence and control their own people and to attempt to undermine the determination of their enemies, using broadcasting, the cinema, and massive stage-managed demonstrations such as the **Nuremberg Rallies**. All governments make use of propaganda of some sort.

Protectionism 1. The placing of duties or quotas on imports, to protect domestic industries against foreign competition.

2. The policy, system or theory of such restrictions. On occasion most industrialised countries have adopted such practices and since WWII the method has been used by trading blocs such as the **EC**, to protect their members' interests. The opposite of protectionism is **free trade**.

Purge The removal of dissidents or opponents from a political party or state, especially associated with events during Joseph **Stalin's** dictatorship in the USSR. These purges (especially in the period 1936–8) resulted in the execution, exile or imprisonment of millions of Soviet citizens after the show trials, when the accused usually pleaded guilty to the 'crimes', frequently after a period of brainwashing or torture.

Putin, Vladmir Vladmirovich (1955–) Former KGB official, he won the Russian presidential elections in 2000. At that time, not much was known about him but his strong image and willingness to take severe measures against Chechen rebels helped him to win the voters' support.

Putsch (*German*) A sudden, violent political uprising.

Q

Quebec Conferences (1943, 1944) Meetings during WWII between British PM Winston **Churchill** and US president F D **Roosevelt** and their chiefs of staff. The 1943 conference discussed the implications of **Mussolini**'s overthrow, the invasion of Europe, and operations in the Far East, particularly the Burma campaign. The 1944 conference discussed the transfer of resources to the Far East after the ending of hostilities in Europe, the Philippines campaign, and the **Lend-Lease Act**, on the assumption that it would continue after the war's end. Henry Morgenthau (1891–1967), US Secretary of the Treasury, put forward a plan for the removal of Germany's means of industrial production. Churchill and Roosevelt agreed to the proposals, but they were later rejected by their ministers as being too costly and impracticable.

Quisling, Vidkun (1887–1945) A Norwegian politician. Quisling was Minister of Defence from 1931 to 1933 but impatience with democratic methods led him in 1933 to form National Unity, a fascist movement which gained little support. On the outbreak of WWII he became involved in German plans for the occupation of Norway, and when the invasion occurred he seized power and ruled the country as a puppet of the occupiers. After the war he was executed for treason. The term 'quisling' is now applied to any person who betrays their country to, and collaborates with, an enemy.

R

Racism 1. The belief that physical and cultural differences between races make some races superior to others.

2. Abusive or aggressive behaviour towards members of another race on the basis of such belief.

Racism was a part of Nazi philosophy and still exists in many parts of the world, though rarely as government policy. (A notable exception since WWII was **apartheid** in South Africa). *See also* **anti-Semitism**; **ethnic cleansing**.

Radar A method of detecting distant objects by the use of radio waves. Its invention and development by Britain in the late 1930s gave the RAF a marked advantage over the Luftwaffe during WWII. In particular, approaching German planes could be tracked by radar and RAF crews were not forced to spend long hours in the air hunting for the enemy. The failure of the German airforce to continue attacking the radar control bases in 1940, and its switch to bombing civilian targets, was a major reason why Germany lost the **Battle of Britain** and had to abandon plans for invading the UK.

Radicalism The aim, beliefs or principles of political radicals, i.e. those wanting major or fundamental changes in economic or social conditions or institutions.

Rahman, Sheikh Mujibur (1920–75) A Bangladeshi politician. Rahman became leader of the Awami League in 1954, whose purpose was to secure the independence

from West Pakistan of East Pakistan as **Bangladesh**.
After the war of independence (1971) and the
establishment of the new state he declined the
presidency but became PM. His attempt to create
parliamentary democracy based on socialist principles
failed and he took dictatorial powers in 1975, which
resulted in his assassination when a military coup
overthrew his government.

Rahman, Tunku Abdul (1903–90) A Malaysian
politician. Rahman became PM of Malaya in 1957 and
of the Federation of Malaysia in 1963. He had worked
hard to achieve cooperation between the country's
different races, but this broke down and he retired from
office in 1970.

Rapallo, Treaty of (1922) An agreement between
Germany and the USSR. Diplomatic relations were
restored, financial claims against each other (arising
from WWI) were withdrawn, and economic
cooperation pledged. It was also secretly agreed that
German soldiers could train in Russia.

Rasputin, Grigori Efimovich (*orig. surname* Novykh)
(1871–1916) A Russian peasant monk and mystic. He
had a magnetic power over the Tsarina Alexandra
Feodorovna (1872–1918), who believed he could help
the condition of her haemophiliac son, Alexis. From
1911 he exerted increasing influence over church and
government appointments, gaining positions for his
nominees and obtaining the dismissal of those of whom
he disapproved, including PM Vladimir Kokovtsov. This
power, coupled with his alcoholism and depraved
private life, earned him the name of 'Rasputin'

(debauched), and made him many enemies. He was
assassinated by a group of noblemen.

Reactionary 1. Opposed to all change, especially
radical political or social change.

2. A person opposed to such changes.

Reagan, Ronald (1911–) A US politician and
Republican president from 1981 to 1989. He followed
generally conservative policies, cutting taxes and welfare
expenditure while massively increasing defence
spending, e.g. on the **Strategic Defense Initiative**.
His hardline attitude towards the USSR moderated
somewhat when Mikhail **Gorbachev** came to power, and
in 1987 he signed the **Intermediate Nuclear Forces
Treaty**. In Central America he attempted to topple the
left-wing regime in Nicaragua by supporting the **Contra**
rebels, despite the opposition of Congress and
condemnation by the UN. He remained popular
throughout his presidency, and this helped his vice-
president, **George Bush**, to win the 1988 election as his
successor.

Red Army The armed land forces of the USSR
established in 1918 by the Bolshevik government. The
word 'Red' was dropped from the title in 1946. After
1990, the Soviet army was reduced in size and then
divided up among the individual states of the former
Union, Russia getting the largest army.

Red Cross Society The international and national
organisation for relief of suffering in time of war and
disaster. It was founded in 1864 as a result of the
inspiration of a Swiss businessman, Jean Henri Dunant
(1828–1910), who had been horrified by the plight of

the wounded at the Battle of Solferino (1859). He was joint winner of the first Nobel Peace Prize in 1901. The society's emblem is a red cross on a white background. The earliest of the agreements of the **Geneva Convention** was closely connected with the society's development.

Red Guards *see* **Cultural Revolution**.

Referendum or **plebiscite** The submission of an issue of national or public importance to the vote of the electorate of a state, region, etc. Referenda have been held by Norway and the UK on the issue of EU membership, in the Republic of Ireland on abortion, and in Denmark on whether to accept the Maastricht Treaty.

Reichstag Fire (1933) The burning of the German Reichstag (parliament building) in Berlin for which a Dutchman, Marinus van der Lubbe, was found guilty of arson and executed. The fire occurred a month after Adolf **Hitler** became Chancellor and he put the blame for it on the Communists – 3 of whom, Dmitrov, Popov and Tanev, all Bulgarians, were tried with van der Lubbe but acquitted. Nevertheless, Hitler took advantage of the incident to give himself and the Nazi government totalitarian powers, including suspension of basic constitutional freedoms, extension of treason to cover any opposition to the regime, and an increased level of penalties for many offences. These measures were soon followed by the abolition of the rule of law and the introduction of a permanent state of emergency.

Reparations The compensation taken as an indemnity from a defeated nation by the victors in war, especially

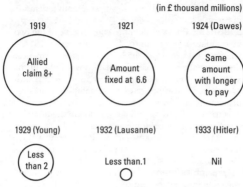

(in £ thousand millions)

1919	1921	1924 (Dawes)
Allied claim 8+	Amount fixed at 6.6	Same amount with longer to pay

1929 (Young)	1932 (Lausanne)	1933 (Hitler)
Less than 2	Less than .1	Nil

Reparations *German reparations 1919–33.*

that taken from Germany and its allies after both World Wars. In 1921 Germany's WWI reparations bill was fixed at £6,600,000,000. Very little of this was paid, and what was paid was mostly covered by American loans. Hitler denounced reparations and refused to pay any more as soon as he came to power. After WWII reparations were mostly in the form of equipment and rolling stock removed from East Germany and taken to the USSR.

Republic A country in which the head of state is an elected or nominated president, not a monarch, and in which the people or their elected representatives possess supreme power. Examples include France, Italy and the

USA. The USSR and Yugoslavia were both federations of republics.

Republican Party The more conservative of the two main political parties in the USA. Founded in 1854, its strength is drawn from the higher-income, business and professional classes based in small towns and suburbs across the country, and the rural areas of the NE and Middle West. It supports economic imperialism, protectionism in trade, private enterprise, lower government spending and a reduction in the powers and responsibilities of central government. Internationally it once favoured isolationist policies but after WWII it followed the principle of **collective security** to combat Communist expansionism.

Resistance Movements Underground organisations engaging in sabotage and secret operations against collaborators and enemy occupying forces, especially in France, Norway, etc. during WWII. *See also* **partisan**; **Maquis**.

Revisionism The shift away from the strict ideals of Communism in order to adapt to a current situation. Lenin could be regarded as the first revisionist for introducing the **New Economic Policy**. Hardline communists called anyone a revisionist who in any way differed from the party line; Stalin regarded **Tito** as a revisionist; Mao persecuted revisionists in the **Cultural Revolution**, and revisionism was the main accusation by Mao against **Krushchev**.

Revolution 1. A far-reaching political change, especially the overthrow of a government, ruler or system, and the substitution of another by the governed.

2. A violent change from one system of production in a society to another, as from feudalism to capitalism, and from capitalism to Communism. Such change is to be expected, according to **Marxist** theory.

Rhineland The area of Germany on both banks of the Rhine bordering France and the Low Countries. After WWI the Treaty of **Versailles** provided for the demilitarisation of the region and its occupation for 15 years by Allied troops. The Treaties of **Locarno** agreed to continue the demilitarisation of the Rhineland but the British and French occupation forces were withdrawn (1926 and 1930 respectively).

Germany occupied the Rhineland in 1936, breaking the terms of the treaties, declaring that it was required as a fortified security zone against possible French aggression. The British and French response was weak because of their policy of **appeasement** towards Germany and the diplomatic crisis caused by Italian aggression against Abyssinia.

Rhodesia *see* **Zimbabwe**.

Rhodesia and Nyasaland, Federation of The union between 1953 and 1963 of Northern and Southern Rhodesia (now Zambia and Zimbabwe) and Nyasaland (now Malawi), supported by Sir Godfrey **Huggins** and Sir Roy **Welensky**. They considered that the copperbelt industries of Northern Rhodesia, the more advanced economy of Southern Rhodesia and the agriculture of Nyasaland would benefit from political union. The union failed largely because African nationalists saw it as hindering moves towards independence, and because right-wing whites in

Southern Rhodesia objected to the Federation's policies of improving the status of black Africans.

Ribbentrop, Joachim von (1893–1946) A German Nazi politician. Ribbentrop was ambassador to the UK (1936–8) and was Foreign Minister from 1938 to 1945. He negotiated the **Anglo-German Naval Agreement**, the **Nazi-Soviet Pact**, and the Tripartite Pact (1940) which allied Germany, Italy and Japan. He was executed as a war criminal.

Romania A republic of SE Europe. Area: 237,500 sq km. Pop: 22,680,000. Language: Romanian. Religion: Christianity (Romanian Orthodox, RC, Calvinist and Lutheran). Cap: Bucharest.

Until the end of WWII Romania was a kingdom, ruled in turn by Carol I, Ferdinand, Carol II and Michael. It was involved in the **Balkan Wars** and during WWI fought on the Allied side, more than doubling its territory postwar as a result, even though it was almost completely overrun by German forces in 1916.

Between the World Wars political corruption was widespread and anti-Semitic in character, under the influence of a fascist organisation called the Iron Guard, led by Ion **Antonescu**. During WWII Romania joined the Axis powers and took part in the invasion of the USSR. After being forced to retreat during the Soviet counteroffensive the Romanians made peace with the Allies and declared war on Germany.

Because it had changed sides, Romania received favourable treatment when the peace treaties were agreed, but it soon fell under Soviet influence. King Michael was forced to abdicate in 1947 and a People's

Republic was declared, dominated by the Communist-inspired Democratic Front. The state was declared a socialist republic in 1965 but later followed an independent course under the leadership of Gheorge Gheorghu-Dej (1901–1965) and Nicolae Ceausescu (1918–89), at the same time remaining a member of the **Council for Mutual Economic Assistance** and the **Warsaw Pact**. Ceausescu was overthrown and executed in December 1989.

In 1990 the former Communist Ion Iliescu became president and the National Salvation Front formed a government. Iliescu was defeated in 1996 by Emil Constantinescu of the Democratic Convention. Under both administrations privatisation proceeded slowly, the transition to a market economy was difficult, and strikes and unrest by miners and others were frequent.

Rome, Treaties of (1957) The agreements setting up the **European Economic Community** and the **European Atomic Energy Community**, effective from 1958. They were signed by Belgium, France, West Germany, Italy, Luxembourg and the Netherlands. The treaties aimed to establish a closer and lasting union between European peoples; **free trade** between the members and common external tariffs for all goods; common policies for agriculture, transport, labour mobility and important sectors of the economy; and common institutions for economic development. Overseas territories and possessions of member states were to be associated with the new community. The essential aim was to improve the life and work of the peoples of the member countries.

Roosevelt, Franklin Delano (1882–1945) A US politician and Democratic president from 1933 to 1945. He was elected president four times, a unique achievement made possible only by the special circumstances of WWII. Disabled by poliomyelitis in the early 1920s, he was nevertheless elected governor of New York (1928–32) before defeating President Herbert **Hoover**.

The USA was in the grip of the **Depression** when Roosevelt took office, and his **New Deal** programme was intended to tackle the crisis. However, the progress of the programme was slowed down by the Supreme Court which ruled against some of the New Deal legislation, and when Roosevelt attempted to reorganise the court to secure sympathetic judges, he met with fierce and successful opposition.

In foreign affairs Roosevelt struggled to overcome his country's traditional **isolationism**, and although the USA was neutral until the end of 1941, he supported the European Allies during the early period of WWII with such measures as the **Lend-Lease Act** and the **Atlantic Charter**. After the US entry into WWII he attended the **Casablanca**, **Quebec**, **Cairo**, **Tehran** and **Yalta Conferences**. He has been criticised for his distrust of the French leader Charles **de Gaulle**, his readiness to give in to the USSR's Joseph **Stalin**, his exaggerated idea of **Chiang Kai-Shek**'s authority over China, and his failure to press on in the US drive across Europe to occupy Berlin, Prague and Vienna before the Soviet forces. He was a strong supporter of the idea of the UN and died three weeks before it was founded.

Roosevelt, Theodore (1858–1919) A US politician
and Republican president from 1901 to 1909. He
became vice-president to William McKinley (1901),
becoming president after McKinley's assassination. He
sought to increase US influence abroad and develop
industry and commerce at home. He insisted on a
strong navy, restrictions on monopolies and trusts, and
the ending of corruption in the civil service. In foreign
affairs he helped bring about peace in the **Russo-
Japanese War**, for which he received the Nobel Prize.

After three years away from politics, he failed to win
the 1912 Republican presidential nomination from
William H **Taft**, whom he then opposed in the election,
standing as an Independent Progressive. His
intervention allowed Woodrow **Wilson**, the Democratic
candidate, to win, and caused the withdrawal of
Roosevelt's followers from the Republican Party, which
took several years to recover from the split. Roosevelt
disapproved of US neutrality in the early years of WWI,
strongly opposing Wilson's isolationist policy.

Roumania *see* **Romania**.

Rowntree, Seebohm (1871–1954) A Quaker and
chocolate manufacturer in York, England. Like his
father and grandfather, Rowntree was concerned for the
welfare of his employees and for the sufferings of the
working classes in general. His surveys of poverty in
York (1897–8 and 1936) made him nationally famous;
and his work was widely quoted at the time and remains
an important contemporary source for historians. Those
who expected his 1936 survey to show a big
improvement in the living standards of the poor were

shocked to find that after nearly forty years of the 20th century, poverty was almost as widespread in 1936 as it had been in the 1890s.

Ruhr The chief manufacturing and mining area of NW Germany. It was occupied by France from 1923 to 1925 because Germany had not made **reparations** payments. During WWII the region suffered severely from Allied bombing raids.

Rumania *see* **Romania**.

Russia (now **Russian Federation**) Area 16,838,855 sq km. Pop: 149,469,000 (1992). Language: Russian in Europe, various in Asia. Religion: Christianity (Russian Orthodox) and mostly atheist/ agnostic in Europe, Muslim and minority religions in Asia. Capital: Moscow.

See also **Union of Soviet Socialist Republics**.

By the beginning of the 20th century, the Russian Empire, ruled by the autocratic Tsar Nicholas II, was becoming an industrialised nation but its inhabitants were not allowed political freedom. There was no form of parliament until the establishment of the **Duma** in 1905. The Tsar failed to carry out political reform beyond this, and did little either to deal with the terrible poverty resulting from poor harvests and industrial unrest, or to rebuild the country's confidence after the humiliating defeat of the **Russo-Japanese War**. Widespread dissatisfaction with his rule led to the **Russian Revolutions**, the first of which was suppressed in 1905.

Russia's alliance with **Serbia** took it into WWI following the assassination of Archduke Franz

Ferdinand in **Sarajevo** (1914), and it was immediately joined by France and Britain (*see* **Triple Entente** *and* **Anglo-Russian Entente**). Military defeat and worsening conditions at home led to the revolutions of 1917. After the February Revolution the Tsar abdicated, and following the Bolshevik October Revolution led by **Lenin**, the Communists came to power, making peace with Germany at **Brest-Litovsk**. Civil war broke out, but by 1920 the Communist forces under Leon **Trotsky** were victorious and in 1922 Russia and the republics under its control became the **Union of Soviet Socialist Republics**. Russia dominated the USSR, and Russia's history from 1922 to 1991 is that of the USSR.

In the autumn of 1991 the USSR collapsed. Russia now became the dominant state in the new **Commonwealth of Independent States** under the leadership of Boris **Yeltsin**. In 1993 ex-Communist members occupied Russia's parliament in an attempted anti-Yeltsin coup, but were removed by the army. A new constitution in 1993 established a mixed presidential-parliamentary system, but economic reform in the country was slow. Russia took military action against separatists in Chechnya in 1994, devastating the Chechen capital Grozny, and again (after a series of terrorist bombs in Moscow) in 1999. The Communist Party continued to win significant electoral support until the emergence in 1999 of a new grouping around Vladimir **Putin**, who became acting president when Yeltsin resigned at the end of 1999.

Russian Revolutions (1905 and 1917) Internal upheavals which radically changed the political system

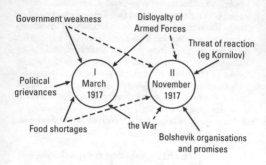

Russian Revolutions *The revolutions of 1917.*

of Russia, ultimately replacing the autocratic monarchy of the tsars with a Communist dictatorship.

The *1905 Revolution* started when a peaceful workers' demonstration was fired on while petitioning the tsar, Nicholas II, resulting in widespread demonstrations and strikes throughout the country. These developed into a general strike, peasant uprisings and a terrorist campaign by socialist revolutionaries. Unable to control the situation, the government permitted limited trade-union activity together with freedom of the press and of speech. These concessions, combined with the ending of the **Russo-Japanese War** which freed troops to crush the revolution, brought the violence to an end. The revolution did, however, lead to land reforms and a period of semi-constitutional government.

The *February 1917 Revolution* (in March by the modern calendar) arose from the military disasters of WWI, which had undermined the authority of the monarchy. Widespread opposition to the war was made worse by the bitter winter and the breakdown of the transport system, which resulted in soaring food prices and severe fuel shortages. Strikes and bread riots broke out and the populace of Petrograd (later Leningrad, now St Petersburg) crossed the frozen River Neva and advanced on the government buildings in the fashionable quarter. The police called on the army for assistance but the troops, in sympathy with the workers, mutinied and soon took control of the city.

Similar unrest occurred in other parts of the country and reached such a peak that the **Duma** elected a provisional government which forced the tsar's abdication, but continued the war. Meanwhile, the Petrograd socialists set up a **soviet** which challenged the authority of the provisional government.

The *October 1917 Revolution* (in November by the modern calendar) arose from continued opposition to WWI and the determination of **Lenin** and the Bolsheviks to seize power (*see* **Bolshevism**). Lenin had little difficulty in winning over the mass of the people, already short of food and facing another severe winter. His promises of peace, land and bread met with popular support, and his well-organised revolutionaries overthrew the provisional government in Petrograd and quickly established Bolshevik authority. Private trading was abolished, factories were handed over to workers' control, property of counter-revolutionaries and the church was confiscated, a cease-fire was arranged with Germany, and Bolshevik administrations established in all the principal cities, with a Council of People's Commissars as the country's executive authority. However, counter-revolutionary ('White') forces continued to fight the Bolsheviks, and the resulting civil war lasted until the Bolshevik victory in 1920. In 1922 the **Union of Soviet Socialist Republics** was established.

Russo-Japanese War (1904–05) A conflict caused by attempts by both countries to gain control of **Manchuria** for purposes of economic and territorial expansion.

Hostilities were started by a Japanese naval attack on the Russian Pacific Fleet at Port Arthur without a declaration of war, and ended by the overwhelming victory of the Japanese over the Russian Baltic Fleet in a naval battle in the Straits of Tsushima. On land the Russians also suffered considerable losses before managing, in Manchuria and along the Yalu river, to check the Japanese advance.

The war was brought to an end by the Treaty of Portsmouth (1905), with US president Theodore Roosevelt acting as mediator. Russia lost the South Manchurian Railway, S Sakhalin, the Liaodong Peninsula and considerable prestige at home and abroad. The war helped to create conditions that led to the **Russian Revolution** of 1905.

Rwanda A republic in E Africa. Area: 26,388 sq km. Pop: 7,347,000 (1992). Languages: French (official). Religion: Christian (RC). Cap: Kigali

Ethnic conflict between the Tutsi aristocracy and Hutu majority dominated Rwanda from independence (1962). In 1994–7 some 700,000 people were killed in massacre, civil war and a refugee crisis.

S

SA (Sturmabteilung) A German organisation founded in 1921, and also known as the *Brown Shirts*, Storm Division or Storm Troopers. It was a paramilitary organisation, using intimidation against the opponents of the Nazi Party. Under Ernst Röhm's leadership (1931–4) it came more and more into conflict with the **SS** and the army, until Hitler decided to put an end to its activities and have it absorbed by the SS. He did this by killing Röhm and the rest of the SA leadership in what came to be known as the *Night of the Long Knives* (1934). *See also* **National Socialism**.

Saarland An area of Germany bordering France and Luxembourg with important mining and iron and steel industries. It was placed under the control of the League of Nations in 1919, France being granted permission to exploit the coalmines for 15 years as part of its **reparations** claim against Germany. The Saarland was returned to Germany in 1935, after a plebiscite (**referendum**). After WWII it was under French occupation until restored to West Germany in 1957.

Sadat, Anwar El (1918–81) An Egyptian politician. He succeeded **Nasser** as president in 1970, and continued Egypt's confrontation with Israel, leading to the 1973 **Arab-Israeli War**. After Egypt's failure to overcome the Israelis, Sadat began a policy of improved relations with the West and ended the country's military dependence on the USSR. The Suez Canal, blocked during the war, was reopened in 1975, and then Sadat, in a bold initiative, went to Jerusalem in 1977 for talks with Israeli ministers and to address the Knesset (parliament). This remarkably courageous act led to the **Camp David Agreement** and a peace treaty with Israel (1979), which restored to Egypt some territory previously occupied by Israel. He was awarded the 1978 Nobel Peace Prize jointly with Israeli PM Menachem **Begin**. However, Sadat was bitterly attacked by radical Arab states and the PLO. He was assassinated in 1981.

Saint Germain, Treaty of (1919) The WWI peace settlement between the Allies and Austria. It limited the Austrian Army to 30,000 men, forbade Austria to unite with Germany and provided for the payment of reparations. Austria's territorial and population losses were enormous: Bohemia and Moravia were transferred to Czechoslovakia; the Trentino and South Tyrol to Italy; Galicia to Poland; Bukovina to Romania; and Bosnia-Herzegovina, Dalmatia and Slovenia to Yugoslavia.

Salazar, Antonio de Oliveira (1889–1970) A Portuguese dictator, PM from 1932 to 1968. Although fascist in character, his government carried out many reforms, including improvements in education, industrial development, living conditions and public works. However, independence movements in the Portuguese colonies and political opposition at home were suppressed, the only permitted party being Salazar's own, the Portuguese National Union.

SALT see **Strategic Arms Limitation Talks**.

Sanctions The actions (usually in the form of trade bans) taken by one or more states against another guilty of breaking international law. As sanctions can be difficult to enforce, they have often proved ineffective, notably when imposed by the League of Nations on Italy after it invaded **Ethiopia** in 1935, and by the UN on Rhodesia to oppose its policy of unilateral independence and white-minority rule (1966–80) (*see* **Zimbabwe**).

Sandinistas *see* **Nicaragua**.

Sarajevo The capital of **Bosnia-Herzegovina**. Sarajevo was the place where in 1914 Archduke Franz Ferdinand (1863–1914), heir to the **Austro-Hungarian Empire**, and his wife were assassinated. The assassin was a Bosnian Serb student, Gavrilo Princip (1894–1918), a member of the Young Bosnia secret nationalist movement committed to the liberation of the province from the Empire. His weapon was supplied by the Black Hand, a secret terrorist organisation based in Serbia that aimed to unite the ethnic Serbs of the Austro-Hungarian and Ottoman empires with independent Serbia.

Austria-Hungary immediately sent an ultimatum to Serbia. Although most of its terms were accepted, Austria-Hungary was not willing to negotiate the remainder and declared war, backed by its alliance with Germany. As Russia supported Serbia it was only a matter of days before the remaining European powers were involved (through their various interlinking alliances) and WWI began.

After Bosnia-Herzegovina broke away from **Yugoslavia** in 1992 there was bitter fighting between Muslims and Bosnian Serbs (aided by the Serbian army) in and around Sarajevo.

Satellite State A country economically, militarily and politically controlled or dominated by another more powerful state. The Warsaw Pact countries were regarded as satellite states of the USSR.

Saturation Bombing A heavy and sustained air attack with the object of destroying the target in a single decisive operation; it was frequently practised during WWII by the Luftwaffe, RAF and USAAF.

Scapa Flow A large natural anchorage in Orkney, used as a British naval base in both World Wars. A large part of the German fleet was interned there at the end of WWI and scuttled in 1919 on the orders of Admiral Ludwig von Reuter. During WWII the battleship HMS *Royal Oak* was torpedoed and sunk there by a German U boat (1939). The base was closed in 1956.

Schlieffen Plan (1905) A detailed scheme prepared by General Count Alfred von Schlieffen (1833–1913) who was German Chief of General Staff 1891–1905. It was intended to ensure a German victory over a Franco-Russian alliance by holding up any Russian advance westwards with minimal strength while speedily defeating France by a massive flanking movement through the Low Countries, then southwards to cut off Paris from the sea.

At the outbreak of WWI, Helmuth von Moltke, Schlieffen's successor as Chief of General Staff (1906–14), put into effect a modified form of the plan which nearly succeeded. It was defeated by an Allied counter-offensive on the Marne in 1914, poor liaison between the German HQ and the field commanders, the withdrawal of forces to stem the rapid Russian drive through E Prussia, unexpected Belgian resistance and the French commander Joseph Joffre's skilled and nerveless transfer of substantial reserves from Alsace while his armies were in full retreat.

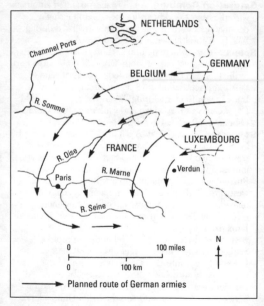

Schlieffen Plan

Schmidt, Helmut (1918–) A West German Social
Democratic politician. Schmidt was Federal Defence
Minister from 1969 to 1972, Finance Minister from
1972 to 1974 and Chancellor from 1974 to 1982. He
followed the policy of **Ostpolitik** begun by his
predecessor, Willi **Brandt**, together with full
commitment to the EC and NATO. He was succeeded
by the Christian Democrat Helmut **Kohl**.

Schröder, Gerhard (1944–) A German Social
Democrat politician. Schröder led his party to victory
over Helmut **Kohl**'s government in the 1998 election,
becoming Chancellor. He has pursued moderate 'Third
Way' socialism attuned to the policies of Tony **Blair** in
the UK and Bill **Clinton** in the USA.

Schuman Plan (1950) A proposal put forward by the
French Foreign Minister, Robert Schuman (1886–1963),
for pooling the coal and steel resources of Western
Europe. It was put into effect when the **European Coal
and Steel Community** was established.

Schuschnigg, Kurt von (1897–1977) An Austrian
Christian Socialist who was Chancellor from 1934 to
1938. He followed a middle-of-the-road policy based on
reliance on Italy against German threats of **Anschluss**.
Italian support ceased with the signing of the Rome-
Berlin **Axis**, and Schuschnigg, from a much weakened
position, vainly tried to appease Germany. This isolated
Austria diplomatically and led to Nazi sympathisers
joining his government. Hitler then delivered an
ultimatum (1938) instructing Schuschnigg to form a
Nazi-dominated government; when Schuschnigg
proposed to let the people give their opinion in a

plebiscite (**referendum**), Hitler put pressure on him to resign in favour of Artur von **Seyss-Inquart**. Schuschnigg was imprisoned by the Nazis until the end of WWII.

SDI *see* **Strategic Defence Initiative**.

SDLP *see* **Social Democratic and Labour Party**.

SDP *see* **Social Democratic Party**.

SEATO *see* **Southeast Asia Treaty Organisation**.

Second World War *see* **World War II**.

Secretary of State The minister in charge of a senior government department in the UK. In the US he or she is the minister in charge of foreign affairs.

Self-determination The right of a nation or territory to decide the form of government or political status it wants.

Senate *see* **Congress**.

Separation of Powers The constitutional principle (effective in most democracies) that the three branches of government – **legislature**, **executive** and **judiciary** – should be independent of each other. This principle does not apply in the UK, but in the US it is clearly laid down in the Constitution.

Serbia The largest republic of the Yugoslav Federation. Area: 87,879 sq. km. Pop: 9,660,000 (1986). Language: Serbo-Croat. Religion: Christianity (Greek Orthodox). Capital: Belgrade.

Previously part of the **Ottoman Empire**, Serbia became an independent state in 1878, and a kingdom in 1882. After WWI it became one of the federal units of **Yugoslavia**. Serbia was involved in both **Balkan Wars**, and Serbian desire to 'liberate' Serbs still under Austro-

Hungarian rule led to the confrontation (*see* **Sarajevo**) that brought about WWI, in which Serbia fought on the Allied side. The independence of Slovenia, Croatia and Bosnia in 1991 and 1992 left Serbia and Montenegro as the only states in the Yugoslav Federation. Serbian politics were dominated throughout the 1990s by the former Communist Slobodan Milosevic, President of Yugoslavia from 1987, with increasingly disastrous consequences. From 1992 to 1995 Serbia supported the Bosnian Serbs in the bloody war in Bosnia, resulting in UN sanctions against the country. In 1999, brutal attempts to suppress Albanian separatists in Kosovo led to concerted NATO air attacks on Serbia itself, causing devastation to infrastructure and economy alike.

Sèvres, Treaty of (1920) One of the post-WWI settlements following the Paris Peace Conference. Turkey was to give Greece extensive rights on the W side of the **Dardanelles**, and to give most of European Turkey and most of the Aegean Islands to Greece. The Straits connecting the Aegean and Black Seas were to be demilitarised and internationalised under a ten-power League of Nations commission, and to be opened to merchant vessels and warships of all nations in times of peace and war. Armenia was granted independence, Kurdistan was allowed **autonomy**, and the Arabian peninsula achieved independence as the Kingdom of Hejaz. Mesopotamia and Palestine were to become **mandates** of Britain, and Syria a mandate of France. Turkish finances were placed under British, French and Italian supervision.

These arrangements were rejected by the Turkish republican movement and led to the **Chanak Crisis**, the rebellions against the Sultan by Mustapha Kemal (**Atatürk**), and the downfall of David Lloyd George's coalition government in the UK. The settlement was later revised by the Treaty of **Lausanne**.

Seyss-Inquart, Artur von (1892–1946) An Austrian politician. Seyss-Inquart hoped that he would be appointed Chancellor after the **Anschluss**, and he used his friendship with Chancellor Kurt von **Schuschnigg** to keep Hitler informed of the Chancellor's every move to retain the country's independence. In support of Hitler, he used his influence as a Counsellor of State (1937) to encourage public disorder by Nazi extremists. Hitler pressured **Schuschnigg** into making Seyss-Inquart Chancellor in 1938, an office he only held for two days but which gave him time to invite Germany to occupy the country to suppress the disorders. After the Anschluss he was appointed Governor of Austria. During WWII he was appointed Commissioner for the Netherlands (1940) where he ruthlessly recruited slave labour and ordered the deportation of Jews to concentration camps. After WWII he was tried for war crimes and executed.

Shah *see* **Pahlavi**.

Sharpeville A South African town in the Transvaal where a massive demonstration took place in 1960 against the Pass Laws which required identity cards to be carried by all non-whites as part of the country's **apartheid** policy. The demonstration was organised by the Pan-African Congress. Police opened fire with automatic weapons and 67 blacks were killed and 186 wounded. This caused worldwide condemnation and was one reason why South Africa withdrew from the Commonwealth to become an independent republic in 1961, rather than risk being expelled.

Shastri, Lal Bahadur (1904–66) An Indian Congress Party politician, PM from 1964 to 1966. Shastri was responsible for the introduction of laws against caste and separatism, and against language and religious discrimination and he refused to commit the country to the development of nuclear weapons.

After the outbreak of hostilities between India and Pakistan over **Kashmir** in 1965, Shastri attended the **Tashkent Conference** (1966). Agreement was reached on a truce but at the end of the conference Shastri died of a heart attack.

Shevardnadze, Eduard (1928–) A Soviet and Georgian statesman. As Foreign Minister under Mikhail **Gorbachev** he was involved in the thawing of East-West relations. After the break-up of the Soviet Union he became interim president of Georgia in 1992 and was formally elected in 1995. He survived assassination attempts in 1995 and 1998.

Show Trials *see* **purge.**

Siegfried Line A series of German fortifications built during the 1930s from N of the Ruhr, up the Rhine to the Swiss frontier, named after the mythical German hero. It seriously delayed the Allied advance into Germany from the W in 1944. *See map at* **Maginot Line** *(p. 211).*

Sikhs A community of about eight million people living mostly in the Punjab, N India. Their religion opposes intolerance and is based on the teaching of their great guru (teacher) Nanak and on the customs and organisation of Guru Govind Singh. They accept the truths of other religions and have no caste distinctions, but do have special rites and customs. Their most important temple, the Golden Temple at Amritsar, was attacked by Indian troops in 1984 in an effort to suppress Sikh demands for a separate state within India.

Sinai A peninsula of NE Egypt at the N end of the Red Sea between the Gulfs of Aqaba and Suez. In 1955–6 Egyptian and Israeli ill-feeling intensified because of a series of terrorist raids launched across the frontier into Israel and the closure of the Strait of Tiran by Egypt, effectively preventing access to the Israeli port of Eilat at the head of the Gulf of Aqaba. These actions helped to bring about the 1956 **Arab-Israeli War** in which Israel seized a large part of the peninsula, including the area around Sharm el-Sheikh, the base at the S end of the peninsula from which the strait had been closed. Israel withdrew after a UN force was stationed at Sharm el-Sheikh with the duty of keeping open the strait.

A similar operation occurred when **Nasser** obtained the withdrawal of the UN force and again closed the strait, leading to the 1967 **Arab-Israeli War** in which Israel seized the whole of Sinai. Following the **Camp David Agreement** (1978), Israel returned Sinai to Egypt in stages, completing its withdrawal in 1982.

Sinn Féin (*Gaelic* – we ourselves or ourselves alone) An Irish political party founded at the beginning of the century by Arthur Griffith (1872–1922), which became closely associated with the republican forces fighting for

Irish independence in the first two decades of the 20th century (*see* **Ireland**). Eamon **de Valera** became leader in 1922, and led the hardline republican faction (*see* **Irish Republican Army**) which opposed both the acceptance by Griffith's group of the formation of the Irish Free State with dominion status in the Commonwealth, and the separation of Northern Ireland from the rest of Ireland. Sinn Féin won an overwhelming victory in the 1918 general election but its MPs refused to take their seats at Westminster, setting up instead their own alternative parliament (Dáil) in Dublin. The two major political parties in the Republic of Ireland, de Valera's **Fianna Fáil** and **Fine Gael**, arose out of this split in Sinn Féin.

Sinn Féin remains closely linked to the IRA, and is now active almost entirely in Northern Ireland. It has been involved since 1997 in the attempt to find a political solution to conflict in the province (*see* **Ireland**, **Anglo-Irish Agreement**, **Irish Republican Army**).

Sino-Japanese War (1937–45) The conflict that developed from Japan's seizure of Mukden in 1931 and its annexation of **Manchuria** in 1932. In 1935 the Japanese began a further advance into N China and full-scale war developed. Japanese progress was rapid, Shanghai, Nanjing, Guangzhou (Canton) and Hankou all being captured in quick succession. Eventually Japan's entry into WWII took the conflict with the Chinese into a wider sphere. There were over two million Japanese troops fighting in China, which became a valued friend of the Allies in the fight against the **Axis** powers, with the UK and the US transporting supplies for the Nationalists along the Burma Road to the wartime capital of Chongquing.

Sino-Soviet Split A major political division that developed between Communist China and the USSR from 1956. When Nikita **Khrushchev** denounced Stalin at the 20th Soviet Communist Party Congress, China complained that it and other Communist states should have been consulted beforehand. From this there developed conflicts over domestic, foreign and defence policies, economic relationships, and ideological differences.

The Soviet Union opposed China's **Great Leap Forward**, the revival of its campaign against Taiwan and its frontier problems with India. China was alarmed by the Soviet efforts at **détente** with the USA and annoyed that technical information on atomic weapons was denied to China in 1959. There were frontier clashes along the Amur and Ussuri rivers, and at international Communist Party conferences angry words were exchanged, with criticism of each other's policies.

World Communism was split, all European national parties except that of Albania taking the Soviet side (Yugoslavia remained neutral), and all Asian parties except those of India and Mongolia (and later Vietnam) siding with China. The **Cultural Revolution** led to further bitterness, and diplomatic relations were broken (1967–70). The 1980s saw a shift by both countries towards a compromise on many of the points in dispute.

Six-Day War *see* **Arab-Israeli Wars**.

Slump *see* **depression**.

Smith, Ian (1919–) A Rhodesian politician. With the

break-up of the **Federation of Rhodesia and Nyasaland**, Smith became a founder of the Rhodesia Front Party in 1962 and PM from 1964 to 1978. Determined to secure immediate independence without African majority rule in Southern Rhodesia, his government made a unilateral declaration of independence (UDI) in 1965 in defiance of the UK decision to delay independence until there was black majority rule. *See* **Zimbabwe**.

Smuts, Jan (1870–1950) A South African soldier and politician. Smuts was an Afrikaner (Boer) general in the Boer War, entered the House of Assembly (1907), and held several ministerial offices while helping towards reconciliation with Britain. That this was achieved by 1914 was largely due to his efforts, and it ensured that South Africa joined the UK against Germany in WWI.

Smuts was a member of the Imperial War Cabinet (1917–18), and PM of South Africa from 1919 to 1924 and 1939 to 1948. He was Deputy PM (1933–9) in James **Hertzog**'s coalition government of the National Party and his own United Party. He was made a field marshal in 1941, became a close adviser of Churchill and other Allied leaders during WWII, attended the **Cairo Conference** and was treated as an elder statesman. In South Africa, however, Smuts was regarded as a traitor by Afrikaans Nationalists for his pro-British attitude, and was disliked by the left and opponents of segregation because of his active support of white supremacy.

Social Democracy The beliefs, practices, principles or programme of social democrats or a social democratic party, based on the changing of capitalism into socialism by gradual reform within a parliamentary system. In Britain social democrats are near the political centre and temper capitalism with mildly socialist policies. In most other countries they are somewhat further to the left.

Social Democratic and Labour Party (SDLP)
A Northern Ireland political party founded in 1970. The policies are centre-left and moderate nationalist. It has campaigned for a just distribution of wealth, civil rights, understanding and reconciliation between the Republic of Ireland and Northern Ireland, and the eventual unification of Ireland with the consent of the majority of the people.

Social Democratic Party (SDP) A British political party of the centre. It was founded in 1981 by four former Labour ministers (sometimes called the *Gang of Four*): Roy Jenkins (leader 1981–3), David Owen (leader 1983–7), Shirley Williams and William Rodgers. In the same year it joined the Liberal Party in a political alliance, fighting the 1983 and 1987 elections on this basis. In 1987 the party voted to negotiate a merger with the Liberal Party. David Owen and a breakaway group tried to keep an independent SDP in existence, but in 1991 it was disbanded for lack of support.

Socialism 1. An economic and political theory proposing state control over the means of production, distribution and exchange. Its aims include equality of wealth, the absence of competitive economic activity, production for use rather than profit and government determination of the level of investment, prices and production norms.

2. A transitional period, in **Marxist** theory, in society 's development from capitalism to **Communism**. There are many kinds of socialist, varying from those democratic socialists who would wish to see capitalism restrained by some socialist ideas, but not overturned, to the extreme Communists who would get rid of all traces of capitalism.

Solidarity An independent Polish trade union founded in 1980. Led by Lech **Walesa** (1943–), Solidarity received widespread popular support for its demands for wage increases and political freedom. It was banned following the imposition of martial law in 1981, but continued its activities underground. Walesa was awarded the 1983 Nobel Peace Prize. In 1989 Solidarity was made legal and given a share in the government, but its influence had waned by the late 1990s.

Somme, Battle of the (1916) A 20-week engagement of WWI fought along a 32-km front N of the River Somme in N France. Well over a million soldiers died, and the Allied territorial gain was a mere 16 km. It had been assumed that the mass New Armies recruited in Britain since 1915 would at last break the German defences; a secondary objective was to relieve pressure on the French at **Verdun**. Despite its huge casualties and lack of obvious success, the battle is now thought to have fatally weakened the German Army, even though the War lasted a further two years. The Somme is considered by some historians to have been the turning point of the war in France.

South Africa A republic of S Africa. Area: 1,140,519 sq km. Pop: 42,327,458. Languages: Afrikaans and English (the official languages), and a number of

African languages. Religion: Christianity (chiefly Protestant). Cap: Pretoria.

Following the Boer War, the Union of South Africa was formed in 1910 from the former British and Dutch colonies of the Cape of Good Hope, Natal, the Orange Free State and the Transvaal. It remained a Commonwealth member until 1961.

Although South African forces fought loyally on the Allied side in both World Wars there was an underlying Afrikaner nationalist sentiment which openly appeared in WWII when leading National Party members declared themselves to have Fascist sympathies.

When the National Party gained power in 1948, elected by the small white minority, these sympathies were put into practice. A strict system of racial segregation (*see* **apartheid**) was enforced, which cut off the country from most of the rest of the world in cultural, political and sporting activities, although not economically. World disapproval had little effect on South Africa, conscious of its strategic importance to the West, which was demonstrated when the Suez Canal was closed during the **Arab-Israeli Wars** and tankers had to transport oil via the Cape of Good Hope. In the 1960s the illegal **African National Congress** (ANC) started to launch sabotage attacks on industrial targets from within the country and from neighbouring black African states. However, some of these states relied on the South African transport system for their exports and imports and dared not permit the ANC to become too militant for fear of reprisals; South African forces frequently crossed frontiers to destroy ANC bases.

After the 1976 riots in the black township of **Soweto** there was an increase in violent unrest among the black and coloured population. This, combined with increasing international pressure, brought about some limited reforms of apartheid, including the granting in 1984 of a degree of parliamentary representation for coloureds. In 1990 the ban on the ANC was lifted and its leader Nelson **Mandela** was released from prison.

In 1991 President F W de Klerk repealed the remaining apartheid laws, and international sanctions began to be lifted. A new constitution in 1992 provided for all-race majority rule, and the ANC won a landslide election victory in 1994. Mandela became president of South Africa in 1994, to international acclaim for his long struggle against racism. He was succeeded as president in 1999 by Thabo M'Beki, his deputy as ANC leader.

Southeast Asia Treaty Organisation (SEATO) A defensive alliance established in 1954 in Manila by Australia, France, New Zealand, Pakistan, the Philippines, Thailand, the UK and the USA. Pakistan withdrew in 1973, followed by France in 1974; the remaining members then disbanded the organisation because of changing circumstances in the region.

Southern Rhodesia *see* **Zimbabwe**; and **Rhodesia and Nyasaland, Federation of**.

Sovereignty 1. The absolute unlimited political power of a state.

2. The source of political power.

Soviet An elected administrative or governmental council in the USSR at either local, regional or national level. The highest was the Supreme Soviet.

Soviet Security Service An organisation which included the secret police. It had several bewildering name changes since it was established by the Bolshevik government. Known as the Cheka from 1917 to 1922, it was reorganised as the GPU (1922–3). It was the OGPU (1923–34) and the NKVD (1934–41). The NKVD was split from 1941 to 1946 into the NKVD and NKGB, and these were renamed MVD and MGB (1946–54). The MGB became the KGB in 1954.

The heads of all these organisations have been responsible for **purges** (most notoriously in the 1930s), political trials, banishment to forced labour camps, executions, censorship, investigations and searches. The **Gulag** (that part of the Security Service which administered corrective labour camps) used forced labour for such activities as forestry, mining and canal, railway and road construction. Much more has been learnt about the activities of these secret organisations since the collapse of the USSR in 1991.

Soweto A black township in the Transvaal, South Africa, where rioting occurred in 1976 after it had been announced that Afrikaans would be the compulsory language of instruction in schools. The trouble lasted three days and a further three days elsewhere in the Transvaal, 236 blacks being killed and over 1,100 wounded when the police opened fire. The proposed compulsory teaching in Afrikaans was abandoned a few weeks later.

Spain A kingdom of SW Europe. Area: 504,879 sq km. Pop: 39,623,000 (1990). Language: Spanish. Religion: Christianity (RC). Cap: Madrid.

Until 1931 Spain was a kingdom, in which political conflict often led to violence. The last monarch of this early period of the century was Alfonso XIII (1886–1941) who tried to solve the problem by encouraging General Miguel Primo de Rivera (1870–1930) to stage a coup and establish a right-wing dictatorship in 1923. For a time this expedient was successful but opposition to his authoritarian regime gradually grew and he resigned in 1930.

In 1931 the king abdicated and a republic was proclaimed, but this did little to solve the country's problems. Although the left-wing government had received substantial support in the 1936 elections, it found its reform policy faced strong right-wing opposition led by the **Falange** and an assortment of aristocracy, the military, monarchists and politically motivated members of the RC church. These groups supported the rebellion organised in Spanish Morocco by General Francisco **Franco** (1936). This spread to the mainland and developed into the **Spanish Civil War**.

Following the rebel victory in 1939, Franco became head of state, a position he held until his death in 1975. One of the important achievements of his regime in foreign policy was the conclusion of an agreement by which air and naval bases were granted to the USA in 1953 in exchange for economic and military assistance. He was succeeded by King Juan Carlos de Bourbon (1938–), grandson of Alfonso XIII. Juan Carlos had been nominated by Franco as his successor in 1969, Franco having promised, in 1947, a restoration of the monarchy after his death.

With the return of the monarchy came the reestablishment of political parties, relaxing the one-party system of the Franco regime. In the first general election for 21 years, the Democratic Centre Party was elected to power in 1977. In 1982 a moderate socialist government was elected. Spain joined NATO in 1982 and the EU in 1986.

One of the problems which faced the new democracy was the demand for provincial autonomy. Basque and Catalan parliaments were established in 1980 although this did not satisfy extreme Basque separatists who continued their terrorist activities through the ETA organisation.

Spanish Civil War (1936–9) A conflict between the Republican government and Nationalist rebel forces. Alarmed by the land reforms and anticlerical and left-wing tendencies of the **Popular Front** government of the Republic, a group of high-ranking army officers launched a rebellion in Spanish Morocco and the Canary Islands. The rebels were supported by the landowning aristocracy, wealthy industrialists, the RC Church, nationalists, monarchists and the **Falange** (Fascist party), while the Government drew support from socialists, Communists, anarchists and those seeking regional autonomy, especially in the Basque country, Catalonia and Galicia. Command of the rebels soon fell to General Francisco **Franco**, who declared that he would establish a fascist state on the Italian model. The rebels received increasing amounts of military aid from Italy and Germany, which used the opportunity to exercise their military forces in

Front line Dec. 1937
Front line Dec. 1938

Areas controlled by Franco and the Nationalists
by the end of 1936

Areas captured by Franco and the Nationalists 1937-38

Spanish Civil War

anticipation of wider war; the German bombing of the Basque town of Guernica in 1937 caused an international outcry. The European democracies maintained a policy of non-intervention, refusing to help the Spanish government, and the USSR's aid to the Republicans required the suppression of anarchist elements on the Republican side. Individual European and US volunteers also defied their governments to form the **International Brigades**. Internal divisions among the government forces, combined with their inability to obtain essential supplies, helped to bring about Franco's eventual victory in 1939.

Spartacist Rising (1919) A week of street violence in Berlin organised by radical socialists of the Spartacus League, which was named after the leader of a slave revolt in ancient Rome. The movement was founded in 1916 and was reorganised as the German Communist Party in November 1918. All its leaders were either arrested or killed in the rioting of January 1919, including the founders Karl **Liebknecht** and Rosa **Luxemburg**. The Spartacists' aim was the overthrow of capitalism, and they believed this could only be achieved by a revolutionary rising of German workers throughout the country. In the same year, soviets of revolutionary workers, soldiers and sailors were established in several major German cities, but these were similarly suppressed.

Special Areas The four districts of Britain where in the 1930s unemployment was at its worst and which the coalition National Government decided in 1934 to single out for direct government help. The areas were

Tyneside, West Cumberland, South Wales and the whole of Scotland. The appointed commissioners had limited money and powers so could do little for the areas at first, but by the late 1930s they were able to attract some industry. The Conservative-dominated National Government was not keen on direct state intervention in the economy, and many of its critics regarded its Special Areas scheme as little more than a propaganda exercise.

Sri Lanka An island republic off the SE coast of India; known as Ceylon until 1972. Area: 66,000 sq km. Pop: 17,464,000 (1992). Languages: Sinhalese, Tamil. Religions: Buddhism, Hinduism. Cap: Colombo.

Annexed by the British in 1815, the country became independent in 1948. PM Solomon **Bandaranaike** was assassinated in 1959 after establishing Sinhalese as the country's official language, which aroused Tamil resentment. Many of the minority Tamils, originally from India, want to set up a separate state in the N and E of the island; from about 1980 a liberation movement spearheaded by the Tamil Tigers militia began to wage a terrorist war against the government. India, which has a large Tamil population in the SE, tried to play a mediating role, with little success. An Indian military intervention in 1988–9 failed to defeat the Tigers and aroused resentment among the Sinhalese majority. The Sri Lankan army inflicted heavy defeats on the Tigers in 1991, but inter-ethnic tensions remained unresolved at the end of the 20th century.

SS (Schutzstaffel) (*Ger.* – protection squad) An organisation founded in 1925 as a bodyguard for Adolf

Hitler. When Heinrich **Himmler** took command in 1929 he transformed the black-uniformed troopers into a militarily trained and ideologically indoctrinated Nazi elite (*see* **National Socialism**). The SS was used to suppress its larger rival the **SA** in 1934. It absorbed the police force in 1936 and became the most feared and powerful movement in the country. It carried out the Nazi policy of exterminating all opposition, especially in the **concentration camps** which it controlled. In the later part of WWII, elite SS units also played a major and notably brutal part in Germany's military effort.

Stakhanov, Alexei (1905–77) A coal-miner in the USSR who cut 100 tons of coal in a single work-shift in 1935. He became a Soviet hero, and Stalin took advantage of his example to try to boost output in his **Five-Year Plans**. Workers who consistently beat output targets or broke output records were called Stakhanovites, and given special privileges in pay, housing and holidays as a reward. These privileges soon came to be much resented by other workers.

Stalin, Joseph (*orig.* Josif Vissarionovich Dzhugashvili) (1879–1953) A Soviet Communist politician and dictator. He spent some years in exile before the 1917 Revolution, and formed close ties with Lenin and the Bolsheviks. From 1919 Stalin managed to gain control over the power centres in party and state, leading to his election as First Secretary of the Communist Party in 1922, a post he held until his death. In a few years in the 1920s he ruthlessly disposed of all his rivals, and with the exile of Leon **Trotsky** in 1929 his ruling position was unchallenged.

He then set about reorganising the economy with
Five-Year Plans, but they suffered many setbacks and
were far less successful than he had hoped. Agriculture
was the poorest performer, **collectivisation** proving
highly unpopular with the wealthier peasants (kulaks).
In 1929, Stalin began a programme of extermination of
the kulaks. He then turned on the officer corps, many
thousands of whom were killed because they were
alleged to have pro-German sympathies. The result of
this slaughter was a shortage of experienced army
officers to meet the German invasion of the USSR in
WWII. In all, at least five million people are believed to
have died in the purges of the 1930s.

During the war Stalin directed the campaigns against
the invaders and had great influence over other Allied
leaders, which created postwar problems for the West
and led to the creation of the **Iron Curtain** and the
beginning of the **Cold War**. Stalin was denounced
publicly by Nikita **Khrushchev** at the 20th Party
Congress in 1956.

Stalingrad A city of the USSR, renamed Volgograd in
1961. It was the scene of a huge Soviet victory after the
Germans besieged the city (1942–3). The battle marked
the decisive end of German territorial advance on the
Eastern Front.

Star Wars *see* **Strategic Defense Initiative**.

Statute *see* **Act of Parliament**.

Statute of Westminster (1931) An **Act of Parliament**
by which the self-governing Dominions (Canada,
Newfoundland, the Irish Free State, South Africa,
Australia and New Zealand) gained complete freedom

to make their own laws, confirming resolutions
approved at the 1926 and 1930 **Imperial Conferences**.

Stern Gang A Zionist underground movement,
founded in 1940 by Abraham Stern (1907–42) when he
left **Irgun Zvai Leumi** because of its decision to suspend
anti-British activities in **Palestine** during WWII. The
gang was responsible for various acts of terrorism
including the assassination of the UN mediator in the
first **Arab-Israeli War**, Count Folk Bernadotte (1948).
The movement was dissolved in 1948.

Strategic Arms Limitation Talks (SALT)
A succession of meetings during the years 1969–72 and
1974–9 between Soviet and US representatives, with the
aim of limiting the nuclear arms race. In 1972 a treaty
(SALT I) was signed restricting anti-ballistic missile
defensive systems. The second round of talks (SALT II)
concentrated on types and numbers of nuclear missiles
possessed by the two states and, though agreement was
reached, the US Senate refused to ratify (approve) the
proposals.

Strategic Defense Initiative (SDI) A proposed US
system of artificial satellites armed with lasers to destroy
enemy missiles in space. It was popularly known as *Star
Wars*. Before the **Cold War** ended it threatened to bring
about a renewed arms race.

Stresemann, Gustav (1878–1929) A German
politician. In 1917 he became leader of the National
Liberal Party, which was re-formed as the German
People's Party in 1919. During WWI he was a hardline
nationalist but moderated his views under the **Weimar
Republic**, of which he was Chancellor for three months

(1923). He was Foreign Minister from 1923 to 1929, pursuing a conciliation policy towards Germany's former enemies. He negotiated the **Dawes Plan**, the Treaties of **Locarno**, and Germany's admission to the League of Nations in 1926. He was awarded the Nobel Peace Prize jointly with Aristide **Briand** (1926).

Sudetenland An area of N and NW Bohemia. It was taken from the Austro-Hungarian Empire and given to the newly formed state of Czechoslovakia by the Treaty of **Saint Germain**. A large part of the population was German-speaking, and this led Hitler to demand that the territory be absorbed into Germany. With this aim the German-Sudeten Party, financed by Germany, began

Sudetenland

a campaign of agitation and civil disturbances. By the **Munich Agreement** (1938), Germany was allowed to annex the area, which it retained until 1945. It was then returned to Czechoslovakia. which deported the German-speaking population.

Suez Crisis (1956) The international tension aroused when Israel invaded Egypt, supported a few days later by an Anglo-French force. The Israeli move was to halt Egyptian raids across the frontier and the Anglo-French expedition was in retaliation for the nationalisation by Egypt of the Suez Canal Company, the shares of which were held by the British government and French investment interests. President **Nasser** argued that Egypt required the Canal dues to pay for the construction of the Aswan High Dam, which the UK and the US had refused to finance.

The Anglo-French invasion, concentrated around Port Said, met with initial success but aroused worldwide condemnation, including threats of Soviet intervention, as well as much home-based opposition. The most determined opponent of the action was the USA (represented by President **Eisenhower** and the Secretary of State, John Foster **Dulles**), which exerted diplomatic and economic pressures. This, together with the condemnation of other Western states, resulted in a halt to the action and the withdrawal of all forces.

Israel, which withdrew its forces from Sinai (1957), probably gained most from the incident; a UN force was sent to act as a buffer against Egyptian raids; the Straits of Tiran, which the Egyptians had closed, were opened to give access to the port of Eilat; and the defeat of the

Egyptians in the field, although limited, acted as a morale booster. Egypt, having suffered a military setback, nevertheless strengthened its claims to leadership of the Arab world by its defiance of two strong Western powers, but it became much more dependent on the USSR for financial and military aid (e.g. for the construction of the Aswan High Dam). UK and US relations became very strained, and the British PM, Anthony **Eden**, lost his reputation for diplomacy and resigned in 1957. *See also* **Arab-Israeli Wars**.

Suffrage *see* **Women's Suffrage**.

Suffragettes *see* **Women's Suffrage**.

Sun Yat-sen (1866–1925) A Chinese politician. He was educated in the West and became a Christian. Because of revolutionary activities against the Manchu dynasty he had to flee the country in 1895. He spent the early years of the 20th century in organising revolution from outside China. His growing support as leader of the **Kuomintang** within the country eventually led to the revolution which overthrew the Manchus in 1911.

Sun Yat-sen was briefly president (1912), but handed over to a military regime, with Yuan Shihkai as president (1912–16). The regime was later opposed by Sun Yat-sen himself. After Yuan's death the country collapsed into civil war between rival warlords. Sun attempted to unify the country by establishing a military government in 1923, but unification was not achieved until after his death. Meanwhile he led a series of governments in S China, though they only controlled a small area. Becoming disenchanted with Western policies, he turned to the USSR for aid and cooperated with the Chinese communists.

Although little respected during his lifetime, he later became admired by both left and right – as the 'father of the country' by the Nationalists and as the 'pioneer of the revolution' by the Communists.

Superpower A dominant world power. After WWII most states were so exhausted in resources and manpower that world leadership was in the hands of the USA with its vast wealth, and the Soviet Union with its huge military power. The USA soon built up its nuclear strength and the Soviet Union made every effort to catch up. Their rivalry was the main factor in the **Cold War**. Many countries were drawn to take sides and regarded a friendly superpower as a necessary protector. Those who did not, the 'non-aligned', were mostly from the **Third World** (*see* **Non-aligned Movement**). No other country reached superpower status, although Communist China came close in power and influence. After the Soviet Union broke up in 1991 the USA was left as the only superpower, but some Europeans see a close-knit **European Union** as a superpower of the future.

Syria A republic of the Middle East. Area: 185,680 sq km. Pop: 14,798,000. Language: Arabic. Religion: Islam. Cap: Damascus.

Until 1918 Syria was part of the **Ottoman Empire**, afterwards becoming a French **mandate**. Before achieving independence in 1944, it was invaded by the British and Free French forces to prevent the establishment of German air bases and to remove **Vichy** French government authorities in 1941.

Politically Syria has been dominated by the Pan-Arab **Ba'ath Socialist Party** which hoped to extend its influence by uniting the country with Egypt as the United Arab Republic (1958–61). Economic and political friction soon developed between the two countries and the union was ended by a military seizure of power in Syria.

A member of the **Arab League**, Syria maintained a hardline refusal to recognise the existence of Israel. This led to involvement in the **Arab-Israeli Wars**, Syrian support for guerrilla activities against Israel and Syrian opposition to Anwar **Sadat**'s attempts at détente.

Syrian forces invaded Lebanon in 1976 supposedly to stop the civil war there by backing the **PLO** and Lebanese Muslims in their struggle against the Lebanese Christians (Phalangists). This move provoked the Israelis to invade Lebanon to protect their country against PLO guerrilla attacks and possible Syrian invasion.

Until the end of the **Cold War**, Syria remained friendly toward the USSR. After the Gulf War of 1991, however, and as a result of Syria's mediation for the release of Western hostages by Muslim fundamentalist groups in Lebanon, the country began to emerge as one of the more pro-Western of the Arab states. Syrian forces had joined the Gulf War coalition against Iraq, and its government began to support US-sponsored moves toward Middle East peace. Negotiations to normalise relations with Israel were discontinued after the assassination of Yitzhak Rabin in 1995, and in 2002 have yet to be resumed.

T

Taff Vale Case (1901) A law case in which the Amalgamated Society of Railway Workers was sued for damages by the Taff Vale Railway Company to compensate for loss of revenue suffered during a strike. Compensation of £323,000 was awarded to the company, the Society being considered responsible for its members' actions. Union anger at the judgement helped the early development of the Labour Party, and led to the passing of the Trade Disputes Act, 1906, which meant that unions were no longer liable to compensate employers for strike losses.

Taft, William Howard (1857–1930) The US Republican president from 1909 to 1913. Although able in government, he was a conservative and cautious politician, having uneasy relations with Congress even though both Houses had Republican majorities. This, together with Theodore **Roosevelt**'s standing as an independent presidential candidate, led to a party split that resulted in Taft's overwhelming defeat by the Democratic candidate, Woodrow **Wilson**, in the 1912 presidential election. Taft became chief justice of the Supreme Court in 1921, an office he held until his death.

Taiwan *see* **China**.

Taliban A group comprised of Afghans trained in religious schools and former Islamic fighters, they retained power in Afghanistan until late 2001. Their aim is to set up the purest Islamic state. In 2001 a war was started by the US against the Taliban, whom they considered responsible for harbouring Osama **Bin Laden**. The spiritual leader of the Taliban is Mullah Mohammed Omar.

Tannenburg, Battle of (1914) A battle between German and Russian armies in East Prussia early in WWI when, helped by poor Russian communications, a small German force destroyed one of two invading Russian armies. Shortly afterwards, the other was severely defeated near the Masurian Lakes in the same region. Russian forces never again entered Germany in WWI.

Tariffs Government taxes levied on imports (and occasionally on exports), for the purpose of protecting domestic industry (*see* **protectionism**), strengthening the balance of payments, or raising revenue.

Tashkent Conference (1966) A meeting between President **Ayub Khan** of Pakistan and PM Lal **Shastri** of India, arranged by the Soviet PM Alexei Kosygin following the 1965 Indo-Pakistan War. The war had arisen over the disputed territory of **Kashmir**, where border incidents and disturbances led to full-scale conflict. At the conference both countries renounced the use of force in the settlement of the Kashmir dispute, and agreed to withdraw their armed forces.

Tehran Conference (1943) The first meeting during WWII between **Churchill**, **Roosevelt** and **Stalin**. Agreement was reached for a Russian offensive to coincide with the opening of a second front in W Europe; on a declaration of war at a convenient time by the USSR on Japan; on the postwar extension of the

USSR frontier to the **Curzon Line** and, in compensation for this, for Poland to receive German territory along the **Oder-Neisse Line**; and on the setting-up of a postwar peace-keeping organisation.

Teng Hsiao-ping *see* **Deng Xiaoping**.

Tennessee Valley Authority (TVA) A federal agency created in 1933 as part of F D Roosevelt's **New Deal**. Its immediate purpose was flood control and it therefore improved existing dams and constructed new ones. However, it also became a major employer in seven states, with hydroelectric schemes, projects to deal with soil erosion and major planting of forests. It was able to improve agricultural prosperity in the Tennessee Valley and to give a boost to industry in the area. The TVA had almost unlimited Federal funds and attracted much opposition, particularly from the power companies, but it was one of the success stories of the New Deal.

Terrorism The systematic use of terror, i.e. violence or intimidation intended to cause fear or panic, in order to achieve political or other objectives. Terrorism has been used by groups wishing to put pressure on governments, and also by dictatorships or other autocratic governments to overcome opposition.

Test Ban Treaty *see* **Nuclear Test Ban Treaty**.

Thant, U (1909–74) A Burmese diplomat who was Secretary-General of the UN from 1961 to 1971. He played a leading role in ending the **Cuban Missile Crisis**; drew up a plan for the ending of the Congolese civil war (1962); sent a peace-keeping force to Cyprus (1964); put forward the cease-fire arrangements after the 1967 **Arab-Israeli War**; and obtained the acceptance of

Communist China as a member of the UN with a seat in the Security Council.

Thatcher, Margaret (1925–) A British Conservative politician, who was PM from 1979 to 1990. She was Secretary of State for Education and Science (1970–4), and was elected leader of the Conservative Party in 1975. She was the first woman in the UK to lead a political party and to hold the post of PM.

Her government's economic policies were for unrestricted free enterprise, which involved cutting taxes and public spending, **privatisation** of major state industries and legislation to reduce the power of the trade unions. Her government followed monetarist policies in finance which strictly controlled the supply of money in the country and meant that the government also had to deal with high levels of unemployment. She took a hard line in relations with the Soviet bloc, and believed in strengthening the UK's nuclear forces. She won the general elections of 1983 and 1987; her 1983 success was in part due to the UK victory in the **Falklands War**. Differences over Europe and criticisms of her personal style of leadership led to her replacement as party leader and PM by John **Major** in November 1990.

Third Reich The name given by the Nazis to their regime in Germany from 1933 to 1945, which **Hitler** boasted would last for a thousand years. According to the Nazis the First Reich was the Holy Roman Empire (962–1806) and the Second Reich was the German Empire (1871–1918).

Third World The name that came into use in the 1960s

to distinguish the rest of the world from the two power blocs of the USA and USSR. It is now loosely applied to the developing countries, especially those of Africa, Asia and Latin America, which are largely non-industrialised and therefore poor. Such countries were generally considered neutral in the East-West alignment (*see* **Non-aligned Movement**). They frequently suffer from mass illiteracy and have political systems dominated by small, often Western-educated elites. Because of their past history as colonies they are usually strongly opposed to **imperialism**.

Tibet A region of W China. Area: 1,221,600 sq km. Pop: 2,160,000. Language: Tibetan. Religion: Buddhism. Cap: Lhasa.

On suspicion that Russia was gaining a foothold in Tibet, and that such a presence would be a danger to India, a British expeditionary force under the command of Col. Francis Younghusband was sent to Lhasa in 1904. Many of the inhabitants were killed by the invading force and no evidence was found of Russian penetration. However, a trade treaty was negotiated between India and Tibet.

China occupied the country from 1910 to 1913, forcing Tibet's spiritual ruler, the Dalai Lama, to seek refuge in India. He returned when the Chinese left, and the country became isolated from the rest of the world.

China reoccupied Tibet in 1951 and eight years of Chinese control caused a widespread rebellion in 1959, involving heavy fighting and the flight of the new Dalai Lama to India, accompanied by many thousands of his subjects. At first Chinese rule was harsh, but in the

1980s and 90s there was some relaxation of oppression: hospitals and schools were opened, highways constructed, air links established with China, frontiers opened for trade, agriculture expanded and reformed, irrigation, mining, forestry and industrial projects started and closed monasteries reopened. Even so, Tibetan nationalists remain strongly opposed to the Chinese occupation.

Timor An island in SE Asia, colonised by Portugal in the 16th century, then by the Netherlands from 1613; a border between the two was only finally agreed in 1914. Japan occupied the island in 1942, and in 1950 Dutch Timor became part of independent Indonesia. Portuguese (East) Timor declared its independence in 1975, but was immediately invaded by Indonesia. Indonesian rule brought poverty and hardship, and severe repression in the face of a guerrilla campaign for liberation (1975–98). In 1999 a referendum voted for independence, and Indonesian militias devastated the country; a UN force finally restored order and Indonesia withdrew, leaving E Timor under UN rule.

Tindemans Report (1976) An investigation into European union prepared by the Belgian PM, Leo Tindemans, at the request of the **Council of Europe**. The report proposed a common foreign policy; progress towards economic and monetary union; a directly elected **European Parliament**; and the granting of greater powers to the European Commission. Some of these proposals were subsequently put into operation.

Tirpitz, Alfred Friedrich von (1849–1930) A German grand admiral. Tirpitz was Minister of Marine

(1897–1916) and built up the strength of the German navy, with the construction of large capital ships to rival the British **dreadnoughts**. He was naval commander-in-chief (1914–16) but resigned when Kaiser Wilhelm II opposed his policy of unrestricted **U-Boat** warfare and prevented the fleet's use in offensive operations in European waters. He turned to politics and was a Nationalist Deputy in the Reichstag from 1924 to 1928.

Tito (*orig. name* Josip Broz) (1892–1980) A Croatian marshal and politician. Tito became a Communist after being captured by the Russians while serving in the Austro-Hungarian army during WWI. He fought in the Russian Revolution and on returning to Yugoslavia spent six years in prison as a political undesirable and enemy of the monarchist régime.

During WWII Tito organised the National Liberation Front of **partisans** to fight the invading German forces (1941). He headed a provisional government from 1943, and had managed to liberate much of the country before the arrival of Soviet forces. He was such a successful leader that he was a popular choice as PM (1945–53). He led Yugoslavia in its break with the Soviet bloc (1948) and became president in 1953. He denounced the Soviet invasion of Hungary (1956) and the Warsaw Pact invasion of Czechoslovakia (1968), and by developing independent policies raised Yugoslavia to an important position in the **Non-aligned Movement**.

Tobruk *see* **North Africa Campaigns**.

Todd, Garfield (1908–) A Rhodesian politician. Todd was president of the United Rhodesia Party and PM from 1953 to 1958. His government legalised trade unions and extended the franchise to an increasing number of black citizens. He co-founded the Central Africa Party (1959) and founded the New African Party (1961). After the Unilateral Declaration of Independence (**UDI**) in 1965 he spent many months in prison or under house arrest because of opposition to Ian **Smith**'s illegal regime.

Tojo, Hideki (1884–1948) A Japanese general and politician. He was leader of the militarist party from 1931 and chief of staff of the Kwantung Army (1938–40). His appointment as Minister of War (1940–41) and PM (1941–44) gave the final control over the country's political affairs to the military and changed the state into a dictatorship. US successes in WWII eventually persuaded Emperor **Hirohito** that Tojo was leading Japan to disaster, and Tojo ultimately resigned. He was executed as a war criminal by the Americans.

Total Warfare The waging of unrestricted warfare against an enemy, including the civilian non-combatant population. Such warfare was not conducted on a large scale until WWII, when *c.*14 million civilians are thought to have died.

Totalitarianism A one-party political system in which the state has absolute power over the lives of its citizens. Examples include the USSR, Nazi Germany and Fascist Italy.

Trade Union An association of employees, formed for the purpose of protecting and promoting its members' interests in connection with benefits, wages and working conditions, by collective bargaining with an employer.

Trades Union Congress (TUC) The central

organisation of UK trade unions, founded in 1868.
Policy is decided by the General Council which is in
contact with government departments and takes an
interest in proposed legislation affecting organised
labour. It holds an annual conference which gives union
representatives the opportunity to consider matters of
concern to members. It has close ties with the Labour
Party, which it helped to establish and for which it was
long the principal source of funds.

Transkei *see* **apartheid**.

Trench Warfare Military action in which opposing
armies face each other from fortified trenches. In WWI,
soon after the outbreak of war, both sides dug
themselves into massive lines of trenches stretching
along the whole of the Western Front. So strongly were
these trenches defended that attacking infantry could
generally only capture them with the support of huge
concentrations of artillery, and after enormous loss of
life. This meant that much of the fighting on the
Western Front resembled a stalemate.

Trianon, Treaty of (1920) The Allied peace settlement
with Hungary after WWI, which resulted in the transfer
of two-thirds of Hungary's prewar population and
territory to Austria, Czechoslovakia, Italy, Poland,
Romania and Yugoslavia. The treaty also provided for
reparations to be made and the army to be limited to
35,000 men.

Trieste A port in NE Italy on the Gulf of Trieste at the
head of the Adriatic Sea. Under Austrian rule from 1382
to 1918, it became Italian after WWI despite
Yugoslavian claims. At the end of WWII it was awarded

to Yugoslavia but this was disputed by Italy. It was established as the Free Territory of Trieste (1947–54), and by a compromise in 1954 the city passed to Italy and the neighbouring countryside to Yugoslavia.

Triple Alliance *see* **Central Powers**.

Triple Entente (1914–17) An alliance in WWI between Britain, France and Russia arising from three separate understandings developed in the period 1894 to 1907, partly to deal with the threat of the Triple Alliance (*see* **Central Powers**). These were the Franco-Russian Alliance (1894), the **Entente Cordiale** between the UK and France (1904), and the **Anglo-Russian Entente** (1907). The first of these agreements was for joint mobilisation if the Triple Alliance mobilised, and that if either state was attacked by Germany alone or with an ally then the other would provide all possible military

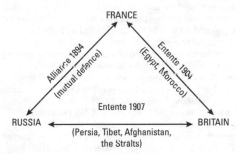

Triple Entente *The ententes between France, Britain and Russia.*

aid. The second and third agreements added to the first meant that Britain, France and Russia would defend each other against aggression from members of the Triple Alliance. Russia left the Alliance in 1917 following the Bolshevik Revolution.

Trotsky, Leon (*orig. name* Lev Davidovich Bronstein) (1879–1940) A Russian politician and revolutionary. Trotsky spent many years in exile, returning to take part in the unsuccessful 1905 **Russian Revolution**. After another period in exile, he returned to Russia in 1917, joined the Bolsheviks, and played a leading role in their seizure of power. He became Commissar for Foreign Affairs (1917–18), and as Commissar for War (1918–25) he created the **Red Army** and was largely responsible for its success in the civil war (1918–20).

After Lenin's death, **Stalin** undermined Trotsky's authority and gained control of Party administration. Trotsky was deprived of all his offices, expelled from the Communist Party in 1927 and exiled in 1929, but continued to agitate, intrigue and condemn Stalin's autocratic ambitions. He was alleged to have organised. with the help of foreign governments, a vast plot to overthrow the Soviet regime, was sentenced to death in his absence (1937), and assassinated by a Soviet agent in Mexico City in 1940.

Truman, Harry S (1884–1972) A US Democratic politician, who was president from 1945 to 1953. He became president following the death of F D Roosevelt. He attended the **Potsdam Conference** with Churchill and Stalin. and his decision to drop atomic bombs on Japan helped end WWII. He played a leading role in the establishment of the UN and of NATO. He was also responsible for carrying out the **Marshall Plan**, and altered US policy towards the USSR (*see* **Truman Doctrine**) following the WWII alliance. In the **Korean War** he sent troops to aid South Korea as part of the UN contingent, and after public disagreement he dismissed General Douglas MacArthur from command of the UN forces in Korea.

Truman Doctrine The policy put forward by President Harry S **Truman** in a message to Congress in 1947 stating that the USA should be committed 'to support free peoples who are resisting attempted subjugation by armed minorities or by outside pressures'. The message was in support of his request for economic and military aid to Greece and Turkey to help them stand up to Communist pressure. It showed a change to a committed anti-Communist strategy by the Truman Administration with the onset of the **Cold War**. The **Marshall Plan** (proposed in 1947) put into practice the Doctrine's objectives.

TUC *see* **Trades Union Congress**.

Tunisia A republic of N Africa, on the Mediterranean. Area: 164,150 sq km. Pop: 9,380,404. Languages: Arabic and French. Religion: mostly Islam. Cap: Tunis.

Ruled by Carthage until the 2nd century AD, Tunisia became a Roman province before passing to the Berbers, then to Turkey. It was occupied by Geman troops in late 1942 and was the scene of heavy fighting in 1943. It gained independence in 1955 under Habib ben Ali Bourguiba after a period of French occupation dating from 1881. Economic difficulties in the 1970s led to political unrest and an attempt, aided by Libya, to unsettle the country. Tunisia concluded special treaties with the EU between 1969 and 1982; it remained a force for moderation among Arab states.

Turkey A republic of SE Europe and W Asia. Area: 779,452 sq km. Pop: 58,584,000. Language: Turkish. Religion: Islam. Cap: Ankara.

From the 14th century, Turkey ruled the extensive **Ottoman Empire**. In 1914 it joined the Central Powers, and after defeat in WWI, the empire fell apart (*see* **Sèvres, Treaty of**).

A war of independence (1919–22) saw **Atatürk** successful in defeating a Greek invasion and in overthrowing the Ottoman sultanate, and in 1923 he proclaimed the country a secular republic (i.e. one with no official religion). At the Treaty of **Lausanne**, the new republic succeeded in revising the terms dictated at Sèvres. After Atatürk's death, his former PM Ismet Inönü (1884–1974) became president (1938–50), continuing the transformation of Turkey into a modern state and introducing political reforms.

Turkey joined NATO, but then endured a succession of civil and military governments, coups and periods of martial law. Even the widely supported invasion of **Cyprus** (1974) failed to overcome this instability. Governments alternately led by Bülent Ecevit and Süleyman Demirel held power in the late 1970s, but in 1980 widespread unrest led to a coup by General Kenan Evren, head of state until 1989.

PMs in the 1990s included Tansu Çiller (1993), the country's first woman leader. An economic crisis in 1995 accompanied the rise of the (Islamist) Welfare Party, which formed Turkey's first government for 75 years that was not wholly secular. Its links with radical Islamic states led in 1998 to a ban on the party, and Ecevit returned to lead a Democratic Left Party government. By the late 1990s, the Kurdish war for independence had claimed 30,000 lives, but began to subside with the capture of the Kurdish leader Abdullah Ocalan.

U

U-2 Incident (1960) The shooting down by the USSR
of a US Lockheed U-2 high-altitude photographic
reconnaissance aircraft over the Soviet city of
Sverdlovsk. The pilot, Francis Gary Powers, was
captured and confessed to being on an espionage
operation. Similar missions had been going on for
several years without Soviet protest, but this time
Khrushchev demanded an apology from US president
Eisenhower at the Paris summit conference a fortnight
later, and when it was not given withdrew from the
meeting. After this such flights ceased and Powers was
exchanged for a Soviet spy in 1962.

UAR *see* **Egypt**.

U-boats German submarines, used effectively in WWI
and WWII to put economic pressure on Britain by
sinking large numbers of merchant ships carrying food
and other vital supplies. *See* **Atlantic, Battle of the**.

UDI *see* **Zimbabwe**.

UK *see* **United Kingdom**.

Ulbricht, Walter (1893–1978) An East German
Communist politician. Ulbricht went into exile from
1933 to 1945 on Hitler's rise to power, spending most of
this time in the USSR. After his return to East Germany
he became deputy PM of the GDR and Party Secretary-
General by 1950. He was chairman of the Council of State
(1960–71) and effectively the country's dictator, believing
in Stalinist repressive measures but without the extreme
terrorist methods of the USSR. He was responsible for the

building of the Berlin Wall (1961), and supported the Warsaw Pact invasion of Czechoslovakia (1968).

Ulster *see* **Ireland**.

Ulster Loyalists Protestants who want to maintain Northern Ireland's link with the UK (*see* **Ireland**). Many Loyalists are members of the **Orange Order** and the majority were represented by the Ulster Unionist Party, the largest political group in the province. The party was the ruling body of Stormont, the Northern Ireland parliament (1921–72), until direct rule was imposed by the UK government. The imposition of direct rule, together with demands for reform and tensions caused by the Troubles, caused the splintering of the party into differing factions and new parties. After the **Anglo-Irish Agreement**, the main Unionist group, the *Official Unionist Party*, became a supporter of attempts to find a peaceful settlement in the province, and its leader David Trimble became First Minister in the Northern Ireland Assembly in 1999. The smaller Loyalist paramilitary parties also supported this process, but the *Democratic Unionist Party*, led by Ian Paisley, continued to oppose cooperation with the Nationalist **Sinn Féin**.

UN *see* **United Nations Organisation**.

UNCTAD *see* **United Nations Conference on Trade and Development**.

Underground Movements *see* **resistance movements**; **Maquis**; **partisan**.

Unemployment **1.** The condition of being out of work or unemployed.

   2. the number of an area country's working population unemployed at a given time. (*See figure overleaf.*)

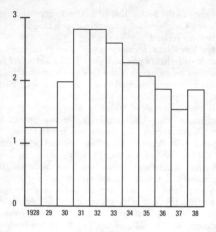

Unemployment

UNESCO *see* United Nations Educational, Scientific and Cultural Organisation.

UNHCR *see* United Nations High Commission for Refugees.

UNICEF *see* United Nations International Children's Emergency Fund.

Unification The joining together of states or parts of divided nations, usually for a common defence, or for economic or political benefit. Nationalism is often a powerful motive for unification.

Unilateral Declaration of Independence *see* Zimbabwe.

Unilateralism *see* Disarmament; **Campaign For Nuclear Disarmament**.

Unionist Party *see* Ulster Loyalists.

Union of Soviet Socialist Republics (USSR)
A Communist federal republic of E Europe and N Asia, which existed from 1923 to 1991. *See also* **Russia**.

The USSR had 15 republics and was governed by the Supreme Soviet consisting of two chambers (the Soviet of the Union and the Soviet of Nationalities) with equal legislative rights and each elected for a five-year term. The highest executive body was the Council of Ministers, appointed by the Supreme Soviet. Between sessions of the Supreme Soviet the state authority was the Presidium, responsible for all its activities to the Supreme Soviet, which elected its membership. In reality, most of the power was held by the leadership of the Communist Party.

The Union of Soviet Socialist Republics came into being in 1923 although a soviet constitution had been established in 1918 after the Bolshevik revolution (*see* **Russian Revolutions**). Following riots and the **Kronstadt mutiny**, **Lenin** had introduced the **New Economic Policy** (NEP) in 1921. He began the process of turning the USSR into a totalitarian dictatorship, ruthlessly eliminating all opposition, a process continued after his death in 1924 by **Stalin** (*see* **purge**). In 1928 Stalin introduced the first of the **Five-Year Plans**, which proposed rapid industrialisation and the **collectivisation** of agriculture. Following the signing of the **Nazi-Soviet Pact** (1939), Germany invaded Poland, an act that led to the outbreak of WWII. The USSR invaded Poland two weeks later. In 1941 Germany attacked the USSR, but at the cost of millions of lives the Germans were eventually driven back across E Europe and defeated. In many respects, the Soviet contribution to the Allied war against Germany was greater than that of any other power.

In the countries of E Europe liberated by the Red Army, the USSR set up Communist governments and subsequently maintained the countries as **satellite states**, allied militarily in the **Warsaw Pact** and economically in the **Council for Mutual Economic Assistance**. Attempts by these countries to break away from the Soviet bloc led to Soviet military intervention, as in **Hungary** (1956) and **Czechoslovakia** (1968). WWII was followed by the **Cold War** between the Soviet bloc and the West, arising out of ideological differences and mutual suspicion, and coming to a climax in the **Korean War** (1950–3). The Cold War lessened somewhat following Stalin's death and Nikita **Khrushchev**'s denunciation of him in 1956, but flared up again from time to time, notably with the **Cuban Missile Crisis** in 1962. Khrushchev was removed in 1964 by Leonid **Brezhnev** and Andrei **Kosygin**. The 1970s were marked by attempts at **détente** between East and West, leading to the **Strategic Arms Limitation Talks**, but following the Soviet invasion of **Afghanistan** (1979) a Cold War atmosphere returned, along with a renewed arms race. The USSR's relations with Communist China also deteriorated, a process starting in the 1950s (*see* **Sino-Soviet split**). After Stalin's death the repressive nature of the state apparatus became less harsh, but the country always lacked basic freedoms and life remained shadowed by secret police activities (*see* **Soviet Security Service**). Shortages of food, housing and consumer goods were largely due to the inefficiencies of a centrally controlled economy run by a vast and often corrupt bureaucracy.

The coming to power of Mikhail **Gorbachev** (1985) saw remarkable (though cautious) moves towards social, political and economic reform (*see* **glasnost** and **perestroika**), together with improved relations with the West. In 1989 the first partially free elections took place, and Gorbachev announced economic reforms designed to lead to a limited market economy. Fearful for their monopoly of power, some members of the political and military establishment attempted a coup in August 1991. It was a badly led and half-hearted attempt, but Boris **Yeltsin**, president of the Russian Republic, organised prompt resistance in Moscow, which ultimately took much of the credit for the coup's defeat. The coup discredited the Communist Party and the central political establishment, and placed the union under irresistible pressure. The USSR began to break up as other republics followed the example of the **Baltic States** in declaring independence. Gorbachev resigned, and the **Commonwealth of Independent States** was created as a loose federation of independent states to replace the USSR in 1991.

United Arab Republic *see* **Egypt**.

United Kingdom of Great Britain and Northern Ireland (UK) A monarchy of NW Europe. Area:

244,027 sq km. Pop: 58,784,000. Language: English. Religion: Protestant, RC. Cap: London.

The UK includes England, Scotland, Wales and Northern Ireland but excludes the Channel Islands and the Isle of Man which are crown dependencies with their own legislative and taxation systems. Legislative power lies with Parliament, but the monarch has to give royal assent to bills before they become Acts of **Parliament**, and law. The House of Commons is elected by universal adult suffrage (everyone over 18) for a maximum five-year term. Much information on the UK's history will be found under the entries for individual PMs, a list of whom is given below. This is followed by a brief survey of British history in the 20th century.

British Prime Ministers 1902–01:
Balfour (Con.) 1902
Campbell-Bannerman (Lib.) 1905
Asquith (Lib.) 1908
Asquith (Coalition) 1915
Lloyd George (Coalition) 1916
Bonar Law (Con.) 1922
Baldwin (Con.) 1923
MacDonald (Lab.) 1924
Baldwin (Con.) 1924
MacDonald (Lab.) 1929
MacDonald (National) 1931
Baldwin (National) 1935
Chamberlain (National) 1937
Churchill (Coalition) 1940
Attlee (Lab.) 1945

Churchill (Con.) 1951
Eden (Con.) 1955
Macmillan (Con.) 1957
Douglas-Home (Con.) 1963
Wilson (Lab.) 1964
Heath (Con.) 1970
Wilson (Lab.) 1974
Callaghan (Lab.) 1976
Thatcher (Con.) 1979, 1983, 1987
Major (Con.) 1990
Blair (Lab.) 1997, 2001

1900–18 At the beginning of the 20th century the UK
was at the height of its power, governing the biggest
empire the world had seen, and leading the world in
trade and industry. Domestically, conditions were still
poor for the working classes, a situation that led to the
foundation of the **Labour Party** to challenge the long-
established **Liberal** and **Conservative Parties**. At home,
Asquith's Liberal government passed reforms, including
the introduction of old-age pensions and national
insurance, and the **Parliament Act**. Agitation for
women's suffrage increased, and women over 30 were
given the vote in 1918. Tensions in the Empire included
the Boer War and pressure for Home Rule in **Ireland**. In
foreign affairs, Britain drew closer to France and Russia
(*see* **Entente Cordiale** and **Anglo-Russian Entente**) and
saw growing imperial, economic and military rivalry
with Germany that came to a head in WWI.
1918–45 The post-WWI years were marked at home by
the first Labour government (1924), the **General Strike**

(1926), and the **Depression** and mass unemployment of the 1930s. All adults over the age of 21 were given the vote by 1928. Most of Ireland was granted independence, and agitation for independence in **India** grew throughout the period. The **Statute of Westminster** (1931) gave legal authority to the legislative independence of Canada, Newfoundland, the Irish Free State, South Africa, Australia and New Zealand. The UK was founder member of the **League of Nations**, but in the 1930s followed a policy of **appeasement** towards Italian and German aggression, which did nothing to prevent the outbreak of WWII.

1945–2002 The successful conclusion of WWII was largely brought about by the involvement of the USSR and the USA, which in the postwar years established themselves as the world's two **superpowers**. The UK was no longer a world power. As the developed worlds split between East and West powerblocs, the UK sided with the USA becoming a founder member of NATO and the UN. The UK's international decline was shown by problems such as the **Suez Crisis** (1956).

The process of **decolonisation** began in 1947 with the granting of independence to India and Pakistan, and by the mid-1960s the UK had granted independence to most of its larger colonies (*see also* **Commonwealth**). The country now looked more towards Europe, and after two unsuccessful attempts, eventually joined the **EU** in 1973. In Northern Ireland (*see* **Ireland**), religious and cultural divisions led to violence which erupted in the late 1960s; a tentative political solution was pursued after the **Anglo-Irish Agreement** in 1994, but remained uncertain at the end of the century.

At home, the postwar Labour government extended the **welfare state** along the lines suggested in the **Beveridge Report**, and began the **nationalisation** of many industries. The Conservative Party opposed nationalisation, believing in free enterprise, and when in government has denationalised several industries; this process was to some extent continued by the Labour government after 1997. The result has been a mixed economy (with both publicly owned and privately owned sectors), similar to that of most other Western nations. Arguments between the parties also continue over issues such as private healthcare which are, broadly speaking, supported by the Conservatives and opposed by Labour.

The UK's possession of nuclear weapons has provided another major area of debate. The Conservatives consistently supported the UK's possession of such weapons, arguing that nuclear deterrence has maintained peace in Europe since WWII. Labour's attitude varied, sometimes approving nuclear weapons (it was a Labour government that ordered the development of the UK's first atomic bombs), and at other times holding a unilateral stance, believing that nuclear weapons should be banned from the country because they increase the risk of the UK's involvement in a nuclear war. The ending of the **Cold War** in the early 1990s made this problem less urgent. *See also* **disarmament**.

One of the major social problems the UK has faced over the last 30 years is racial integration in the face of opposition from a reactionary minority of white citizens. Over this period, immigration from the Commonwealth has turned the UK into a multiracial society with a variety of different cultures. Other major concerns at the end of the 20th century included the extent of Britain's future integration into the EU and its euro currency.

United Nations *see* United Nations Organisation.

United Nations Conference on Trade and Development (UNCTAD) An organisation with HQ in Geneva, established in 1964 to protect the interests of developing countries. It consists of the Trade and Development Board and four committees. The board meets twice a year and its committees on Commodities, Manufacturing, Shipping, and Invisibles and Finances Related to Trade meet annually. Every four years the conference meets to consider and pass judgement on the board's activities.

United Nations Educational, Scientific and Cultural Organisation (UNESCO) An agency with HQ in Paris, established in 1945 to promote cooperation in communications, culture, education and science, and to develop universal respect for justice, the rule of law and human rights without distinction of language, race, religion or sex.

United Nations High Commissioner for Refugees (UNHCR) An agency with HQ in Geneva, established in 1951 to provide international protection for refugees, and to seek permanent solutions to their problems through voluntary repatriation, resettlement in other countries or integration into the country to which they have fled.

United Nations International Children's Emergency Fund (UNICEF) An organisation with HQ in New York established in 1946 to aid child health and welfare projects in countries badly affected by WWII. Since 1950 it has also been concerned with the expansion of maternal and child health services and educational and vocational training schemes in developing countries. The fund relies for financial assistance on voluntary contributions from individuals and UN member governments. It was awarded the 1965 Nobel Peace Prize.

United Nations Organisation (UNO) An association of states with HQ in New York, established in 1945 as successor to the **League of Nations**. Its main aims were decided at conferences held during WWII at Moscow, **Dumbarton Oaks**, **Yalta** and San Francisco. They are the maintenance of peace and security and the promotion of international welfare by economic, political and social means. Membership totalled 160 at the end of the century.

There are six main bodies in the UN: the General Assembly, the Security Council, the Economic and Social Council, the Trusteeship Council (*see* **mandates**), the **International Court of Justice** and the Secretariat. The General Assembly consists of all members, and its work is divided between several committees. The Security Council is the executive of the UN and has 15 members, 10 of which are elected for a 2-year term, and 5 of which are permanent – the People's Republic of China, France, the UK, the USA and formerly the USSR, now Russia, each of which has the right to veto

any decision of which it disapproves. The chief
administrative officer is the Secretary-General who is
appointed for five years by the Assembly on the
recommendation of the Council. The Secretary-Generals
have included Trygve **Lie** (1945–52), Dag
Hammarskjöld (1953–61), U **Thant** (1961–71), Kurt
Waldheim (1972–82), Javier Perez de Cuellar (1982–92),
Boutros Boutros Ghali (1992–6; he was forced out after
disagreements with the USA), and Kofi Anan (1996–).

Unlike the League of Nations, the UN has the power
to call for military action by its members, as well as the
power to impose sanctions. In settling international
disputes, the UN has had a limited success, e.g. in the
Arab-Israeli Wars, the **Korean War** and in **Cyprus**.

The UN has a large number of specialised agencies,
including **General Agreement on Tariffs and Trade,
International Bank for Reconstruction and
Development, International Labour Organisation,
International Monetary Fund, United Nations
Conference on Trade and Development, United
Nations Educational, Scientific and Cultural
Organisation, United Nations High Commission for
Refugees, United Nations International Children's
Emergency Fund, United Nations Relief and
Rehabilitation Administration, United Nations Relief
and Works Agency** and the **World Health Organisation**.

**United Nations Relief and Works Agency
(UNRWA)** An organisation with HQ in Vienna,
established in 1950 for the resettlement of Palestinian
Arab refugees and the provision of relief services and
work opportunities for them. The refugees mostly live in

camps in the Gaza Strip, Jordan, Lebanon and Syria, and funds are provided mainly by Canada, Sweden, Germany, the UK and the USA.

United States of America (USA) A federal republic of N America. Area: 3,543,883 sq km. Pop: 248,709,873. Language: English. Religion: Protestant and RC. Cap: Washington, D.C.

The Union of 50 states and the District of Columbia is governed by Congress, the legislative body. The president and vice-president are elected in the November of every leap year and take power the following January. Executive power is with the president who is also commander-in-chief of the armed forces. The Democratic and Republican parties are the main political organisations, from which the president, vice-president and congressional members are elected.

Information on the USA's history will be found under entries for individual presidents, a list of whom is given below. This is followed by a brief survey of the main currents in US history in the 20th century.

American Presidents 1901–2001:

T Roosevelt (Rep.) 1901
Taft (Rep) 1909
Wilson (Dem.) 1913
Harding (Rep.) 1921
Coolidge (Rep.) 1923
Hoover (Rep.) 1929
F D Roosevelt (Dem.) 1933
Truman (Dem.) 1945
Eisenhower (Rep.) 1953
Kennedy (Dem.) 1961

Johnson (Dem.) 1963
Nixon (Rep.) 1969
Ford (Rep.) 1974
Carter (Dem.) 1977
Reagan (Rep.) 1981
G Bush (Rep.) 1989
Clinton (Dem.) 1993
G W Bush (Rep.) 2001

1900–45 By the turn of the century, the USA was
beginning to establish itself as one of the world's leading
industrial nations, but in world affairs it followed a
policy of **isolationism**. This kept it out of WWI until
1917, when it declared war on Germany because of the
Zimmermann Telegram and the unrestricted U-boat
campaign (*see* **Lusitania**). After WWI the USA returned
to an isolationist policy, refusing to join the **League of
Nations** and failing to ratify the Treaty of **Versailles**.

The war was followed by an economic boom, but this
collapsed with the **Wall Street Crash** (1929). President F
D Roosevelt's **New Deal** did much to tackle the
problems of the Depression and mass unemployment
that followed in the 1930s.

The USA did little to prevent the growth of Fascism in
Europe and only entered WWII because of the Japanese
attack on **Pearl Harbor** (1941). However, US
involvement helped to ensure the eventual Allied
victory, after which the USA and the USSR became
established as the world's **superpowers**.

1945–2002 After 1945 the USA abandoned isolationism
in favour of determined opposition to Communist
expansion, based on the **Truman Doctrine**. WWII was

followed by the **Cold War** between the West and the Soviet bloc, leading to US involvement in the **Berlin** airlift, the **Korean** and **Vietnam Wars**, the **Cuban Missile Crisis** and the growth of military alliances such as NATO. A period of **détente** with the USSR began in the late 1960s, marked by the **Strategic Arms Limitation Talks**, but following the Soviet invasion of **Afghanistan** (1979), a Cold War atmosphere returned. After 1985, relations with the USSR improved again to a limited degree, until the Cold War ended in the early 1990s. The USA played a leading role in the liberation of **Kuwait** from Iraqi occupation in 1991, and mounted various military operations against perceived terrorist threats worldwide throughout the 1980s and 1990s. The destruction by terrorists of the New York Trade Center towers on 11 September 2001 intensified US opposition to terrorism.

At home, the early 1950s saw anti-Communist feelings at their height in **McCarthyism**. In the 1960s there were **Civil Rights Acts** aimed at eliminating racial discrimination, and also social reforms intended to deal with poverty. The US economy is largely free enterprise, and there is a strong tradition of opposition to government interference, combined with a belief in self-help that tends to oppose government welfare provisions.

UNO *see* **United Nations Organisation**.

UNRWA *see* **United Nations Relief and Works Agency**.

USA *see* **United States of America**.

USSR *see* **Union of Soviet Socialist Republics**.

U Thant *see* **Thant, U**.

V

Verdun, Battle of (1916) A WWI engagement which raged for most of the year around the fortress town of Verdun in NE France. Enormous casualties were suffered by both sides but after early German gains, the French under **Pétain** recaptured most of the lost ground. The British offensive on the **Somme** and the **Brusilov Offensive** on the Eastern Front helped the French in the later stages of the battle.

Versailles, Treaty of (1919) The settlement signed at the end of WWI between the Allied powers and Germany at the Paris Peace Conference.

Germany lost some 10 per cent of its population with 12½ per cent of its territory, including **Alsace-Lorraine** to France, and parts of East Prussia and Upper Silesia to Poland (*see also* **Danzig**). Germany's overseas possessions became **mandates** of the **League of Nations**, whose covenant was included in the Treaty. The union of Austria and Germany (**Anschluss**) was prohibited, the **Saarland** was to be occupied by French troops and the **Rhineland** was to be demilitarised and occupied by Allied forces. Germany was forbidden to manufacture heavy armaments, military service was abolished, and the armed forces were to be limited in equipment and manpower. Provision was made for the trial of German war leaders including Kaiser **Wilhelm II**, though this never took place, and Germany was obliged to accept guilt for causing the war. German waterways were to be open to international navigation and severe **reparations** were to be imposed, the amount of which was decided in 1921.

The loss of territory, manpower and control of waterways restricted Germany's ability to pay the reparations, and means were found of getting round the disarmament clauses. The bitterness and frustration caused by the treaty helped to strengthen German **nationalism** and to make possible **Hitler**'s rise to power. Hitler denounced the treaty, and his attempt to recover the territory lost to Poland was a direct cause of WWII.

Verwoerd, Hendrik F (1901–66) A South African politician. A member of the Nationalist Party, Verwoerd opposed South Africa's entry into WWII. As Minister of Native Affairs (1950–8) he was able to put into practice his firm belief in the principles of **apartheid**. He was elected leader of the party and PM (1958–66), and made the country a republic when South Africa left the Commonwealth in 1961. He was assassinated in the House of Assembly by a Portuguese East African.

Vichy Government (1940–4) The French semi-fascist government set up after the fall of France in WWII. It took its name from the town in the unoccupied centre of the country where it was established by Henri **Pétain**, its other important leaders being Admiral Jean Darlan and Pierre **Laval**. After the armistice with Germany, it ended the Third Republic, introduced anti-Semitic legislation, banned strikes and dissolved trade unions.

When Germany occupied the whole country in 1942, the government became openly collaborationist, secretly cooperated in the sending of forced labour to Germany and made no attempt to stop French agricultural and industrial products being seized by Germany. It was opposed by the **Free French** and by underground **resistance** movements.

Victor Emmanuel III (1869–1947) King of Italy from 1900 to 1946. Against the wishes of parliament, he took Italy into WWI on the Allied side (1915), and appointed Benito **Mussolini** as PM (1922). Mussolini made him Emperor of Abyssinia (1936) and King of Albania (1939), but during the Fascist regime he was little more than a constitutional puppet, although he was strong enough to dismiss Mussolini when the Allied success in WWII became obvious (1943). He abdicated in 1946 and died in exile in Egypt.

Viet Cong The name given in the 1960s and 1970s to the Communist-led armed forces of the Front for the Liberation of South Vietnam. In the **Vietnam War** they waged a guerrilla campaign against the South Vietnamese regime and US forces, and were supported and increasingly controlled by the communist regime in North Vietnam.

Viet Minh The Revolutionary League for the Independence of Vietnam, a political movement founded in 1941 by the Indo-Chinese Communist Party in North Vietnam to resist the Japanese attack on Indo-China in WWI. It operated with the Workers' Party and the army in expelling the French from the country and its authority N of the 17th parallel of longitude (i.e. in North Vietnam) was recognised by the 1954 Geneva Agreements. The movement's leading members were **Ho Chi Minh**, Pham Van Dong and Vo Nguyen Giap.

Vietnam A republic of SE Asia. Area: 329,566 sq km.

Pop: 68,488,000 (1990). Language: Vietnamese.
Religion: Taoism and Buddhism. Cap: Hanoi.

The country was formed in 1949 by the merger of
Annam, Cochin China and Tonkin, formerly parts of
Indo-China. After a war of independence led by **Ho Chi
Minh** the French were finally defeated at **Dien Bien
Phu**, and Vietnam became independent from France
(1954) although divided at the 17th parallel of latitude
into North and South as a result of agreements reached
at the 1954 Geneva Conference.

Vietnam remained divided until 1975 when the
Communist North conquered the South (which had
been backed by the USA) after US forces withdrew
from the **Vietnam War**. The unified country has been a
communist state since 1976. It joined the **Council for
Mutual Economic Assistance** in 1978 and signed a 25-
year treaty of friendship and cooperation with the
USSR. These moves, together with the Vietnamese
invasion and military domination of **Cambodia**,
damaged relations with China, leading to a border war
in 1979. In 1989 large numbers of 'boat people' left the
country, creating a major refugee crisis in nearby Hong
Kong. In the 1990s, economic reforms allowed Vietnam
to join the booming 'Tiger' economies of SE Asia.

Vietnam War The conflict in SE Asia fought between
the US-backed anti-Communist forces of South Vietnam
and the **Viet Cong**, who were supported by North
Vietnam's Communist government and Soviet
armaments.

After the partition of **Vietnam** in 1954, communists in
the South had waged a guerrilla campaign to reunify the

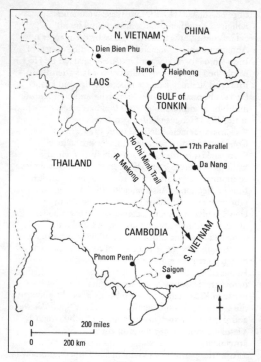

Vietnam

country, and in 1961 the USA began economic and military aid to the South to prevent the spread of communism in the region. An attack on the US destroyer *Maddox* in the Gulf of Tonkin by North Vietnamese torpedo boats in 1964 caused the USA to launch retaliatory air raids on naval bases and oil refineries in the North. Following increased Viet Cong activity, President Lyndon **Johnson** ordered a huge build-up of US forces in South Vietnam (from 1965), which in turn led to more direct involvement by North Vietnamese forces. Australia, the Philippines, South Korea and Thailand also sent forces to aid the South.

The successes and the heavy casualties of North Vietnam's Tet Offensive (1968), together with growing opposition to the war in the USA, encouraged both sides to begin negotiations at the **Paris Peace Talks**. However, bitter fighting continued, spreading to neighbouring Laos and **Cambodia**, and US bombing of the North was resumed. Eventually in 1973 a peace agreement was made in Paris. All US forces were withdrawn by 1975, resulting in the occupation of the South by the communists and the reunification of Vietnam. The USA thus suffered a disastrous and expensive military defeat, and saw the failure of its communist containment policy.

Vishinsky *see* Vyshinski.

Vorster, Balthazar Johannes (1915–83) A South African politician. Vorster was interned in 1942 and 1943 during WWII because of his involvement in a fascist Afrikaner movement. He joined the National Party and became Minister of Justice (1961–6), party

leader and PM (1966–78), and president (1978–79). He
followed **apartheid** policies, strengthening repressive
measures against blacks and coloureds, but received
overwhelming support for his actions from the white
electorate.

Vyshinski or **Vishinsky, Andrei** (1883–1954)
A Soviet politician. Vyshinski was the hardline
prosecutor of the show trials of the 1930s (*see* **purge**).
He became deputy Foreign Minister (1940–9 and
1953–5), permanent delegate to the UN (1945–9) and
(1953–4), and Foreign Minister (1949–53), in which
roles he played a prominent part in the policies of the
Cold War.

W

Waldheim, Kurt (1918–) An Austrian diplomat. Waldheim was Foreign Minister (1968–70) and UN Secretary General (1972–82). He was elected to the Austrian presidency in 1986, but attacks on his war record led him not to seek re-election in 1992.

Walesa, Lech *see* **Solidarity**.

Wall Street Crash (1929) A financial collapse of the US economy, which experienced an artificial boom in the 1920s caused by wild speculation on the stock market. Doubt about the security of certain major business enterprises caused panic selling on the New York Stock Exchange (sited in Wall Street), and millions of shares changed hands in four days. Banks and businesses failed, unemployment rose rapidly to *c.*17 million, and there was a recession throughout the country which eventually spread to Europe, causing the **Depression** of the early 1930s.

War Communism The policy introduced by **Lenin** after the Bolshevik seizure of power in late 1917, to try to save the country from economic chaos. It involved the nationalisation of land, industry and banking and the running of factories by worker managers. It was not successful in the countryside where it meant state confiscation of food supplies, and led to terrible famine. Widespread discontent at its ruthlessness led to the **Kronstadt mutiny** in 1921, and Lenin decided, for the time being, to abandon the immediate introduction of Communism and to try more gradual methods. Thus, he

replaced War Communism with a partial return to
capitalism by introducing the **New Economic Policy**
(NEP) in 1921.

War Crimes Acts committed in wartime by civilians or
members of the armed services against the accepted
customs and rules of war, e.g. as set out in the **Geneva
Convention**. After WWII German Nazi leaders were
convicted of war crimes and 'crimes against peace and
humanity' at the Nuremberg Trials (1945–6) by an
Allied military tribunal, several being sentenced to
death. Japan's war leaders were also convicted in similar
trials in Tokyo.

Warsaw Pact The Eastern European Mutual
Assistance Treaty (1955), signed in Warsaw by Albania,
Bulgaria, Czechoslovakia, East Germany, Hungary,
Poland, Romania and the USSR. The Pact was signed
following West Germany's entry into NATO. It set up a
unified military command with each country agreeing
not to use, or threaten to use, force in relationships with
each other, and to give immediate assistance by all
means it might consider necessary to any member
threatened by attack. It also pledged its members to
work for a general reduction in armaments and the
outlawing of nuclear weapons, and to respect each
other's independence and sovereignty by non-
intervention in internal affairs. Albania was excluded
from the Pact's activities in 1961, and withdrew in 1968.
It was dissolved in 1991.

Washington Conference (1921–2) An international
meeting held with the aim of reducing naval armaments
and relaxing tension in the Far East. The countries

taking part were Belgium, China, France, Italy, Japan, the Netherlands, Portugal, the UK and the USA. The agreements reached included:

a. a guarantee of China's independence;

b. the continuance of the 1899 Open-Door Policy, a system for China's economic development by which the political unity and independence of the country were assured and all nations guaranteed equal commercial and tariff rights there;

c. a Japanese pledge for the eventual return to China of the bay of Jiaozhou taken by them from Germany (1914) which had leased it from China (1897);

d. the intention by the USA and the UK not to strengthen naval bases between, and including. Hawaii and Singapore;

e. a guarantee by France, Japan, the UK and the USA of each other's existing Pacific possessions;

f. a naval convention of which all the states undertook not to build capital ships for ten years. together with agreement on the numbers of battleships in the navies of France, Italy, Japan, the UK and the USA.

Watergate Affair The incident during the US 1972 presidential election campaign when agents employed by President Richard **Nixon**'s re-election organisation were caught breaking into the Democratic Party's HQ in the Watergate Building, in Washington, DC. The subsequent scandal was made worse by attempts to conceal the fact that senior White House officials had approved the burglary. Eventually the president was implicated in the cover-up and in 1974 he was forced to resign to avoid impeachment.

Wehrmacht The armed services of the German **Third Reich** (1935–45).

Weimar Republic (1919–33) The post-WWI German republic that took its name from the town where the National Constituent Assembly met after Kaiser Wilhelm II's abdication. Its constitution provided for two elected chambers, proportional representation, a seven-year presidential term of office and federal rights. The republic suffered from economic problems caused by WWI, especially hyperinflation in 1923, and **reparations**. The **Dawes Plan** helped with reparations, but the Depression after 1929 led to mass unemployment and a worsening of the economic situation, and paved the way for the advance of the Nazi Party, which came to power in 1933 and introduced a new constitution.

Weizmann, Chaim (1874–1952) An Israeli politician. He played a major part in securing the **Balfour Declaration**. The plight of East European Jewry led him to fight for a Jewish homeland in **Palestine**, with the help of the Declaration. He was president of the World Zionist Organisation (1920–30 and 1935–46) and of the Jewish Agency in Palestine from 1929. On the formation of the state of Israel in 1948 he became its first president, an office he held until his death.

Welensky, Sir Roy (1907–84) A Rhodesian politician. He founded the Northern Rhodesia Labour Party in 1938, and on the formation of the Federation of **Rhodesia and Nyasaland**, which he had worked hard to bring about, he became Minister of Transport and Communications (1953–56) and PM (1956–63). When the Federation was dissolved, white Rhodesians abandoned his party in favour of Ian **Smith**'s Rhodesian Front, and although he supported the Front's opposition to a trade boycott, he was against the Unilateral Declaration of Independence in 1965.

Welfare State The system by which a government takes the main responsibility for the economic and social wellbeing of the population by such means as unemployment insurance, pensions of various kinds, health services and housing. *See also* **Beveridge Report**.

West Bank The part of Jordan to the W of the River Jordan occupied by Israel since the 1967 **Arab-Israeli War**. The provision of the **Camp David Agreement** (1978) that Israel should grant a degree of Palestinian autonomy in the West Bank was finally carried out in 1994, but in the interim the area was increasingly settled by Israelis. This led to acts of civil disobedience, rioting and guerrilla activities by the PLO and the local Arab population (*see* **Palestine Liberation Organisation**) which continued after the establishment of a Palestinian authority.

West Germany *see* **Germany**.

Western European Union (WEU) An organisation established in 1955 to replace the Brussels Treaty Organisation, a military alliance formed in 1948 with the same membership as the WEU apart from Italy and Germany. Its members are Belgium, France, Italy, Luxembourg, the Netherlands, the UK and Germany. The foreign ministers form a Council, and there is an assembly of representatives of the WEU in the Consultative Assembly of the **Council of Europe**. and an Armaments Control Agency which works with NATO. The union's objectives are cooperation on cultural, economic, military and social matters.

Westminster, Statute of *see* Statute of Westminster.

WEU *see* Western European Union.

White House The official Washington DC residence of the US president. The term is also used loosely for the president and his executive.

White Supremacy A theory based on the ignorant belief that white races are naturally superior to other races, especially black Africans, a view basic to the **apartheid** policies of South Africa.

Whites *see* Russian Revolutions.

WHO *see* World Health Organisation.

Wilhelm II (1859–1941) Emperor (*Kaiser*) of Germany from 1888 to 1918. He had visions of German world domination and set out to strengthen the country's military and naval forces even though this damaged relations with Britain, France and Russia. Though he was a grandson of Queen Victoria, a personal hostility existed between him and his uncle, Edward VII. His actions and arrogant personality helped bring about WWI in which, however, he was largely dominated by his military leaders. He abdicated two days before the Armistice (1918) and went into exile in Holland.

Wilson, Sir Harold, Lord Wilson of Rievaulx and Emley (1916–95) A British Labour politician, who was PM from 1964 to 1970 and 1974 to 1976. In 1963 he was elected leader of the Labour Party, and became PM in 1964, increasing Labour's majority in the 1966 election. Rhodesian **UDI** and the rejection of the UK's second application to join the **EU** both occurred during his first premiership and during both of his terms of office there were difficult **balance of payments** crises and high inflation. From 1966 he attempted to deal with inflation by legal limits on prices and incomes, and from 1974 by the 'Social Contract' with the trade unions, aimed at a voluntary limitation on wage increases. He resigned in 1976 and was succeeded as PM by James **Callaghan**.

Wilson, Woodrow (1856–1924) The US Democratic president from 1913 to 1921. He kept the US out of WWI until 1917 when the **Zimmermann Telegram** and the unrestricted U-boat campaign (*see* **Lusitania**), together with aroused public indignation, forced him to allow US intervention.

His famous **Fourteen Points** were a peace programme for a new world order after WWI, but apart from the establishment of the **League of Nations** his ideas were not fully put into practice. Isolationists gained the upper hand in Congress, which rejected the terms of the Treaty of Versailles and refused membership of the League, against Wilson's advice. His administration introduced **Prohibition** (a ban on alcoholic drink) and **women's suffrage** in 1920, reorganised the federal banking system and introduced important anti-trust measures. He suffered a stroke in 1919 which made it very difficult for him to cope in the last years of his presidency.

Women's Suffrage The right of women to the franchise, i.e. to vote in public elections.

The chief British movement in support of this cause was the radical Women's Social and Political Union (WSPU) founded in 1903 by Emmeline **Pankhurst**; its members became known as *suffragettes*. As it grew rapidly in numbers and wealth so its members increasingly were imprisoned for attacks on property, refusal to pay taxes, and demonstrations. Many went on hunger strikes in prison and were forcibly fed. In a dramatic demonstration on behalf of the cause of votes for women, *Emily Davidson* threw herself under the king's horse running in the Derby and was killed (1913).

The fact that women took over what had been considered as 'men's work' during WWI. combined with growing political pressure, resulted in women over 30 being given the vote subject to educational and property qualifications (1918). All women were granted the vote in 1928.

A moderate, nonviolent movement with the same objectives as the WSPU was the National Union of Women's Suffrage Societies (NUWSS) founded in 1897 by *Millicent Fawcett* (1847–1929).

Emancipation of women in other parts of the world has been varied, some countries granting women voting rights before Britain but most later, while some still withhold the franchise.

Wood, Edward Frederick Lindley, Baron Irwin and Earl of Halifax (1881–1959) A British Conservative politician. He was appointed Viceroy of India (1926–31) at a time of unrest on the North-West Frontier. As Foreign Secretary (1938–40), he at first supported **appeasement**, but played an important part in persuading Neville **Chamberlain** to take a stronger line with Nazi Germany after March 1939. He was ambassador to the USA from 1941 to 1946.

World Bank *see* **International Bank for Reconstruction and Development**.

World Health Organisation (WHO) A UN agency with HQ in Geneva, established in 1948 to develop international cooperation in the control of diseases and drug addiction; in medical and drug research; and in environmental and family health resources, including education, nutrition, family planning, housing, sanitation and working conditions.

World War I or **First World War**, formerly **Great War** (1914–18) The conflict in which the Allied powers, principally Britain, France, Russia (*see* **Triple Entente**) Serbia, Belgium, Japan, Italy (from 1915), Rōmania (from 1916) and the USA (from 1917) were engaged against the **Central Powers**, principally Austria-Hungary, Germany, the Ottoman Empire and Bulgaria (from 1915).

The causes of the war included economic, colonial and naval rivalry between the power blocs, with fears of German expansion; the division of Europe into mutually suspicious alliances; the tension in the Balkans between Austria-Hungary and Russia (Russia supported the Serb nationalism that threatened the Austro-Hungarian Empire), which reached breaking-point with the assassination of Archduke Franz Ferdinand at **Sarajevo**; and the consequent Austro-Hungarian attack on Serbia. Once this had taken place, the network of alliances meant that Germany was at war with Russia

World War I *The Western Front,*
December 1914–March 1918.

and with France, which it attacked through Belgium.
Belgian frontiers had been guaranteed by Britain, which
then entered the war to defend them.

The Western Front On land, the rapid German
advance in the W was stopped near Paris at the Marne

(1914) and was followed by prolonged stalemate with concentrated **trench warfare**. Attempts to break the stalemate, at e.g. **Ypres**, **Verdun** and the **Somme**, only resulted in enormous loss of life and little territorial gain, despite the introduction of poison gas, tanks, and the development of aerial warfare, including the bombing of military and civilian targets. In the spring of 1918 the Germans launched a massive offensive which again took them close to Paris, but an Allied counter-offensive drove them back again.

Other European fronts In the E, the Germans checked the initial Russian advance at **Tannenberg** (1914), and the war saw a succession of major breakthroughs. Notable Russian successes included Galicia (1914) and the **Brusilov Offensive** (1916), and German successes of Gorlice Tarnow (1915) and Romania (1916). Russia was less able to endure the exhaustion of men and materials, and opposition to the war helped bring about the **October Revolution** (1917) after which the Bolsheviks arranged an armistice with Germany.

Fierce fighting also occurred in the Balkans, where Serbia was overrun until the Allied breakthrough of 1918, and on the Austro-Italian border, where there was largely stalemate until the Austrian victory at **Caporetto** (1917) and an Italian counter-offensive of 1918.

The Middle East In the Middle East, British and Imperial forces were eventually successful against the Turks in Palestine and Mesopotamia, and in Arabia T E **Lawrence** organised a revolt against Ottoman rule. In 1915 the Allies launched the **Dardanelles** campaign to open the straits to Russia, but after prolonged fighting were defeated by the Turkish defenders.

Naval operations The war at sea saw only one major naval battle (**Jutland**) but a campaign of German **U-boat** attacks against merchant shipping, which led to the introduction of the convoy system and contributed to the USA's entry into the war in 1917 (*see* **Lusitania**). Eventually the Allies gained command of the seas and were able to maintain a blockade of Germany that brought the country near to starvation in 1917–18.

The battles on the Western Front finally wore down German resistance, but at an enormous cost to both sides in men and materials, and it was these wasteful battles rather than loss of territory that led to the German surrender. An armistice was signed in November 1918, and at the Paris Peace Conference (1919), harsh terms were imposed on the defeated powers.

World War II or Second World War (1939–45)

A worldwide conflict between the Allied powers and the Axis powers. The Allied powers were principally the British Commonwealth, the USSR (from 1941), the USA (from 1941) and several European nations overrun by enemy forces. The Axis powers were Germany, Italy (from 1940) and Japan (from 1941), supported by Bulgaria, Finland, Hungary and Romania.

The causes of the war included the failure of the WWI peace settlements; the aggressive expansionist policies of **Hitler**'s Nazi Germany and of Japan; the **appeasement** policies of France and the UK (*see* **Munich Agreement**); and the **isolationism** pursued by the USA.

The occupation of W Europe The **Nazi-Soviet Pact**

opened the way for Germany's invasion of Poland (1939), which caused Britain and France to declare war on Germany. After a few months of **Phoney War**, Germany's **Blitzkrieg** offensives rapidly overran Denmark, Norway, the Low Countries and France. The British Expeditionary Force was evacuated from France at Dunkirk (1940), and Hitler stood poised to invade the UK. This was prevented by the defeat of the Luftwaffe by the RAF in the **Battle of Britain**. German aerial bombing of civilian and industrial targets (*see* **Blitz**) failed to break British morale, and similar raids were carried out by the Allies with increasing intensity against Germany and later Japan. Italy invaded Greece in 1940 but was driven back. In 1941 Germany overran Yugoslavia, Greece and Crete, and British troops took control in the Middle East (e.g. Iraq) to prevent attempts to capture the oilfields. In the **North Africa Campaigns** the fighting moved backwards and forwards across the deserts, but eventually Allied forces pushing W from Egypt joined US forces advancing E from Algeria (1943).

The invasion of Italy In 1943 Allied forces invaded Italy from N Africa. Mussolini was overthrown and Italy joined the Allies. However, German forces entered the country and were only forced northwards after heavy fighting, eventually surrendering in 1945.

The Russian Campaign Hitler's invasion of the USSR in 1941 took German forces close to Moscow and Leningrad, and into the Caucasus and Ukraine. The tide was halted by the Soviet victory at **Stalingrad** (1942–43) and turned back by the titanic struggle at

Kursk (1943), after which Soviet armies forced the Germans back across E Europe, entering Germany in 1945.

The liberation of W Europe British, Commonwealth and US forces invaded W Europe at the **Normandy Landings** (1944). Progress was temporarily halted by the German **Ardennes Offensive** (1944–45), but Allied troops advanced into Germany in 1945, linking up with Soviet forces. After the Russians entered Berlin. Hitler committed suicide and Germany surrendered unconditionally.

Naval operations German surface raiders, aircraft and especially U-boats inflicted huge losses on Allied shipping, threatening to cut off entirely the military supplies from the USA that enabled Britain to remain at war. The convoy system introduced in the Atlantic, the Mediterranean and the North Sea, and on the Arctic route to the USSR, and eventually growing Allied air and naval superiority prevailed (*see* **Atlantic, Battle of the**).

The war with Japan Japan entered the war in December 1941 by attacking the US Navy at **Pearl Harbor** in Hawaii, and then occupied Hong Kong, Thailand, Malaya, Singapore, Indo-China, the Philippines, the East Indies and many of the Pacific islands. Although notable victories were won by the Allies in Burma and in naval and air engagements in the Pacific, large areas still remained in Japanese hands until after the dropping of two atomic bombs on Japan (*see* **Hiroshima** and **Nagasaki**) which forced unconditional Japanese surrender (1945). The War's cost in lives was the

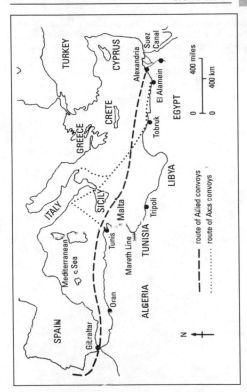

***World War II** North Africa.*

route of Allied convoys

route of Axis convoys

greatest of any conflict in human history. Estimates are
about 55 million dead (approximately 20 million
military and 35 million civilian); about 20 million of
these were from the Soviet Union alone, 13.5 million
from China, 7.3 million from Germany and 5.4 million
from Poland.

Y

Yahya Khan, Agha Mohammed (1917–80)
A Pakistani soldier and statesman. He became
commanding general of the army in 1966 and replaced
Ayub Khan as president from 1969 to 1971, imposing
martial law. He decided to settle political problems by
allowing the first universal male suffrage elections in the
country (1970–1). Civil war broke out as a result of his
refusal to accept the verdict in favour of the Awami
League independence movement in East Pakistan
(**Bangladesh**). India's military intervention on behalf of
Bangladeshi independence (1971) led to Pakistan's
defeat and Yahya Khan's enforced resignation. He was
replaced by Zulfikar Ali **Bhutto**.

Yalta Conference (1945) The second and more
important of the WWII meetings between Churchill,
Roosevelt and Stalin (the first was the **Tehran
Conference**). Principal agreements reached included:

   a. Germany's division into four occupation zones and
      the establishment of an Allied Control Commission
      in Berlin following the expected Allied victory;
   b. Germany's disarmament and obligation to pay
      reparations, together with the trial and punishment
      of war criminals;
   c. Poland's reestablishment within new frontiers, the
      E part of the country to be ceded to the USSR
      along the **Curzon Line**, with the W part extended
      into German territory along the **Oder-Neisse Line**
      as compensation;

   d. the establishment of democratic governments in liberated countries on the basis of free elections;

   e. a declaration of war on Japan by the USSR;

   f. the establishment of **Korea**'s independence after a period of American and Soviet occupation;

   g. support for the **Atlantic Charter** as the basis of Allied postwar policy;

   h. the calling of a conference for the purpose of founding a **United Nations Organisation**.

Several of these points were restated at the **Potsdam Conference** after the Allied victory in Europe.

Yaoundé Agreements (1963 and 1969) Conventions signed in the Cameroon capital between the EEC and former Belgian, Dutch, French and Italian colonies which wanted to continue their trading association with the EEC after independence.

Following the enlargement of the EC in 1973, former British colonies entered the agreements, which were superseded by the **Lomé Convention** in 1975.

Yeltsin, Boris (1931–) A Russian politician and former Communist. He criticised Mikhail **Gorbachev**'s policy of **perestroika** for not moving fast enough, and was elected to the Russian parliament in 1989 with a massive popular vote. In August 1991 he went on to the streets to help defeat the coup against Gorbachev, who resigned a few months later. Yeltsin became undisputed Russian leader. He was a Russian nationalist and did little to save the USSR from break-up in 1991–2, but he did support the creation of the **CIS** to replace it. He was replaced by his deputy **Vladimir Putin**.

Yom Kippur War *see* **Arab-Israeli Wars**.

Young Plan (1929) A scheme for the settlement of Germany's WWI reparations proposed by a committee chaired by a US businessman, Owen D Young (1874–1962).

It replaced the **Dawes Plan** and reduced Germany's payments by some 75 per cent, the remaining debt to be paid off in annual amounts to an international bank until 1988. It ended foreign control over Germany's finances; returned German securities that had been held by the Allies; abolished the Reparations Commission; and ended Allied rights to apply sanctions should payments be in default.

Payments were suspended for three years in 1932 owing to the **Depression**, and Hitler blocked further payments after 1935. The plan was, therefore, of little value since only one payment was made under its terms.

Young Turks A Turkish reform movement of the early 20th century which organised a rebellion against the Ottoman Empire by liberal army officers in Salonika in 1908, followed by the founding of a Committee of Union and Progress in Constantinople (now Istanbul).

The revolt was in support of a demand for the restoration of the 1876 constitution, and the committee was headed by three officers who had been urging the country's modernisation for several years. A parliament was summoned, the constitution restored, Sultan Abdul Hamid deposed, and a policy of radical reform of government and society was begun. The movement broke up because of internal disagreements.

Ypres, Battles of Four engagements in WWI centred around the Belgian town of Ypres, which was

completely destroyed but never captured by the
Germans. The first battle (1914), resulted in the
German capture of Messines Ridge. The second battle
(1915) was the first occasion on which gas was used on
the Western Front. The third battle (1917) involved a
combined Australian, British and Canadian offensive
against Messines Ridge and the village of Passchendaele.
The fourth battle (1918), also known as the Battle of the
River Lys, was a part of the huge final German offensive
of the war. In total the Germans suffered some $1/4$
million casualties while the Allied losses amounted to
about twice that figure.

Yugoslavia A socialist federal republic of SE Europe.
Area: 255,804 sq km. Pop: 21.690,000 before breakup.
Languages: Macedonian, Serbo-Croat and Slovene.
Religions: Orthodox, RC and Islam. Cap: Belgrade.

The states of the republic were, from 1929 to 1992,
Bosnia-Herzegovina, Croatia, Macedonia, **Montenegro**,
Serbia and Slovenia; there were also two self-governing
provinces – Kosovo and Voivodina. Of these Slovenia,
Croatia, Bosnia-Herzegovina and Macedonia had
declared their independence by the mid-1990s, and
Serbia and Montenegro remained within a federal
Yugoslavia. The 'Kingdom of Serbs, Croats and
Slovenes' (renamed Yugoslavia in 1929) was established
in 1918 under the terms of the Corfu Pact (1917),
concluded by leaders of Serbia and of Slav refugees
from Austria-Hungary. The variety of religious beliefs in
the various republics caused considerable political
difficulties in the unification of the new state, reaching a
climax with the assassination of a Croat agrarian leader,

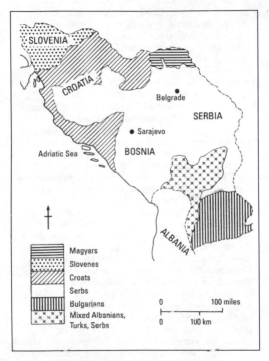

Yugoslavia *Racial (not religious) divisions.*

Stefan Radic, in the Constitutional Assembly in 1928. This resulted in the repeal of the constitution and the taking of dictatorial powers in 1929 by King Alexander (1888–1934). Alexander was a Serb and his actions aggravated the divisions within the country. Croats and Slovenes in particular alleged that the state was too Serb-orientated, and in 1934 Alexander was assassinated by Croatian extremists.

Alexander was succeeded by his son, Peter II, but as he was a minor Alexander's cousin, Prince Paul (1896-1976) acted as regent. In 1941 Paul was dismissed in a military coup for being too much under German and Italian influence. Ten days later Germany invaded Yugoslavia, and king and government went into exile in the UK. Resistance movements fought on and eventually **Tito** and his followers deposed the king in 1944 and established the Republic in 1945.

Under Tito, Yugoslavia became a leader of the **Non-aligned Movemen**t. Although a communist state, it followed an independent course from that approved by the USSR and its allies, having broken with them in 1948. It condemned the invasions of **Hungary** and **Czechoslovakia** and was not a member of the **Cominform**, **COMECON** or the **Warsaw Pact**. Foreign investment was encouraged, the tourist industry was expanded, land reforms without **collectivisation** occurred, and industrial development covered a wide range of manufactures.

After Tito's death in 1980, ethnic divisions caused increasing unrest, and successive ministers had difficulty in holding Yugoslavia together. The collapse of

Communism in E Europe gave the opportunity for both Croatia and Slovenia to withdraw from the federation and to declare independence. The new states gained international recognition in 1991 and this encouraged Bosnia-Herzegovina to declare independence in 1992. The dominant partners in what was left of Yugoslavia, the Serbs, fought a war against Croatia, claiming that this was to prevent the break-up of Yugoslavia, and against the Bosnian Muslims in order to acquire as much of Bosnia for ethnic Serbs as possible. After the Dayton Accord (1995) ended the Bosnian conflict tension began to grow in Kosovo, a self-governing province of Serbia where ethnic Albanians were being driven from their homes by the Serbian army and Kosovan Serb militias. An aerial bombing campaign against Serbia by US and UK forces in 1991 led the Serbs to abandon Kosovo, which became a UN-policed enclave of ethnic Albanians. In 2000 the (Serbian) Yugoslav president, Slobodan Milosevic, was overthrown by the people of Belgrade after trying to annul the results of the elections he had lost. In 2001 Milosevic was delivered for trial as a war criminal at The Hague. Yugoslavia (Serbia and Montenegro) continues to exist, but indications that Montenegro might also wish to secede raise the question of how long it can survive.

Z

Zhou Enlai or **Chou En-lai** (1898–1976) A Chinese Communist politician. Zhou was a founder member of the French Communist Party when he lived in Paris (1920–4). On returning to China he organised revolts against the warlords in Shanghai, Nanjing and Canton, spent two years in the USSR, and then became **Mao Zedong**'s urban revolutionary affairs adviser. During WWII he was the Communists' liaison officer in the wartime capital, Chongqing. He was PM (1949–76) from the time the Communists took power, also holding the office of Foreign Minister until 1958. He became the best known of China's leaders, travelling widely on diplomatic missions, and as leader of détente with the USA (1972–3).

Zhukov, Georgi (1896–1976) A Soviet marshal and politician. An outstanding commander of WWII, Zhukov directed the defence of **Leningrad**, the defence of Moscow (1941), the victory at **Stalingrad** (1943) and the advance from the Ukraine in 1944 that ended with the capture of Berlin in 1945. He was Minister of Defence from 1955 to 1957. Soon after becoming a member of the Presidium (1957) he was dismissed from government and party posts for encouraging his own personality cult and of undermining the party's position within the armed forces.

Zia ul-Haq, Mohammad (1924–88) A Pakistani general and politician. After WWII Zia rose rapidly through the ranks to become chief of staff (1976). He led the coup deposing Zulfikar Ali **Bhutto** (1977) and succeeded him as president in 1978. Martial law was in force and political parties banned (1977–8). Partial democracy was restored after a general election in 1985, but the country remained under Zia's military-backed rule. He introduced an Islamic code of laws while relying on the USA for defensive requirements and the West in general for economic and financial support. He died in a plane crash, the cause of which has never been fully established.

Zimbabwe A Commonwealth republic of SC Africa. Area: 390,308 sq km. Pop: 10,205,000 (1992). Official language: English. Religions: animist, Christianity. Cap: Harare (formerly Salisbury).

Governed by the British South Africa Company from 1893, the country became the British colony of Southern Rhodesia in 1923, and part of the **Federation of Rhodesia and Nyasaland** (1953–63). In 1965 the Rhodesian Front government of PM Ian **Smith** sought to ensure the continuation of white minority rule by making a unilateral declaration of independence (UDI) from the UK, which wished to delay independence until black majority rule was achieved. Talks with Britain broke down, the UN applied sanctions, and in 1970 Rhodesia was declared a republic.

Rhodesia's international isolation, and increasing guerrilla activities by the African liberation movements of Robert **Mugabe** and Joshua **Nkomo**, forced Smith to form a joint black and white government in 1978, with Bishop Abel Muzorewa becoming PM in 1979. Meanwhile, the guerrilla war continued and in 1979

talks in London led to independence and the
establishment of black majority rule in 1980. The
Zimbabwe African National Union (ZANU) won the
election that followed, and Mugabe became PM.

In 1984, Mugabe made Zimbabwe a one-party state
and commenced an increasingly autocratic and erratic
rule. By the end of the century, Zimbabwe's economy
was in tatters, and the country was politically divided
(and diplomatically isolated) by a government-
sponsored programme of forcible eviction of white farm
owners, opposed by the country's courts.

Zimmermann Telegram (1917) A coded message
from the German Foreign Minister, Arthur
Zimmermann (1864–1940), to the German minister in
Mexico. It was intercepted by British naval intelligence,
which disclosed its contents to the US Government.

The main point of the message was that if the USA
declared war on Germany, Mexico should attack the
USA with German and Japanese assistance in return for
the American states of Arizona, New Mexico and Texas.
Japan had entered WWI on the Allied side in 1914, and
Germany was seeking unsuccessfully to persuade it to
change sides.

In the event neither Japan nor Mexico collaborated
with Germany, but the outrage aroused by the telegram
in the USA played a major part in the country's decision
three months later to enter WWI.

Zinoviev Letter (1924) A communication which
helped to bring about the Labour Party's defeat in the
1924 UK general election.

The letter was supposedly from the chairman of the

Comintern, Grigori Zinoviev (1883–1936). It was addressed to the British Communist Party and called for the spreading of propaganda among the armed services in preparation for a rebellion against capitalism. The letter was published by the *Daily Mail* four days before the election, together with a Foreign Office protest to the USSR.

Proof that the letter was genuine was never established and it has been suggested that it was forged in Berlin by White Russians, as many such documents were being circulated by émigré organisations at the time in an effort to discredit socialism.

The Labour Party considered that many marginal voters swung to the Conservatives because they had been led to believe, quite wrongly, that not only the Communists but also the Labour Party held similar views to those expressed in the letter.

Zionism A political movement founded in 1897 for the setting up of a national homeland for Jews in what was **Palestine**. The movement is now concerned with the development and prosperity of **Israel**.